D0934917

Resource Allocation in Higher Education

THE ECONOMICS OF EDUCATION

Paying the Piper: Productivity, Incentives, and Financing in U.S. Higher Education, by Michael S. McPherson, Morton Owen Schapiro, and Gordon C. Winston

Resource Allocation in Higher Education, edited by William F. Massy

Resource Allocation in Higher Education

William F. Massy, Editor
and collaborators

Ann Arbor
THE UNIVERSITY OF MICHIGAN PRESS

Copyright © by the University of Michigan 1996
All rights reserved
Published in the United States of America by
The University of Michigan Press
Manufactured in the United States of America
⊗ Printed on acid-free paper

1999   1998   1997   1996   4   3   2   1

A CIP catalog record for this book is available from the British Library.

Library of Congress Cataloging-in-Publication Data

Resource allocation in higher education / William F. Massy, editor.
        p.   cm. — (Economics of education)
    Includes bibliographical references and index.
    ISBN 0-472-10686-4 (hardcover : alk. paper)
    1. Universities and colleges—United States—Business management.
    2. Resource allocation.   3. Universities and colleges—United
    States—Finance.   I. Massy, William F.   II. Series.
    LB2341.U6R47   1996
    378'.02—dc20   95-48854
                                                                        CIP

To Sally

Acknowledgments

The list of people who helped bring this book to fruition spans many years—beginning with my colleagues on Stanford University's Budget Group from 1971 onward and ending with Janice Pang, our extraordinarily capable writer and editor at the Stanford Institute for Higher Education Research.

The direct impetus for the book came from Professor Alan Odden, who directed the Finance Center of the Consortium for Policy Research on Education (CPRE) between 1991 and 1995—first from the University of Southern California and then from the University of Wisconsin–Madison. Alan suggested the idea of a CPRE conference on resource allocation, during an in-flight conversation between Baltimore and Chicago in 1992. The conference did in fact take place, thanks to Alan's financial and logistical support. Then, however, he wouldn't rest until he had obtained my commitment, and those of the other conference presenters, to produce a book on higher education resource allocation. So this book owes its genesis to Alan's vision and persistence—which I hereby gratefully acknowledge.

I would also like to acknowledge the Consortium for Policy Research in Education and its leader, Susan Fuhrman, and the U.S. Department of Education's Office of Education Research and Improvement (OERI) and our contract monitor, Duc Le To. (Our project was funded through CPRE by OERI under contract number R117610039-91.) Without their financial support, neither the conference on resource allocation nor this book would have been possible.

My collaborators also deserve a strong word of thanks. Jon Strauss, John Curry, Edward Lawler III, Susan A. Mohrman, and Edward Whalen presented papers at the conference and then agreed to revise their work for publication herein. They also exhibited great patience when preparation of the other chapters took longer than expected. Elaine El-Khawas, Harry Atkinson, and David S. P. Hopkins signed on after the project was under way, when it became apparent that help was needed to cover particular subject areas. Gordon Winston provided encouragement for our work and graciously agreed to reprint his article on global budgeting.

Colleagues on the Stanford Budget Group shaped my thinking about university resource allocation in early and important ways. William F. Miller, Stanford's provost in 1971, began the process by extending my duties as vice provost for research to include participation in planning and budgeting. Later, as vice president for business and finance, I worked with Bill and his successors, Albert Hastorf and James Rosse, to refine and reengineer the budget process. Jim, in particular, provided the leadership to move Stanford into the world of decentralization through block budgeting.

Vice Provost Ray Bacchetti headed Stanford's budget staff for many years, and I'm grateful for our many discussions about how to run university resource allocation. I am also grateful to Kent Peterson, director of management and financial planning and later associate vice president for business and finance, and to Kenneth Creighton, associate vice president and controller, for their many years of able assistance, advice, and support.

David Hopkins deserves a special vote of thanks for his work on the budget staff as director of management and financial planning, as my research collaborator and coauthor on *Planning Models for Colleges and Universities*, and as co-teacher of a graduate seminar on planning models during the late 1970s. Finally, the list of Stanford acknowledgments would not be complete without mentioning the two presidents under whom I served: Richard Lyman and Donald Kennedy. The work that led to this book would not have been possible without their support, encouragement, and critical commentary.

Professor Robert Zemsky of the University of Pennsylvania, director of the Pew Higher Education Program and coinventor of Responsibility Center Budgeting, contributed greatly to my evolving insights about resource allocation. Back at Stanford, SIHER Assistant Director Andrea Wilger provided invaluable advice, and Roberta Callaway handled the innumerable details of finance and logistics. Doctoral student Yee-Tien (Ted) Fu provided the impetus for my keynote speech to the APEC International Conference on Higher Education, held in Chinese Taipei during April of 1994: this talk provided the genesis for much of chapters 2 and 3, which represented a critical milestone in preparing the book.

The book could not have materialized without Janice Pang. She took my disconnected writings and produced a coherent manuscript. She edited the papers of my collaborators. She provided invaluable advice and critical commentary, pushed me to set and meet deadlines, and managed our end of the publication process. And she did it all with patience, and with humor. Thank you, Janice!

Finally, I thank my wife, Sally—my toughest-minded critic as well as my delight, inspiration, and support.

Contents

Part 1
Background

CHAPTER 1

Introduction

William F. Massy

American higher education is touted as the envy of the world, yet our country views the academy with increasing suspicion. While institutional leaders proclaim the need for sustained funding to maintain or increase access and quality, political figures and the general public wonder why colleges and universities cannot manage their costs more effectively—why, indeed, they cannot follow industry's lead by improving productivity to reduce the burden on tuition payers and the public purse. Productivity improvement requires that academic and administrative processes be reviewed and, where applicable, restructured, reengineered, or eliminated. Analyses of resource allocation processes are particularly important because they deeply affect and impact most other institutional processes.

What is there to study about resource allocation? Isn't it obvious that one just puts the money where it will do the most good? In the most prestigious universities, isn't it received wisdom that one should hire as many of the best faculty as possible and then step back and let them do their jobs? Can't informed people, who know the academic disciplines and their institution's strengths and weaknesses, simply decide what programs need funding the most and give them the money?

It's not that simple. While resource allocation does boil down to knowledgeable people making informed decisions, the record shows that *process*—the way decisions are made and communicated—powerfully affects outcomes. The same knowledgeable people, blessed with the same information and diligence, can reach a successful conclusion through a good process but end up with failure if they must fight a poor process every step of the way. As we shall see, common sense coupled with knowledge of discipline and institution are not always sufficient to distinguish good process from bad.[1]

---

1. See Stephen A. Hoenack, "Economics, Organizations, and Learning: Research Directions for the Economics of Education," *Economics of Education Review* 13, no. 2

3

The impetus for writing this book stems from two interconnected series of developments: one experiential and the other analytical. The first derives from my experience as university officer, consultant, and participant on higher education committees and panels. This convinced me that deeper understanding of resource allocation principles and processes is in fact badly needed. The second derives from my research on the economics, finance, and management of colleges and universities. The resulting concepts and models provide the basis for a treatment of resource allocation that is at once practical and well-grounded in theory.

The importance of theory can be illustrated by this well-known proposition: "universities will raise all the money they can and spend all the money they raise." Known in the literature as Bowen's law,[2] such behavior is often cited as the "cause" of cost-rise and productivity erosion in academe. Institutions have been called "greedy"[3] or, less provocatively, urged to go on a "revenue diet."[4] The idea that restraint is the key to resource allocation, however, turns out to be only half true. As we shall describe in chapter 3, Bowen's law can be derived from the economic theory of nonprofit enterprises. It represents constructive behavior for higher education institutions, analogous to Adam Smith's "invisible hand of competition." The keys to resource allocation reform lie elsewhere.

Keys to Effective Resource Allocation

The first key to effective resource allocation lies in understanding the system of incentives that guides spending in colleges and universities. The incentives are based partly on intrinsic values and partly on instrumental ones. For example, programs with strong market demand (e.g., from students, research sponsors, and donors) but low intrinsic value may serve instrumentally to cross-subsidize programs with high intrinsic value but low financial potential. A good resource allocation process will allow the institution to achieve a proper balance between its intrinsic values and those of the marketplace. Institutions that ignore the market-

---

(1994): 147–62 for a discussion of research priorities aimed at improving resource allocation and incentives in higher education.

2. Howard R. Bowen, *The Costs of Higher Education: How Much Do Colleges and Universities Spend Per Student and How Much Should they Spend?* (San Francisco: Jossey-Bass, 1980).

3. William J. Bennett, "Text of Secretary Bennett's Address Last Week at a Harvard University Anniversary Celebration," *Chronicle of Higher Education* 33, no. 7 (October 15, 1986): 27–30.

4. "The Other Side of the Mountain," *Policy Perspectives* 5, no. 1 (1991): 2A.

place risk financial dislocation; those that ignore intrinsic values—as bound up in the academic mission and vision, for example—will come to behave like an ordinary business enterprise.

A second key involves recognizing and managing the diversity of intrinsic values that abounds within any higher education institution. The diversity springs partly from professional background (chemists view the world differently than English professors), partly from differences in educational purposes, and partly from self-interest. Economic agency theory examines how resources are diverted away from institutional goals as a result of self-interest. This theory prescribes methods by which a principal (administrators, trustees) can limit an agent's (faculty, employees) resource diversion without disempowering him to the point of ineffectiveness. While resource diversion certainly affects colleges and universities, the more important problem involves good-faith differences in what principals and agents view as intrinsically important. For example, faculty often view academic priorities differently than administrators, trustees, or government funding agencies, and faculty in one department may have different views than their colleagues elsewhere. Each group argues for its view in terms of high principles, often reinforced by the fact that success also furthers self-interest.

Managing complexity represents a third key to resource allocation reform. Colleges and universities are quintessential professional organizations: the expertise needed for effective teaching and research lie almost exclusively in the hands of faculty. This is why we speak of "academic administrators" rather than "academic managers." Resource allocation reform usually involves decentralizing detailed budgeting responsibility away from central organizational units where it has traditionally been lodged in an effort to mitigate principal-agent problems.

Centralization can disempower those who represent the institution's core competencies, undermining the incentives for productivity improvement and making accountability for such improvements impossible. Moreover, centralization falls far short of attaining its stated goals. According to Stephen Hoenack of the University of Minnesota, despite centralized budget control, "academic suppliers have little difficulty in diverting resources away from purposes intended by their clients."[5] Much of our discussion of resource allocation processes involves the question of how to decentralize budget-making authority without abandoning institution-level values and priorities—that is, of unleashing the expertise and motivation residing in schools, departments, and faculty without losing the funding agent's ability to influence outcomes.

---

5. Hoenack, "Economics, Organizations, and Learning," 155.

The Resource Allocation Problem

Efforts to balance values and market forces, cope with value diversity, and manage complexity have traditionally led policymakers to insist upon central control over resources. The most common control method is incremental line-item budgeting, wherein the previous year's budget base (usually adjusted for inflation) is incremented or decreased by sums associated with particular line items of expenditure. Complexity drives the process's incremental character: attention is focused on additions and deletions because the base budget is too hard to analyze. Moreover, concerns about academic quality and faculty morale lead administrators to insulate academic units from market vicissitudes by holding each unit's budget base immune to revenue fluctuations so far as possible. Therefore, after a period of time, operating units tend to assert ownership of base funding levels and come to view most of their costs as fixed. Productivity improvement comes to be regarded as impossible or even malevolent—while costs can be reduced if necessary, such actions are seen as threatening quality.

Traditional budgeting systems may have served in a simpler and more stable time, but they break down when confronted with a combination of complexity and rapid environmental change. Complexity makes it hard for central allocators to make the case for adaptation, and unit managers may have little or no incentive to do so because Bowen's law drives each to maximize expenditures and vigorously protest proposed reductions. Value diversity politicizes efforts to reallocate resources among units, since downsized departments see themselves as victims of an ideologically driven conspiracy. These forces amplify the drive for expenditure growth and tend to produce across-the-board reductions rather than adaptive redistributions when expenditures must be cut. They make productivity improvement problematic, and they can prevent the institution from optimizing either its intrinsic values or its response to market forces.

The antidote lies in resource allocation reform at several levels. The first priority is to dissolve the operating units' sense of base budget ownership and their belief that cost and quality are ineluctably linked. This requires a combination of process change and cultural change to establish the principle that resources will flow in relation to market demand and assessed performance. The second priority is to maintain a dialogue about program relevance, quality, and productivity, and to implement the processes and data needed to make the dialogue meaningful. Resources should be invested according to the so-called high-assay principle. (If one owned several gold mines wouldn't it make sense to invest in the one with the highest assay?) In colleges and universities, *high-assay* means quality relative to institutional mission, vision, and goals, delivered as productively as possible. The final priority is to relax restrictions on how operating units manage resource trade-offs: units should be free to determine for themselves how to meet the agreed objectives within the available budget.

While incremental line-item budgeting leaves the most to be desired, shortfalls occur with other methods as well. For example, budgeting by formula tends to lock in unit costs, making productivity improvement exceedingly difficult and drawing attention away from institutional goals. Block allocation systems that lack good processes for evaluating plans and performance in relation to institutional goals hinder accountability and reinforce the idea that operating units "own" their funding. Every-tub-on-its-own-bottom systems maximize operating units' attention to market forces but make it very hard to influence their behavior when unit goals diverge from institutional goals.

Plan for the Book

This book lays the groundwork needed for institutional leaders and government officials to assess their existing resource allocation processes and plan for improvement. The book is conceptual in character: it does not provide recipes that, if followed faithfully, will produce a high likelihood of success. Higher education resource allocation is too complex to offer such sure guidance. Instead we offer a series of essays about topics bearing on resource allocation—in hopes that the ideas so presented will help readers interpret their own experience and insight for the betterment of their institutions and constituencies.

The book began as a collection of papers on decentralizing resource allocation. A conference on that subject, convened in November 1992 at the University of Southern California, brought together the initiators of revenue responsibility budgeting—also known as responsibility center budgeting and responsibility center management—and others concerned with how to devolve authority, responsibility, and accountability to academic operating units. (As we shall see later, revenue responsibility budgeting makes schools or departments responsible for revenue generation as well as cost control.) We agreed that the our papers should be pulled together and published as an integrated volume, and the conference papers provide the basis for chapters 6, 7, and 12. Subsequently the project was expanded with continuing sponsorship by the Consortium for Policy Research in Education (CPRE) and funding from the U.S. Department of Education's Office of Educational Research and Improvement (OERI).

Background

Chapter 2, "Reengineering Resource Allocation Systems," begins by describing how higher education's external environment has changed in the past decade. Different student needs, the increasing public concern about value for money, the advent of information technology, new financial constraints, and distance learning methods provide the impetus for transforming colleges and universities. Twenty years as Stanford's vice provost for research and vice president for business and finance taught me, among other things, that institutional transformation cannot be accomplished without first developing an appropriate resource allocation process.[6]

As institutions sharpen their priorities and proceed toward restructuring, they find that traditional resource allocation methods obstruct change—that reengineering is needed. After a firsthand account of traditional line-item budgeting, we examine the assumptions that flow from it and the resulting pitfalls. We also briefly compare two other budgeting systems, revenue responsibility budgeting and performance responsibility budgeting, that represent two polar alternatives to line-item budgeting. Revenue responsibility budgeting maximizes marketplace effects while performance responsibility budgeting emphasizes intrinsic-value effects. Both systems rely on decentralization to mitigate the worst drawbacks of line-item budgeting.

Governments also must confront the question of decentralization. Tight centralized control is an accountability killer—and usually the controls don't work well anyway. Privatization, which represents the governmental analog to revenue responsibility budgeting, has become the approach of choice for many states. The alternative, performance-based funding, which is roughly analogous to performance responsibility budgeting, allocates funding according to an institution's score on some kind of assessment system. Although this idea is hardly new, recent initiatives in the United Kingdom and certain Commonwealth countries have generated renewed interest by relying on performance-based funding on a grander scale than ever before.

Chapter 3, "Productivity Issues in Higher Education," continues our examination of the economic workings of higher education institutions. Starting with the definitions of productivity and gross productivity, we discuss the cost disease and the growth force, two often-cited reasons

---

6. This lesson was reinforced through participation in the Pew Higher Education Roundtable Program and at the annual meetings of the Stanford Forum for Higher Education Futures and its predecessor, the Forum for College Financing.

for higher education's increasing costs. We introduce the concept of growth by substitution, an essential mitigant for cost-rise.[7] After considering higher education's inputs and outputs, we discuss the relation between objectives and productivity, and an institution's production, market, and financial constraints.

The economic theory of decision making in nonprofit enterprises ("value theory"), mentioned earlier, provides the chapter's conceptual core. The theory builds on my work with David Hopkins in the 1970s[8] and also on the work of James[9] and Hoenack.[10] Value theory, which provides the conceptual basis for several later chapters, offers important insights about Bowen's law, the balance between values and market forces, cross-subsidies, and operational efficiency. Brief examinations of economic agency theory and economic externalities follow; then they are applied to the several approaches to higher education resource allocation described in chapter 2. Finally, we discuss phenomena that have strong implications for productivity: the administrative lattice, the satisficing of teaching, and the academic ratchet.

Capital

No book on resource allocation would be complete without consideration of strategic decisions involving capital. Chapters 4 and 5 deal with these questions. Chapter 4, "Endowment," focuses on the relation between endowment investment return and spending for operating purposes. Maintaining endowment's purchasing power, an important goal for many institutions, is rooted in the concepts of programmatic support in perpetuity and intergenerational equity. Achieving the goal requires that an institution develop an appropriate endowment spending rule—in particular, a rule that produces long-run financial equilibrium. The chapter traces the history of endowment investment and spending and then

---

7. These concepts derive mainly from the Pew Higher Education Research Program; they represent a distillation of the combined wisdom of the original roundtable participants and subsequent fieldwork with institutions.

8. David S. P. Hopkins and William F. Massy, *Planning Models for Colleges and Universities*. (Stanford, CA: Stanford University Press, 1981).

9. Estelle James and Egon Neuberger, "The University Department as a Non-Profit Labor Cooperative." *Public Choice* 36 (1981): 585–612; Estelle James, "How Nonprofits Grow: A Model." *Journal of Policy Analysis* 2 (1982): 350–66.

10. S. A. Hoenack, "Incentives and Resources Allocation in Universities." *Journal of Higher Education* 45 (1974): 21–37; Stephen A. Hoenack, "Direct and Incentive Planning Within a University." *Socio-Economic Planning Sciences* 11 (1977): 191–204; Hoenack, Stephen A., and David J. Berg, "The Roles of Incentives in Academic Planning." *New Directions for Institutional Research* 28 (1980): 73–95.

develops the equilibrium spending concept in operational terms. We conclude by describing alternative methods for smoothing the impact of investment-return fluctuations without losing the essential discipline on spending. I developed the ideas in this and the next chapter during my tenure as vice provost and vice president.

Chapter 5, "Optimizing Capital Decisions," addresses the strategic management of all an institution's assets including but not limited to endowment. Institutions have two kinds of capital: financial and physical. Financial capital consists of endowments and invested reserves of various kinds. Physical capital consists of plant and equipment used in the course of operations. An institution's capital structure also may include long-term debt—in effect, negative financial capital. How should one decide what resources should be allocated to physical capital additions and how much should be invested as financial capital? How should one determine the amount of financial leverage: that is, how much endowment and how much debt? Working from the principles of decision making in nonprofit enterprises, the chapter develops a paradigm for optimizing capital decisions based on relative benefits, reversibility of strategies, and the time value of money. Decisions about leverage also involve the purpose of borrowing, internal versus external borrowing, and debt capacity. Strategic financial planning requires an institution to manage its endowment support ratio, the fraction of its operating expenditures supported by endowment. This, in turn, leads to the development of a comprehensive strategy for guiding spending and endowment accumulation.

Decentralization

Decentralization represents the necessary condition for resource allocation reform, as noted earlier. Absent decentralization, rigidities and misallocations will build up to the point where the institution cannot remain true to its mission or respond effectively to environmental threats and opportunities. The difficulty is making the devolution a matter of delegation with accountability and not a de facto abdication of responsibility by the central authorities. Chapters 6 and 7 describe the lessons learned from decentralization in the business and academic communities, respectively.

In chapter 6, "Organizing for Effectiveness: Lessons from Business," Edward Lawler III and Susan A. Mohrman of the University of Southern California discuss whether the type of organizational changes that corporations have developed in response to a global economy are applicable to higher education. Becoming a dynamic learning organization, being simultaneously large and small, achieving customer focus, outsourcing while concentrating on what the institution does best, and getting employees more involved in the business of the university are business-developed strategies that can help institutions increase productivity. Most of these changes involve decentralizing decision making from a central authority to teams of employees. Lawler and Mohrman conclude that the flexibility decentralization has given large U.S. corporations such as IBM and Xerox can be useful to higher education institutions in the new competitive environment.

Perhaps the most widely recognized application of decentralization in the academic community is in administrative and budgeting functions. The three authors of chapter 7, "Revenue Responsibility Budgeting," have all had firsthand experience in implementing a decentralized budgeting system in a university setting. Jon Strauss of the Howard Hughes Medical Institute discusses some of the principles of revenue responsibility budgeting and describes how data generated according to these principles can be used to guide budget decisions even if the institution does not practice decentralized budgeting. John Curry, currently at the California Institute of Technology, describes the actual process of adopting a form of decentralized budgeting at the University of Southern California in the early 1980s. Edward Whalen, author of *Responsibility Center Budgeting*, argues the case for the adoption of decentralized budgeting at public higher education institutions. All three pieces contain both practical and conceptual insights.

Other Contexts

The health care industry faces problems similar to those of higher education. Growth of access and the proliferation of new technologies have driven up costs, and reluctance to subordinate intrinsic values to the discipline of the marketplace has confounded the problem. All of us are familiar with the results: dramatic increases in Medicare and Medicaid funding and the cost of private medical insurance have led to a variety of reform efforts—some of which are causing significant dislocations in medical practice. Chapter 8, "Lessons from Health Care," speculates on how the "diagnosis-related groups" concept now being used to pay hospitals for Medicare cases might be extended to public colleges and universities. Cowritten by David Hopkins, a former Stanford Hospital executive, this chapter postulates the development of "program-related groups" to help structure funding for higher education institutions.

The United States is not alone in its concern about the cost and performance of colleges and universities. Britain and certain Commonwealth countries, for example, have recently implemented major reforms under the rubric of performance-based funding. Such systems distribute funding in the form of block grants with no restrictions on how the money is spent to support institutional purposes. These systems also, however, provide explicit performance monitoring and make future funding contingent on the results. The performance assessments, which generally involve teaching and research as separate exercises, are quite labor intensive. The system's proponents believe this is the only way to maintain accountability for outcomes—and that outcomes accountability is essential for effective resource allocation over the long term. In chapter 9, "Britain's 'Performance-Based' System," Elaine El-Khawas of the American Council on Education and I reflect on possible insights the British experience may offer about the possibilities and problems of resource allocation reform.

Models

My familiarity with the British system derives in part from serving on Hong Kong's University Grants Committee. During the last few years, the committee developed a model to help it determine appropriate funding levels for seven very different institutions in Hong Kong. Higher education funding agencies have long been interested in models that predict costs as a function of enrollments and other activity levels. The Comprehensive Analytical Methods for Planning in University Systems (CAMPUS) and Resource Requirements Prediction Model (RRPM) were adopted by many states during the 1960s and 1970s, and the availability of modern computing power has extended both the capacity and accessibility of such models. The ease of model development and use has led to a proliferation of approaches, however, and recent analytical thinking has complicated the terrain further. A model must address many issues, such as whether expenditures for teaching should be separated from those for institutionally funded research, even when such research is not separately accounted for. In chapter 10, "Quantitative Funding Models," Harry Atkinson and I describe the set of design principles he used to develop the Hong Kong funding model. We describe the model in some depth so that readers may understand the complexity of issues that must be addressed in constructing a model.

Modeling and, indeed, any major decisions about resource allocation require good forms of data about an institution. In chapter 11, "Global Accounts," Gordon Winston of Williams College describes a type of accounting designed to give an accurate and easily comprehensible summary of the financial activities and resources of an institution.[11] Unlike fund accounting, which separates this information into many discrete accounts that may distort or conceal important trends, global accounts provide a comprehensive view of an institution's financial health so that trustees and others concerned with governance can make better-informed decisions. Further, global accounts can be used as the basis of a long-run economic planning model.

Chapter 12, "Value Responsibility Budgeting" (VRB), builds on the previous materials to provide a single template for higher education resource allocation. The template is designed around resource allocation within institutions, but the principles are applicable to allocation by systemwide administrations and governmental funding agencies. As the name implies, value responsibility budgeting tries to strike a balance between market-driven discipline, as in revenue responsibility budgeting, and an institution's intrinsic values. Like performance responsibility budgeting, VRB relies heavily upon the quality of academic plans in relation to institutional mission and on accomplishment in relation to plan. The implementation of VRB can be adapted to emphasize intrinsic values more or less heavily in relation to market forces.

The chapter and book conclude with a discussion of how resource allocation processes should intersect the other dimensions of institutional restructuring. The particular question at issue is whether, and under what circumstances, resources should be withheld from schools or departments whose performance lags behind institutional goals. We describe the particular circumstances in which such withholding could result in a "quality trap." Taking maximal advantage of incentives while avoiding the quality trap requires close articulation between resource allocation and the other elements of an institution's restructuring strategy: the grassroots hands-on processes that lead to empowerment and the full acceptance of responsibility.

We hope we have provided in this selection of essays some ideas that will spark new thinking about resource allocation reform. We hope, especially, that our work will enable institutional and governmental policymakers to address resource allocation processes at a systemic level, and to consider significant reengineering where necessary to empower academic program officers and align their incentives with their institution's mission, vision, and goals.

---

11. This chapter is reprinted from Gordon Winston's "The Necessary Revolution in Financial Accounting," in Michael S. McPherson, Morton Owen Schapiro, and Gordon C. Winston, *Paying the Piper* (Ann Arbor, MI: University of Michigan Press, 1993), 279–303.

CHAPTER 2

Reengineering Resource Allocation Systems

William F. Massy

The golden age for American universities and colleges began after World War II, when research and graduate education were established as major sources of institutional funding, visibility, and prestige. The postwar period also produced major gains in access, with participation rates climbing from single digits to 20 or 30 percent in many countries.[1] This was a time of great faith in higher education, a time of growth and prosperity for institutions and their faculties. The best institutions set their own agendas—in terms of intellectual rather than market values—and these agendas guided most other institutions as they searched for excellence. Universities and colleges reaffirmed their right to autonomy, the ability to define and control their own standards of behavior, even as the proportion of public funding increased dramatically. For fifty years, the public and their legislators bought into the idea that academic quality is proportional to funding—and hence that higher levels of expenditure per student (more quality) are better than lower ones. This proposition, however, is now being challenged in the United States, Great Britain, and many other countries.

Rising educational demand and the incentives to expand research and scholarship have collided with financial constraints—limitations caused by competing social requirements that outstrip resources even in the fastest-growing economies. Moreover, criticisms about higher education's quality, relevance, and costliness have become commonplace. The result has been a profound shift in how the public views universities and colleges, a shift that was summed up this way by the California Higher Education Policy Center:

> Institutional quality should not be judged solely on the grounds of conventional ideas such as prestige and high levels of expenditure

---

1. See, for example, participation rates cited in the U.S. Department of Education, *Digest of Education Statistics*, NCES 93–292.

per student, but also on real-world concepts of productivity, student learning, and efficiency in delivering educational services.[2]

What Is Different?

In the fall of 1991, a group of twenty-four university citizens from twelve countries, ranging from St. Petersburg University in the east to Stanford in the west, met to think through the new concerns. The group consisted of rectors and presidents, higher education scholars, and leaders of organizations concerned with protecting and preserving scholarly institutions. We met three times during 1991 and 1992, and over the course of our conversations we came to this conclusion:

> *Proposition:* The changes most important to the university are external to it. What is new is the use of societal demand—in the American context, market forces—to reshape the university.
> *Principal Corollary:* The failure to understand these changes puts the university at risk. The danger is that the university has become less relevant to society precisely because it has not fully understood the new demands being placed on it.[3]

The growing demand for higher education stems from peoples' desires to improve their employment prospects and a conviction that obtaining more education will bring dividends in that regard. Governments' and institutions' efforts to improve access have led to what the Europeans call "massification," an increased participation in higher education by students of all backgrounds, including nontraditional students, most of whom simultaneously work in the labor market. In the United States, 60 percent of currently graduating high school seniors can be expected to enroll in college in the fall, while the total number of students enrolling in some form of secondary education throughout the year has reached about twenty million, or 8 percent of the U.S. population, an all-time high.[4] Massification also has spawned a heightened sense of vocationalism, not in the narrow sense of blue-collar training but, rather, in terms of acquiring skills in problem solving, communication, teamwork, and information technology that will prove useful in the world of employment.

---

2. The California Higher Education Policy Center, *Time for Decision: California's Legacy and the Future of Higher Education* (San Jose, CA: Discussion Draft, March 1994), 17.

3. "A Transatlantic Dialogue," *Policy Perspectives* 5, no. 1 (1993): 1.

4. Arthur Hauptman, "Higher Education Finance Issues in the Early 1990s," working paper, Center for Research in Education Finance, University of Southern California, June 1992.

Massification and vocationalism focus concern on value for money, the degree to which universities and colleges produce relevant learning in effective and efficient ways. Higher education's critics believe that students are paying more and getting less, that educational productivity has declined. Some critics also point out with increasing stridency that schools do not take full advantage of information technology—that while today's applications demonstrate IT's potential, institutional conservatism stifles truly significant innovation.[5]

Data from the Roper Center of the University of Connecticut's Institute for Social Inquiry document the public's concern about college costs (see table 1). For example, 91 percent of respondents in a 1990 survey felt that most people could not afford college without financial aid. In a 1991 survey, only 25 percent of respondents felt that college was affordable, whereas 87 percent felt that "college costs are rising at a rate which will put college out of the reach of most people." Most worrisome, though, is the 77 percent of 1991 *Money* magazine readers who, when asked whether "tuitions are fairly priced or overpriced," responded that they are overpriced. This well-off group, who also indicated that college cost did not pose a major problem for them, were questioning higher education's value for money and also, perhaps, our integrity.

The resulting sense of entrapment—being convinced of the need for a college education but worrying about its affordability—threatens to reach dangerous proportions:

> The real anger at higher education comes principally from the makers and shapers of public policy—governors, legislators, regulators, heads of public agencies, and surprisingly, an increasing number from the world of philanthropy. Certainly not all, but clearly too many, of those responsible for higher education's funding believe that colleges and universities have become too isolated from the economic pressures that are forcing most other enterprises to rethink their purpose and mission.[6]

Governmental actions reflect these concerns as well as the underlying changes in the environmental context for higher education. Institutions are responding, as we shall see. First, though, let us examine the drivers of change in somewhat more detail.

---

5. See for example, Lewis J. Perelman, *School's Out* (New York: Avon Books, 1992).

6. "To Dance with Change," *Policy Perspectives* 5, no. 3 (1994): 6A.

TABLE 1.   Attitudes about College Costs

	Yes: Can Go without Financial Aid	No: Must Have Financial Aid	Don't Know
Do you think most people can afford to go to college today without financial aid, not?[a]	7%	91%	2%

	Agree	Disagree	Don't know
College costs in general are such that most people can afford to pay for a college education.	25%	73%	2%
I would be able to get a college education at this time only with low interest loans or grants.[b]	74%	20%	6%

	Agree	Disagree	Don't know
College costs are rising at a rate which will put college out of the reach of most people.[c]	87%	10%	3%

	Overpriced	Fairly Priced	
Do you think tuitions are fairly priced or overpriced?[d]	77%	21%	

Source: Roper Center of the University of Connecticut's Institute for Social Inquiry.
[a]Gallup National Poll, adults; June 1990
[b]Gallup National Poll, adults; June 1991
[c]Gallup National Poll, adults; June 1991
[d]Willard and Shullman: National, household financial decision makers who worry about money very/fairly often; Autumn 1991

Vocationalism

Nontraditional students now represent the new majority in American higher education. They are defined as: "(1) all currently enrolled undergraduates aged 25 or older; (b) all undergraduates under 25 years old who did not proceed directly from high school to college, who attend part-time, or who have 'stopped out' for more than one year."[7] Accord-

7. "Breaking the Mold," *Policy Perspectives* 2, no. 2 (1990). The calculations are based on data through 1987 and have not been updated, but information from individual institutions suggests that the trend is continuing.

ing to the U.S. Census Bureau's *Current Population Survey*, the figure for new-majority students as a share of all undergraduate enrollments grew from about 43 percent in 1978 to about 49 percent in 1987.[8] If current trends continue, these students will represent some 60 percent of enrollment by the end of the decade. Upward trends also have been observed in the U.K., Australia, and continental Europe.[9]

New-majority students focus especially on vocational objectives, but the fear of not finding a job after college is redefining the college years even for "rite-of-passage" students who proceed directly from high school to college. Even in the most selective residential institutions, vocationalism now affects everything from the choice of major to the demand for job placement student services. While traditional academic programs may contribute to the employment goal, this can no longer be asserted as a matter of principle. In other words, universities are coming to be valued for what they can *do,* not for what they *are.* As we state in "A Transatlantic Dialogue," "The more general consequence of massification is the public's sense that the university ought to be an engine of economic growth and social equilibrium."[10]

The employment motive's impact on U.S. students cannot be overstated. As recently as 1981, nearly 9 percent of the nation's top-paying (upper quartile) jobs were held by blue-collar manufacturing employees with only a high school education. A decade later that figure was 6 percent, which represents an absolute decline of nearly half a million jobs in a labor force that grew by almost twelve million. America's shift toward a service economy raised the relative earning power of baccalaureate degree holders by some 20 percentage points during the past decade. Even those achieving "some college" are enjoying a significant earnings impact, as employers show increasing reliance on the associates degrees and technical certificates to screen prospective job applicants.[11] A 1993 survey of Californians found that "three out of four . . . agree that even in today's tough economic climate, a young person who goes to college has better economic prospects than one who takes a job right out of high school."[12]

---

8. Ibid., extrapolation from figure 4 in "Profiles" section, 3.

9. "Innovations in Australian Tertiary Education" (paper presented at the OECD Conference on Current Issues in Mass Higher Education: Financing and Innovation, Chiba City, Japan, 8–11 March 1994); "A Transatlantic Dialogue."

10. "A Transatlantic Dialogue," 3A.

11. "To Dance with Change," 3.

12. John Immerwahr and Steve Farkas, "The Closing Gateway: Californians Consider Their Higher Education System" (Public Agenda Foundation for the California Higher Education Policy Center, Sept. 1993), iv.

Value for Money

Parents' financial worries and rising levels of educational debt are fueling concerns about value for money. The value being rewarded by the marketplace shows little tolerance for inefficient or indifferent service, and the market pays little heed to traditional scholarly pursuits. According to a recent Pew Higher Education Program *Policy Perspectives:*

> The most dramatic change is in what the consuming public has come to expect from higher education—and the increasingly pragmatic, even cynical, terms in which the public evaluates particular colleges and universities. "Rite-of-passage" students, paying parents, and the growing number of adult learners who constitute higher education's "new majority"—all seek a reasonable limit to what institutions charge, access to programs that will result in meaningful jobs, a reduction to bureaucratic impediments to a degree, and, above all, real assurances that shifting financial and political fortunes will not place a higher education beyond their grasp.[13]

The same pragmatism is reflected in governmental efforts to buy educational services as cost-effectively as possible. Competing demands on the public purse, coupled with a growing cynicism about whether institutions can control their costs, provide impetus for new resource allocation and performance assessment strategies.

The concerns about cost and price are not unfounded. Between 1985 and 1990, the period of peak cost escalation in U.S. universities, median inflation-adjusted educational and general expenditures per full-time equivalent (FTE) student grew by 4.9 percent per year at private institutions, 2.6 percent per year in public institutions, and 3.8 percent overall.[14] The figures were even larger for those universities offering major research programs: 5.5 percent per year for the private research universities, 4.0 percent per year for their public counterparts, and 4.7 percent overall (fig. 1). The impact of these growth rates, simply stated, is that in the space of five years, the cost per FTE student in private research

---

13. "To Dance with Change," 5A.

14. Data source: "A Call to Meeting," *Policy Perspectives* 4, no. 4 (1993): 23B. Community and proprietary colleges are excluded. Educational and general expenditures exclude direct expenditures on sponsored research as well as dormitories and food service, intercollegiate athletics, and similar activities. Research universities are defined as those institutions that belong to the Association of American Universities (AAU); these institutions account for the bulk of the U.S. academic sponsored research. The "overall" figures are the means of medians for all institutional types.

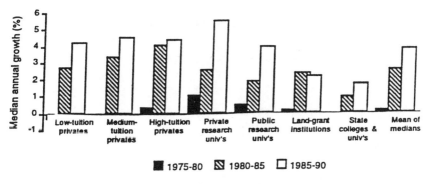

■ 1975-80   ▧ 1980-85   □ 1985-90

Fig. 1. FTE unit costs by type of institution

universities grew by almost one-third. Given the charges about diminishing educational quality during the same period, complaints about productivity loss in higher education have not surprisingly proliferated.

While unit cost increases can inflame public officials and the media, their impact on the general public is multiplied significantly when they drive up tuition (table 2). Private institutions raised tuition at an inflation-adjusted rate of between 3 and 4 percent during the late 1980s, relying on the perceived linkage between cost and quality to immunize them from public reaction. The increases, however, triggered a substantial market and political backlash—indeed, some well-known schools were characterized as "greedy." Private-sector tuition growth has slowed substantially when viewed in nominal rather than inflation-adjusted terms. It declined from 9 percent in 1988–89 to only 6 percent in 1993–94 while remaining essentially constant in real terms—apparently lower inflation has masked the continued increases, but it is doubtful whether such real rates can be maintained when inflation rises again.

Ironically, just as the private-sector pricing pressure seemed to abate, public institutions started raising tuitions at an even faster rate. Beginning in 1991, states tried to mitigate the effects of appropriations cuts on institutional budgets by granting tacit or explicit approval for tuition hikes.[15] In 1990–91, public-sector tuition rose by a startling 9

---

15. State support for higher education declined by 1 percent overall between 1990–91 and 1992–93, according to a recent survey by the Center for Higher Education at Illinois State University. Public appropriations in seventeen states declined between 1 percent and 13 percent, and in an additional twenty states appropriations remained constant or failed to increase enough to keep up with inflation.

TABLE 2. Inflation Adjusted Tuition Growth, 1987–93

Year	Private	Public
1987–88	3%	1%
1988–89	4	0
1989–90	4	2
1990–91	3	9
1991–92	4	7
1992–93	3	7

Source: Data from *Chronicle of Higher Education* annual summary of tuition changes deflated by the Consumer Price Index.

percent, inflation adjusted, and the next two years brought 7 percent increases. State-funded financial aid rose as well, at an average rate of 8.2 percent from 1991–92 to 1992–93, although the gain matched the increases in cost-of-attendance in only ten of the fifty states.[16] As Arthur Hauptman points out, decreases in state appropriations are often the result of slowdowns in the economy, so that tuition increases tend to occur "when students and their families can least afford it, during tough economic times."[17] The market and political backlash has now reached the public sector, and the rate of tuition increases has abated. Nevertheless, America's public universities and colleges now rely significantly less on direct state support than they did even five years ago.

In 1991, my colleagues on the Pew Higher Education Roundtable and I called for institutions to go on a "revenue diet," and curb the appetite for additional real expenditures by reallocating funds from lower to higher priority work instead of asking for additional funds to finance new programs.[18] We feared that continued cost-rise and attendant tuition increases would erode public confidence in higher education. Justified or not, government edict and market action have now imposed the revenue diet.

The resulting cost-price squeeze means that institutions will have to become more efficient. While efficiency has become something of a bad

---

16. Kit Lively, "State Spending on Student Aid Rebounds Sharply," *Chronicle of Higher Education,* April 9, 1993, A24.

17. Hauptman, "Finance Issues," 8.

18. "The Other Side of the Mountain," *Policy Perspectives* 5, no. 1 (1991): 2A

word in academic circles, both theory and empirical evidence demonstrate powerfully that the more efficient an institution can become, the more it will be able to spend on its chosen high-value activities. Many U.S. institutions are pursuing efficiency gains. Bruce Johnstone, then chancellor of the sixty-campus State University of New York, explained the efficiency objective this way:

> Colleges and universities must become more productive: that is, produce more learning, research, and service at lower unit costs— more efficiently. Market and political forces alike are demanding more productivity from all colleges and universities; public and private, undergraduate and graduate, two- and four-year, selective and less selective.

> The challenge is to become genuinely more productive—not just cheaper and shabbier, or less scholarly, or otherwise merely less costly.[19]

To improve efficiency, institutions will have to improve their planning and management systems, tightly focus their activities, and then concentrate on quality—recognizing that they can't afford to do everything while insisting on excellent performance in their chosen areas. Institutions will have to explore continuous improvement and process reengineering methods, which can reduce cost as well as improve quality. Most important, higher education must embrace information technology's potential to transform radically the nature of both academic and administrative work.

Information Technology

Information technology (IT) already represents a significant force in academic life. The Internet, for example, is transforming libraries and scholarly communication. The number of Internet connections has been growing exponentially at 2.9 percent per month, and in early 1993 stood at some 1.8 million sites in 127 countries.[20] Estimating the number of users at 10 per host, this implies 18 million Internet users—and that was in 1993. Vint Cerf, president of the Internet Society since 1991, estimates that the Internet will have 300 million users by the end of the decade.[21]

19. Bruce Johnstone, "Enhancing the Productivity of Learning," *American Association of Higher Education Bulletin* (December, 1993).

20. Mark Lottor, Network Wizards, SRI International, Menlo Park, California.

21. *Wired* 12, no. 12 (December 1994): 154.

Internet access provides for information sharing on a worldwide scale. In the past, libraries tried to collect as much material as possible. But now they can share resources in "real time" (defined according to user needs). By developing sophisticated systems for locating and obtaining user-requested materials, libraries can hold down expenditure growth without eroding service quality by adopting a "just in time," as opposed to a "just in case," acquisitions strategy. Similar economies can be obtained in travel by eliminating the need to employ local experts in arcane subject matter. Via the Internet, the expert in Iceland can be accessed as easily as the one on the other side of the campus. Quality teaching and research can come to depend as much on network connections—of both the electronic and human kind—as on the size of the library and the number of experts on staff.

Distance learning offers another example of how IT can transform education. Multimedia concepts now being developed will improve the quality of distance learning enormously while further reducing its cost. Indeed, the distinction between on-campus and distance education will blur to the point where the term *distance learning* no longer has meaning—the technology will deliver the same services whether the distance is across the campus or across the world. IT will leverage faculty time and dramatically improve teaching and learning. IT also will alter the economics of education and introduce new competition.

Taking full advantage of information technology will require substantial restructuring. Experience from process reengineering tells us that technology enables significant productivity gains but does not guarantee them.[22] So far institutions have made gains in libraries, electronic mail, administration, and distance learning, but the restructuring of core teaching and learning processes is encountering considerable resistance.

But the day will come. In the 1970s, the Carnegie Council on Higher Education celebrated the university's remarkable stability and permanence with the following observation:

> Taking, as a starting point, 1530, when the Lutheran Church was founded, some 66 institutions that then existed in the Western World still exist today in recognizable forms: The Catholic Church, the Lutheran Church, the Parliaments of Iceland and the Isle of Man, and 62 universities. . . .[23]

22. Michael Hammer and James Champy, *Reengineering the Corporation: A Manifesto for Business Revolution* (New York: Harper Business, 1993).

23. Carnegie Council, *Three Thousand Futures: The Next Twenty Years in Higher Education* (San Francisco: Jossey-Bass, 1980).

No wonder change comes slowly to the academy. But now, in the 1990s, we can add the observation that the fundamental technology of information generation, transformation, storage, transmission, and dissemination—the technology of the university—remained substantially the same from the invention of moveable type until the development of ubiquitous, cheap, and powerful information technology a relatively few years ago. It took decades for the electric motor to transform the factory, but the changes were fundamental. The changes in teaching and learning will be just as fundamental.

Institutional Responses

Recent research shows that institutions follow a predictable pattern when confronted with a changing environment and associated financial difficulties.[24] Almost invariably, the first step is to look for new ways to enhance revenue. Tuition may be raised, sponsored research sought, and gifts solicited, for instance.[25] If the financial gap cannot be bridged with new revenue, institutions cut budgets across the board so the pain can be shared as equally as possible. Often such cuts are accompanied by hiring freezes, travel restrictions, and reductions in capital expenditures. Certain exceptions to this "squeezing strategy" do occur, however. Administrators may harbor secret lists of programs that have outlived their usefulness but which would be politically difficult to close in normal circumstances. A budget-cutting climate offers the opportunity to move against these "targets of opportunity," usually in the context of speeches about "making hard choices."

What if these tried-and-true responses are not sufficient to restore an institution's financial health? Two kinds of strategies present themselves: *top-down* and *broad-based*. Top-down strategies start by refocusing administrative and support functions and, if necessary, academic programs. By *refocusing* I mean eliminating or downsizing—ending worthwhile services, popular benefits, or even whole academic departments. Downsizing usually means cutting jobs—making the university less an engine of employment. Hopefully this can be accomplished through attrition, but increasingly, U.S. institutions are resorting to

---

24. Adapted from "A Call to Meeting," 9B.

25. For examples of revenue-enhancement approaches see D. Bruce Johnstone, "The Costs of Higher Education: Worldwide Issues and Trends for the 1990s" in *The Funding of Higher Education: International Perspectives*, ed. Philip G. Altbach and D. Bruce Johnstone (New York: Garland Publishing), 25–44 ; and William F. Massy, "Building a More Entrepreneurial University" (paper presented at the University Operation and Financial Management Conference, Chinese Taipei, March 25, 1994).

outright layoffs. Such actions are painful to all concerned, which leads one to the next response stage: reengineering resource allocation so that future downsizings can be avoided. By improving planning methods as well as associated management information and decision support systems, institutions can improve their elasticity, their ability to adapt to external events without wrenching dislocations.

Broad-based strategies embrace the principles of *continuous quality improvement* (CQI) and *business process reengineering* (BPR). CQI and BPR decentralize quality and efficiency improvement to the individual-worker level. Broadening the base of participation takes longer and requires a different kind of leadership than top-down strategies, but such decentralization is necessary if the university is to become truly efficient and elastic. Employee teams, given the necessary tools and training, are empowered to respond to external events and act on productivity-enhancing opportunities. Performance feedback brings team rewards or, on occasion, a resolve to do better. CQI and BPR now are widely used in business, and universities and colleges are adopting them with increasing frequency.[26] (They are even being used by the Church of England in its efforts to serve members more effectively while making financial ends meet.)[27] The vast majority of higher-education applications are in the administrative and support areas, but initiatives aimed at restructuring academic work are beginning to appear.

This book addresses the lower left-hand box of figure 2, "reengineering resource allocation." The remainder of this chapter will describe the problems with traditional budgeting systems and begin to discuss how institutions and governmental units are decentralizing budget decisions to achieve greater effectiveness, accountability, and responsiveness to the preferences of students and other college and university customers. We shall conclude this chapter by asking how academic values can be balanced with market forces in the new decentralized environment, a question that is central to both the theoretical models and practical applications of this book.

Problems with Incremental Line-Item Budgeting

The traditional university controls resources tightly from the center, using what is called line-item budgeting. The line items usually are con-

---

26. Ted Marchese, "TQM Reaches the Academy," *AAHE Bulletin* 44, no. 3 (November 1991), 3–9; and "TQM: A Time for Ideas," *Change* 25, no. 3 (1993): 10–13; Dean L. Hubbard, ed., *Continuous Quality Improvement: Making the Transition to Education* (Maryville, MO: Prescott Publishing, 1993). The subject also has been the focus of a recent report to England's Committee of Vice-Chancellors and Principals (CVCP).

27. "Nave gazing," *The Economist* 330, no. 7854 (March 12, 1994): 62.

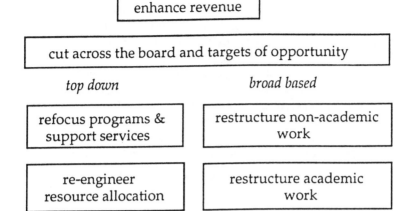

Fig. 2. Institutional responses

sidered on an incremental basis: that is, items proposed as additions (or deletions, in the case of downsizing) are the only ones to be scrutinized. Limits of time and attention prevent the central authorities from continuously reviewing the ongoing budget base. A variant on centralized budgeting uses formulas to determine the level of each expenditure type (e.g., numbers of faculty, expenditures on staff and supplies) according to student enrollments. This ties the ongoing budget base to activity levels, but such formula-based funding also introduces rigidities into the system.

Centralized budgeting generally prohibits operating units from shifting funds among budget categories. For example, eliminating an approved line item might lead to withdrawal of funds on the grounds that the need had vanished. In other examples, moving money from travel to salaries or vice versa might be discouraged and the use of operating money for equipment purchases expressly prohibited. By controlling everything, administrators believe they can ensure that resources will be used effectively.

Nothing could be further from the truth. Centralized resource allocation systems now are generally recognized to be less effective than ones in which goals are shared, operating units empowered to decide how best to attain the goals, and performance feedback maintained through after-the-fact accountability. We shall illustrate the problems with centralized line-item budgeting by the following account based on the traditional system used at Stanford when, as the newly appointed vice provost for research, I joined the Budget Group in the autumn of 1971.

The year's budget process began with the projection of operating-budget revenue, expected inflation and cost-rise on the existing budget, an inventory of "unfunded liabilities," and a call to operating units for their estimates of "new needs." The latter always produced a large compendium of "requirements," items that the deans and support-service managers believed would be needed to maintain or improve quality and to implement desirable new programs. The lists aggregated to hundreds of items, each specified in detail—for example, a new assistant professor or a new secretary, more teaching assistants, new equipment—and each justified by paragraphs or pages documenting "ineluctable need."

The so-called "maintenance budget," the current-year base escalated by inflation and cost-rise, provided a starting point unless we were in a time of budget adjustments. In other words, operating units owned the purchasing power of their existing budget bases unless specific reductions had previously been negotiated. Stanford did adjust its budgets during the late 1960s and early 1970s, eliminating about seventeen percent of the operating base over an eight-year period.[28] Dollar targets were set, faculty committees consulted, and agreements reached to remove particular line-items. This did not negate the principle that a unit owned the purchasing power of its budget base, since items could be removed only after extensive consultation and negotiation.

The annual budget exercise consisted of "closing the gap," because the sum of requirements invariably exceeded the projected available funding by a wide margin. Gap-closing was accomplished with the aid of a device we called a "migration analysis." New requests and unfunded liabilities were "induced to migrate" across a spreadsheet, stopping in one or another column—the last column representing the jackpot: "funded in the operating budget." Stops along the way included "not funded" and, importantly, "funded outside the operating budget base." The latter meant that funding was on a "one-time basis"—that is, the expenditure was authorized for one year, but ownership of the funds was not passed to the unit. Once authorized, however, these items would often acquire a life of their own and come back to haunt us as unfunded liabilities the following year. The word "no" became very difficult to articulate, and efforts to bypass the "not funded" column could reach heroic proportions.

---

28. For a description of tone of these programs see David S. P. Hopkins and William F. Massy, "Budget Equilibrium Program," in *Planning Models for Colleges and Universities* (Stanford, CA: Stanford University Press, 1981).

Another heroic struggle involved the estimation of income. Pressures on the tuition, overhead recovery, and gift projections seemed to grow in proportion to the budget gap. Arguments in favor of higher tuition were marshaled, pencils were sharpened on the overhead calculations, and fund-raising strategies were honed. We extended high praise to members of staff who could find new income sources: one year we described our associate controller as "jumping out of the cake" at the eleventh hour with an unexpected new income projection—and for the next few years we eagerly awaited, and implicitly counted on, his repeat performances.

These efforts were not Machievellian. They did not lack integrity. But they did reflect and reinforce a mind-set that focused on the short run and pushed every income source as hard as possible within that context. We did close the gap, and we did balance the budget. At the end of the day, however, it was hard to see what we had accomplished—other than coping with the year's pressures and maintaining peace among the deans and faculty as best we could. The lists of line items approved, not approved, and funded "one-time" did not add up to a coherent strategy. Worse, we were reinforcing a cycle of growing expectations, thus placing ever-stronger pressures on general-funds revenue sources. Yet it all seemed so rational at the time.

Hindsight illuminates many specific shortcomings of the traditional process. Instead of enumerating these shortcomings in detail, however, let us step back and examine the assumptions implicit in traditional resource allocation. While these assumptions are rarely acknowledged explicitly, their influence on resource allocation within colleges and universities remains powerful. So powerful, in fact, that we will sometimes refer to them as principles rather than assumptions.

The first assumption can be summed up by the phrase, "property rights."[29] Once an operating unit has obtained approval for a program, that program has a right to continue unless circumstances change dramatically. Not unlike a tenured professor—as some have pointed out—these property rights are difficult to withdraw absent financial exigency or some even more dramatic event. Program budgets with tenured faculty lines do involve contractual property rights. Faculty and students are viewed as deserving academic freedom: their programs should not be subject to what might turn out to be capricious or malevolent judgments. The

---

29. Henry Levin, "Raising Productivity in Higher Education," working paper, PEW Higher Education Research Program, 1989.

property-rights principle means that the purchasing power of the existing budget base should be protected as a first priority and that reductions can be imposed only after due process.

The second assumption holds that academic units are too fragile and their work too important to be disrupted by the hurly-burly of the marketplace. Academic time constants—meaning the gestation of academic work and the duration of faculty employment contracts—are simply too long to accommodate short-term financial fluctuations. The central authorities should shield schools and departments from financial fluctuations to the greatest extent possible. Revenue shortfalls should be covered from central reserves, or budget deficits if necessary, until the need for reductions is irrefutable and academic units have been given time to adapt with minimum disruption. The oft-quoted wisdom that "a great department takes a generation to build, but precipitous action can destroy it in a year" reinforces the arguments for caution to hold academic units harmless from market fluctuations.

The third assumption is closely related to the second. It holds that the central administration should *take responsibility* for the financial health of the academic units. Not to maintain adequate funding for a school or department is perceived as an institutional failure—a perception that can be mitigated but not eradicated by blaming external forces. Funding reductions, which administrators want to avoid if at all possible, are perceived as reducing quality. The idea that funding reductions might trigger improved productivity is foreign to the academy. The predominant view is that less funding means "doing less with less." Searching for ways to be more productive, of doing more with less, is not part of the faculty's job description.[30] The institution is responsible for delivering the funding needed to maintain quality using traditional pedagogical methods.

Deeply embedded in the academic culture, the responsibility principle is also reaffirmed in the faculty marketplace. An institution that fails to provide what its faculty feel they need may well find itself on the short end of competitive raiding activities. This concern for faculty morale and the prospect of losing one's best faculty makes "no" difficult to articulate. The result is a vicious circle: administrations believe their job is to protect academic units and faculty from financial vicissitudes, which reinforces the faculty's belief that this is in fact the institution's responsibility, which lowers the tolerance for budget reductions among deans, department chairs, and faculty.

---

30. William F. Massy and Andrea K. Wilger, "Improving Productivity," *Change* 27, no. 4 (July/August 1995): 10–20.

The three assumptions transform resource allocation from an exercise in investment, where scarce resources are put to the best possible uses, to an exercise in coping and conflict management.[31] Such behavior produces a strategy of minimizing the worst breaches of what is seen as administrative responsibility and resulting losses in morale. Since an unadulterated "no" risks serious disruption, this is avoided where possible—unless, of course, the case for funding can be shown to be flawed in some communicable way. Most requests do represent worthwhile endeavors, however, so budget authorities feel besieged. They feel that they have lost control of the process and that the way to reestablish control is to find new sources of income.

Decentralizing Resource Allocation

Decentralization provides an antidote to the negative consequences associated with line-item budgeting. Performance responsibility budgeting (PRB) and revenue responsibility budgeting (RRB) represent successive steps on the decentralization path, and value responsibility budgeting (VRB), introduced in chapter 12, adopts the best aspects of block and revenue responsibility budgeting while mitigating their most serious difficulties.

Figures 3–6 provide process flow diagrams for line-item budgeting and for the aforementioned three varieties of decentralized budgeting. The diagrams provide an overview of where funds are allocated and expended, including how the central authorities, operating units, and support units are connected in terms of authority for initiating transactions. The definitions of these three entities depend on the level of budgeting being discussed. For example, in intra-institutional budgeting the central authority might be a president or provost, the operating entities would be school deans (and possibly department chairs) and support units (other than service centers and auxiliaries). For a state, the central authority would be the system head or perhaps the state budget office, while the operating entities would be campuses or institutions.

In line-item budgeting, which we show to provide a baseline for comparison, the central administration allocates an institution's general funds as indicated at the top of figure 3. In addition, most academic units receive restricted funds in the form of research grants and contracts, gifts, and restricted endowment payouts. Operating units expend funds for personal services (compensation), goods and services from outside,

---

31. Hans DeGroot and Jordan Van der Sluis, "Bureaucracy Response to Budget Cuts: An Economic Model," *Kyklos* 40 (1987): 103–9.

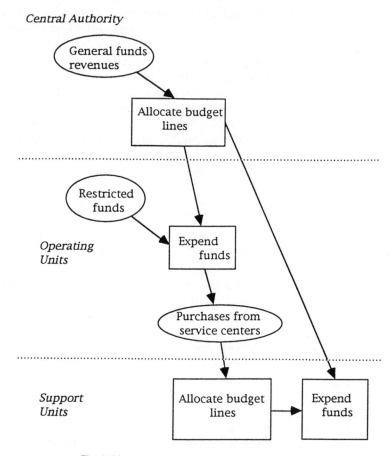

Fig. 3. Line-item budgeting process flow diagram

and outputs from service centers and auxiliaries. Service center and auxiliary spending is determined by the units' ability to sell goods and services to other institutional entities (and to outsiders in the case of auxiliaries): purchasing decisions by customers, based on price and quality, provide for resource rationing. Line-item restrictions usually do not govern these support units; rather, they are free to deploy their available funds in ways they believe to be most effective.

Figure 4 presents the process flow diagram for performance responsibility budgeting. The central authority allocates funding to the operating units in blocks, which can be used as the unit head sees fit. The unit head must allocate resources to lower-level units, which eventually

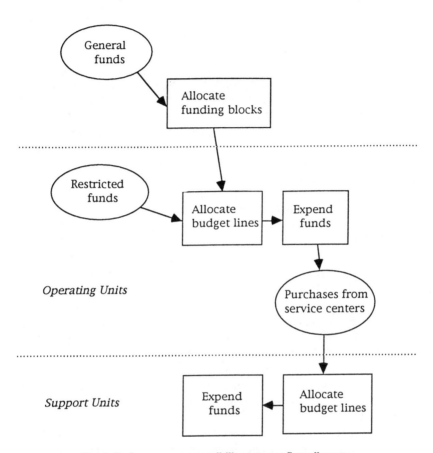

Fig. 4. Performance responsibility process flow diagram

determine individual budget lines against which expenditures can be controlled. The rest of the system works the same as in line-item budgeting, the critical difference being that in performance responsibility budgeting, those closest to the production process—that is, those who possess the best information about the effects of alternative expenditure patterns—make the eventual line-item allocation decisions. Stanford adopted performance responsibility budgeting in the 1980s, when the shortcomings of line-item budgeting became apparent.[32]

---

32. William F. Massy, "Budget Decentralization in Higher Education," *Planning for Higher Education* 18, no. 2 (1990): 39–55.

In PRB, the central authority determines the size of the block grant by first applying a costing formula and then modifying the block according to judgments based on the unit's performance and plans for the future. The costing formula may simply adjust last year's allocation for inflation, or it may take student numbers and other cost drivers into account. (Costing models are examined in chap. 10.) Sometimes the number of tenured faculty appointments is controlled outside the budget process to avoid imprudent long-term commitments, but the number of such regulatory limits tends to be circumscribed. Good performance and plans that advance institutional goals yield added funding—money that can be viewed as a reward for past service or an investment in future prospects. Plans should include information on the unit's revenue enhancement efforts, and less-than-adequate efforts should bring less, not more, funding from the central administration.

In RRB, the central authority allocates revenue lines instead of expenditure lines. Each operating unit is responsible for both its revenues and expenditures. Most revenues are allocated, with only a few truly unattributable lines, such as unrestricted endowment income, placed in the "general revenue" category. General revenues are used to fund central overheads and subventions; alternatively, the general revenues may be allocated by some arbitrary rule (in proportion to assigned revenues, for instance, and then recalled in the form of taxes). As an example of assigned revenues, the tuition "earned" by teaching a certain number of credit-hour enrollment units might be assigned to a school or department, thus comprising "revenue" that the operating unit is free to expend according to its best judgment. The system extends the sensitivity to market forces down through the institution, since operating unit budgets depend on their ability to generate revenue. For example, enrollment shortfalls produce budget consequences, immediately and decisively, the only appeal route being through the difficult subvention route.

The operating units are not generally allowed to expend all their assigned revenue, as demonstrated in figure 5. First, taxes are levied as a percent of revenues, said taxes flowing back to the central authority for redistribution in the form of subventions. The subventions permit the institution to compensate for any market-based revenue shortfalls in relation to cost by applying an "equity judgment." (The equity judgment will reflect the institution's intrinsic values.) For example, a music school that generates little market-based revenue might receive a large subvention, while an affluent business school might pay more in taxes than it gets back in subventions. The taxes also may be used to finance the central authority's own activities, and the activities of support units

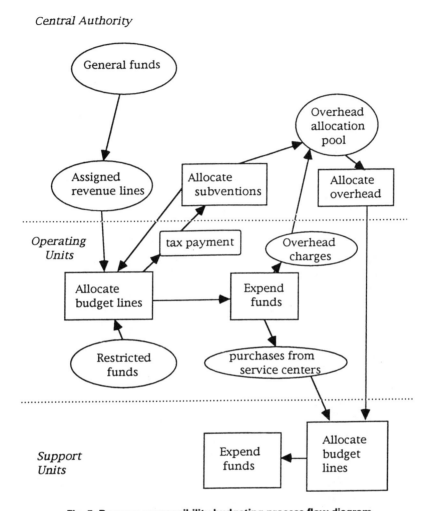

Fig. 5. Revenue responsibility budgeting process flow diagram

(other than service centers and auxiliaries) that do not generate their own revenue. These "income taxes" may be supplemented by "expenditure taxes," overhead payments that also help to fund administrative and support activities.

Revenue responsibility budgeting maximizes entrepreneurship and responsiveness to market forces, but it may prevent the institution from reaching its strategic goals. What the economist calls "externalities" may distort resource allocations, as when one operating unit's decisions adversely affect other units to a powerful extent but the offending unit is immunized from the negative effects by the rules of the budgeting process. An engineering school, for example, might decide to teach its own calculus classes in order to garner the extra income, causing the math department to lose the critical mass of students necessary to fill its classes. Basing the subventions on equity instead of performance limits accountability and fragments planning. Even when externalities are not important, revenue responsibility budgeting may elevate market effects at the expense of institutional values. Institutions try to deal with this problem through subventions, but heavy use of subventions undermines the sense of revenue "ownership" that forms the core of the responsibility center system. Schools tend to resent revenue taxation, and heavy taxation undermines accountability.

At the other end of the spectrum, performance responsibility budgeting significantly dilutes the effect of market forces. The central budgeting authority usually can help smooth over revenue fluctuations, so that the operating units become insensitive to the effects of price and quality on demand. Performance responsibility budgeting also tends to smooth other differences among academic units, including differences stemming from the kinds of performance variations the system is designed to mitigate. Central authorities may defer to the aforementioned property rights principle and forgive performance problems rather than penalize faculty, employees, or students by withdrawing funds. We shall examine this apparent contradiction in chapter 3 and again in chapter 12.

These considerations have led me to propose a hybrid system, *value responsibility budgeting,* which adopts responsibility center concepts for portions of an institution's revenue base and block allocation concepts for the remainder.[33] As shown in figure 6, the system divides an institution's revenue streams into three categories instead of the two used in revenue responsibility budgeting. Assigned revenue lines would be those where: (*a*) the allocation principles are unambiguous and (*b*) externalities are unimportant. For example, tuition from professional masters enrollments or a specialized course in the major might be assigned, whereas general education enrollments might be withheld and placed in

---

33. William F. Massy, "Resource Allocation Reform in Higher Education," (paper presented at the Conference on Resource Allocation and University Management by the Finance Center of the Consortium for Policy Research in Education; University of Southern California, November 19–20, 1992); Value Responsibility Budgeting seems to have elements in common with the system used by De Montfort University (U.K.), described in Michael A. Brown and David M. Wolf, "Allocating Budgets Using Performance Criteria" in P. G. Altbach and D. B. Johnstone, *The Funding of Higher Education* (New York: Garland Publications, 1993): 173–88.

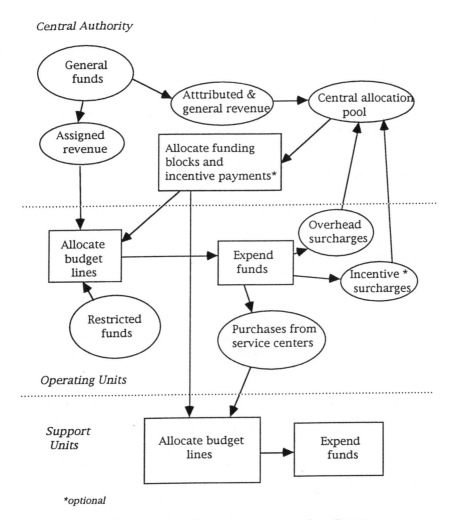

Central Authority

Operating Units

Support Units

*optional

Fig. 6. Value responsibility budgeting process flow diagram

the "attributed revenue" category. Assigned revenues are owned by the operating units as in revenue responsibility budgeting, whereas attributed and general revenues are allocated in blocks as in performance responsibility budgeting. Overhead charges may be assessed, and a new form of transfer, "incentive surcharges," may be invoked to further specific purposes as defined by the central authority. Chapter 12 describes value responsibility budgeting in detail, so we shall not consider it further at this point.

Governmental Responses

Now that we have examined budgeting issues from within the institution, let us turn to similar issues at the level of state and government funding of higher education institutions. Governmental responses to higher education's changed circumstances can be summarized simply: improve accountability. Officials are coming to believe that traditional resource allocation and regulation systems fail to influence significantly, let alone control, the strategic directions of universities and colleges. Without accountability, the argument goes, institutions have tilted too far toward research and scholarship, failed to adapt to student aspirations and needs, and paid too little attention to efficiency.

To improve institutional accountability, governments are moving away from the common incremental budgeting approach and relaxing line-item control if it is being imposed. They are following the decentralization advice given in 1986 by the University of Oregon's L. R. Jones, Columbia University's Fred Thompson, and the University of Washington's William Zumeta:

> it appears that legislators and executive decision makers in government ought to resist the monopoly biases of budgeteers and lend their support to experiments with competitive service supply and per-unit subsidy arrangements in higher education and elsewhere.[34]

The preferred approaches fall into two broad categories: privatization and performance-based funding, both of which strengthen accountability without unduly meddling in institutions' internal affairs. Privatization has much in common with revenue responsibility budgeting as used within institutions. Performance-based funding is somewhat like performance responsibility budgeting but goes further in holding operating units accountable.

Accountability Killers

In incremental budgeting, the government begins by allocating each university and college a certain sum based on past experience and then discusses how much of an increase (or decrease) will be provided in the

---

34. L. R. Jones, Fred Thompson, and William Zumeta, "Reform of Budget Control in Higher Education," *Economics of Education Review* 5, no. 2 (1986): 147–58; see also Mary P. McKeown, "Issues in Higher Education Budgeting Policy," *Economics of Education Review* 5, no. 2 (1986): 159–63 for a discussion of governmental practices and effectiveness circa 1986.

coming year. Unfortunately, focusing on strategic issues or on performance in the context of year-to-year increments is very difficult. Institutions assert property rights to use their current base for existing (or at least their own) purposes, arguing that new state initiatives should be funded as add-ons. The system also has disastrous implications for efficiency, as Derek Bok, Robert Zemsky, and I told the Hungarian government after reviewing their options for higher-education reform:

> [The incremental budgeting] method contains mostly negative incentives. University officials have no reason to save money since doing so is likely to lead to reductions in state appropriations in the following year. Instead, officials will be inclined to spend all the money they receive, whether they need it or not, and to exaggerate their problems and needs in order to receive more money in the future. In addition, the system contains no incentive to consolidate or shut down inefficient programs.[35]

The problems with incremental budgeting are similar to those of line-item budgeting, discussed earlier in the context of institutions' internal resource allocation. Often line-item control is combined with incremental budgeting, which compounds the negative effects of both.

Line-item systems were much more common among U.S. state governments a decade ago than they are at present. For example, in studying one large multicampus university during the 1970s, I found state budget officials had to approve most significant financial decisions. Today that same university operates under a block grant, which gives its officers the freedom *and* the responsibility to expend funds at times and in ways most likely to achieve state and institutional goals. The change was negotiated in the context of severe appropriations cuts: in effect, the chancellor told the governor that he could not be responsible for making the university more efficient without the power to allocate and reallocate resources internally. The state was committed to the cuts, but realized it had to make a choice: continue line-item control and accept deteriorating quality—a "cheaper and shabbier" university—or delegate authority and hold the institution accountable for offsetting the cuts with improved efficiency. The same rule applies when budget cuts are not imminent: accountability and micromanagement don't mix.[36]

---

35. Derek Bok, "Universities in Hungary" (Budapest: Citizens Democracy Corps, October 1992), 10; Derek Bok is president emeritus of Harvard University and Robert Zemsky is professor of higher education at the University of Pennsylvania.

36. William F. Massy, "Measuring Performance: How Colleges and Universities Can Set Meaningful Goals and Be Accountable" in *Measuring Institutional Performance in*

Privatization

In the traditional view of higher education, governments shielded universities and colleges from the pressures of market and political forces. Public policy concerned itself with the health of institutions, on the grounds that universities and colleges are public resources and that education is a public good. The traditional view was founded on the following principles:

> government is the principle provider of public policies relating to universities;
>
> universities provide education to a limited segment of society as a public good;
>
> society influences universities by exerting pressure on the government to change its public policy; and
>
> university traditions of autonomy are designed principally to limit government's capacity to intrude.[37]

Unfortunately, as I noted earlier, government policy and oversight have been unable to assure quality and efficiency to the satisfaction of public officials and their constituents. And if that weren't enough, the same officials are beginning to view the private benefits of a college education (as captured by lifetime salary differentials, for instance) as being more and more important relative to the public benefits of an educated citizenry.

The result has been an increasing "privatization" of higher education by placing greater reliance on tuition and market forces as a substitute for public appropriation. Governments are embracing market principles in hopes that competition will discipline prices, quality, and relevance in ways that bureaucracies cannot, and governments are behaving more like procurers of educational and research services than supporters of institutions. Privatization embraces these principles:

> the role of public policy diminishes as public policy becomes less important for defining universities;
>
> universities, often in competition with other segments of higher education, are expected to provide education and educational services to an ever-expanding segment of society;

Higher Education, ed. William F. Massy and Joel W. Meyerson (Princeton, NJ: Peterson's, 1994), 29–54.
    37. "A Transatlantic Dialogue," 4A.

society influences universities directly through constituency pressures and direct purchases; and

traditional autonomy provides universities less protection from external demands; institutional entrepreneurism rises in response to emerging market opportunities; and the university is less able to integrate demands of external and internal constituencies.[38]

In many parts of America, the public is coming to accept the notion that market mechanisms represent the most practical way to distribute resources, even to the point of determining the relative value of institutional missions according to the enrollments or revenues they garner. Societal demand is being exerted directly on institutions instead of through government mediators.

Privatization need not bring diminished access for disadvantaged students: several mechanisms have been suggested to counteract this trend. Although these mechanisms remain somewhat controversial, most of the controversy stems from a basic disagreement with privatization itself, not the particular mechanism. In at least one state, for example, "serious consideration has been given to ending direct appropriations altogether, replacing them with a voucher system that would make public institutions compete head-on with private institutions for public funds."[39] Even in conventional funding systems, simultaneous increases in financial aid can help offset the effect of tuition hikes on access. "High tuition-high aid" policies target public funds according to financial need, leaving affluent students to pay the full cost of their education.[40] Adopting such policies would end the concern that:

Appropriations for public higher education, particularly at flagship institutions, amount to a public tax for the benefit of the economically advantaged whose children neither need nor deserve such subsidy for their college education.[41]

Performance-Based Funding

Where direct competition isn't practical or desired, governments can simulate market actions by making funding contingent on assessed

---

38. Ibid., 5A.

39. "To Dance with Change," 5.

40. See Michael S. McPherson and Morton Owen Shapiro, *Keeping College Affordable* (Washington, DC: The Brookings Institution, 1991) for a detailed discussion of high tuition-high aid policies.

41. "To Dance with Change," 6.

institutional performance. In other words, government exercises the market function by adjusting its purchase-contract prices and quantities in response to changes in absolute or relative institutional performance.

Performance-based resource allocation has its roots in the so-called assessment movement, which became popular in the United States during the 1980s, but the two are not identical. Assessment now focuses on developing feedback for intra-institutional use as much as on producing externally mandated public "report cards." External assessment represents a necessary but not sufficient condition for simulating market action: a mechanism must be present to translate assessment results into meaningful changes in prices or quantities. Assessment can add value even in the absence of such mechanisms by improving information flow into the real market, but this falls under the heading of privatization. Governments that rely on assessment alone, without privatization or performance-based resource allocation, are likely to be disappointed.

America's assessment movement grew in response to concerns about the quality of higher education. At the beginning of the 1990s, at least fifteen states "used some form of student outcome measure as a basis for evaluation by a state agency." Two states, Tennessee and Colorado, "directly linked budgets to an assessment of university outcome measures," and three other states reported pending recommendations for similar policies. More than a dozen additional states were considering assessment, and all six regional accreditation agencies required "some kind of student outcomes assessment in their review process."[42] The U.S. Department of Education has contracted the development of a battery of comprehensive tests for evaluating college learning outcomes, which may (or may not) prove useful for resource allocation. Despite all the activity, however, one must look abroad for the most comprehensive efforts to implement performance-based funding.

The British government has demonstrated its commitment to performance-based funding by separating the allocations for teaching and institutionally funded research, and by basing each allocation on department-level quality assessments.[43] Funds are provided in block grants, with allocations between teaching and research and among de-

42. Serbrenia J. Sims, *Student Outcomes Assessment* (New York: Greenwood Press, 1992), 56–57.

43. "Tertiary Education in the United Kingdom" (paper presented at the OECD Conference on Current Issues in Mass Higher Education: Financing and Innovation, Chiba City, Japan, 8–11 March 1994); Graeme John Davies, "Successful Revitalization" (paper presented at the Stanford Forum for Higher Education Future Symposium on "Revitalizing Our Institutions," Pacific Grove, CA, October 7–8, 1993); and various circulars published by the higher education funding councils of England and Scotland.

partments being a matter for institutional decision. A similar system has been implemented in Hong Kong,[44] and Australia has introduced a program through which institutions that demonstrate extraordinary teaching quality will be rewarded with additional funds.[45]

The separation of teaching and research contrasts markedly with U.S. practice, where self-funded research usually is comingled with educational funding. Sponsored research, which is kept separate in both systems, accounts for a larger fraction of total research expenditures in America than in Britain because Britain funds academic salaries, laboratory infrastructure, and overhead through block grants rather than projects. The U.S. government's budget pressures, however, have transferred more of the burden to institutions in recent years, so the amount of self-funded research now is substantial. Sponsored research proposals are filtered through a powerful market mechanism, peer review, but self-funded research rarely receives such scrutiny. Self-funded research expenditures manifest themselves mostly in more favorable teaching assignments—for example, reduced loads, fewer preparations, smaller classes, and more teaching-assistant support. Such improvements quickly get built into departmental budget bases and may be regarded as property rights by affected faculty, whether or not they actually do meaningful research.

The antidote to such property rights is a system of performance-based assessments, linked to resource allocation. This is not easy, but experiences in Britain and Hong Kong, and in some U.S. universities, indicate that the job can be done. We will consider the British research assessment process in chapter 9 and the application to funding models in chapter 10.

Evaluating teaching and learning is much harder than evaluating research. The U.K. system remains controversial, for example, even though two different groups (the Funding Council and the Committee of Vice-Chancellors and Principals) currently are actively engaged in evaluation. The task of developing performance measure is not beyond our reach, however. Whereas outsiders have difficulty assessing the delivered quality of teaching and learning, they can fairly easily determine

---

44. The author, as a member of the Hong Kong University and Polytechnic Grants Committee, is an architect of the new system. For a preliminary description, see Nijel J. French, "Higher Education in Hong Kong: Recent Development and Current Issues" (paper presented at the OECD Conference on Current Issues in Mass Higher Education: Financing and Innovation, Chiba City, Japan, 8–11 March 1994).

45. "Financing Mass Higher Education in Australia" (paper presented at the OECD Conference on Current Issues in Mass Higher Education: Financing and Innovation, Chiba City, Japan, 8–11 March 1994).

the presence or absence of departmental quality assurance and improvement processes.[46] Evaluators should look for evidence that faculty systematically assess their own work and that of their peers, and then formulate and act upon improvement strategies. Such processes must operate continuously in order to be effective, so the search for evidence is not difficult. (Alas, few departments can muster evidence of continuous teaching quality improvement.[47]) Institution-level reviews are important because they elicit and discipline department-level processes, but the focus should be on the departments themselves, where the ability to assess and improve educational quality truly resides (fig. 7).

Quality-process audits should not be confused with the evaluation of inputs (for example, expenditure per student or faculty reputation), which have a deservedly bad name in assessment circles. Performance-based measures should never be based on inputs, since that would be circular. Absent good methods for comprehensively measuring student outcomes, the focus should be on how resources are used—that is, on departmental assessments. Such audits can rely on written submissions supplemented with site visits. The approach is rooted in the principles— eminently reasonable in my opinion—that poor teaching is more likely to be caused by inattention and failure to focus on student needs than by incompetence, and that quality will improve if faculty work together to continuously improve their performance. Departmental assessments can ascertain what faculty do and how they do it in addition to capacity and competence.

Values and Market Forces

We have seen how market forces are reshaping the university, making it more responsive, more efficient, and more entrepreneurial. The new focus on societal demand is not merely an attribute of our times but the inevitable consequence of massification and democracy. For institutions to ignore the shift would be fruitless and dangerous. Yet how will market forces affect that most fundamental objective of the classic university—to nurture the community of scholars that since ancient times has conserved and advanced mankind's intellectual and cultural heritage? Under what conditions will academic institutions be able to defend intellectual autonomy in the face of privatization and performance-based funding?

Economic theory can shed some light on this question, and the view

---

46. William F. Massy and Andrea Wilger, "Hollowed Collegiality: Implications for Teaching Quality," *Change* 26, no. 4 (July/August 1994): 10–20.

47. Massy and Wilger, "Improving Productivity," 10–20.

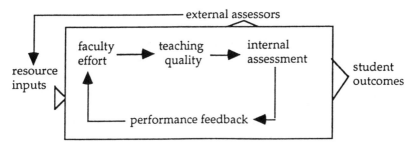

Fig. 7. Departmental process audits

is not encouraging. According to the theory, nonprofit enterprises like universities and colleges choose their activities (that is, their outputs and the associated processes) to maximize the amount of utility produced, where *utility* is defined subjectively by the institution according to its own value system.[48] This contrasts with the for-profit world, where value is defined in monetary terms by stockholders or other private claimants. Nonprofit enterprises also must take account of productivity factors and market forces (production and demand functions in economic parlance), just like their for-profit cousins, and nonprofits must insure that revenues cover expenditures.

I shall describe the theory in chapter 3. For now, let us simply note that universities cross-subsidize activities with high academic value but low market value by using either fixed revenue—that is, funds that do not depend on current institutional performance—or the proceeds from activities that fetch high prices in relation to their costs. This "discretionary revenue" and the cross-subsidies that flow from it distinguish nonprofit enterprises from businesses, where surpluses may be distributed to owners rather than being plowed back into the entity's own activities.

The traditional university received most of its funding in the form of fixed revenue from historically based government appropriations, endowments, gifts, and the like. (Selective private institutions also have been able to charge high tuition without materially eroding student demand.) Thus, they did not have to worry much about market forces. Decisions were dominated by self-defined values, derived (at least in principle) from scholarly deliberations and defended in the name of intellectual autonomy. We have come to equate this kind of independence with the very essence of a university, but that is an oversimplification. The

48. See David S. P. Hopkins and William F. Massy, *Planning Models for Colleges and Universities* (Stanford, CA: Stanford University Press, 1981), chapter 3.

conditions for value autonomy require a high proportion of discretionary revenue as well as high-minded goals and a nonprofit structure.

Privatization and performance-based funding reduce discretionary revenue, thus altering the relative effects of values and market forces in institutional decision making. Both methods do this by design—indeed, making universities and colleges pay more attention to market forces is their primary goal. These forces—transmitted through the price-quantity reactions of real markets or simulated by performance-based funding mechanisms—trigger institutional adaptive behavior. So far so good. But what happens if the process is allowed to go too far?

The aforementioned economic theory predicts what will happen if discretionary revenues vanish and competition drives prices down to rock-bottom levels: *the university will behave like a business.* The loss of discretionary revenue will eliminate cross-subsidies, and with them will go institutions' ability to pursue values not fully shared by the marketplace. One can prove mathematically that, as budget constraints become tighter and tighter, the nonprofit institution's decision rules converge to the form used by for-profit enterprises. That this is not simply a theoretical proposition can be seen from recent developments in higher education in the Peoples Republic of China—where government funding cuts of 50 percent and more have turned some academic departments into essentially for-profit enterprises.[49] In other words, altruistic-oriented not-for-profit entities become slaves to market forces as their viability comes under threat.

Governmental and institutional policymakers must find ways to give effective voice to societal demand while avoiding the limiting case where market forces become completely dominant. Universities must commit to reform, to becoming more efficient and to meeting the rising and more varied demands for postsecondary education *before* being forced to do so by extreme market pressure. Governments must find ways to transmit market signals to institutions without placing them at the mercy of sometimes ill-informed and shortsighted shifts in educational demand.

We need a new social compact, both within colleges and universities and between public institutions and the state funding agencies. The new systems should be designed to give market-derived revenue a significant role in university decision making but still retain enough discretionary revenue to maintain autonomy. The universities, for their part, must

---

49. Personal visits to Beijing; also Yin Qiping and Gordon White, "The 'Marketization' of Chinese Higher Education: A Critical Assessment" (discussion paper 335, Institute of Development Studies, the University of Sussex, 1993).

demonstrate effective stewardship by taking the external society's priorities into account when exercising their autonomy. In the words of "A Transatlantic Dialogue":

> In return for the university's commitment to internal reform, to participating as full partners in the alliance necessary to meet the rising demand for higher education, and to making the provision of social and economic services an integral, indeed equal, part of their missions, public agencies must provide base financial and political support for the university's scholarly functions—which includes protecting and supporting their intellectual and political autonomy.[50]

The compact should extend within universities, to cover schools, departments, and other academic units.

Forging the new social compact will reorient negotiations between governments and universities, and within universities, on a worldwide scale. To quote again from "A Transatlantic Dialogue," the negotiation will take place in the triangular space defined by:

> the rising demand for higher education that has placed a premium on useful knowledge and vocational training;
>
> the university's own demands that its intellectual autonomy and right to define as well as control its own standards and behavior be respected; and
>
> the demands that the university become both more efficient and more accountable, in order to limit its draw on public resources.[51]

Institutions that can demonstrate relevance, efficiency, and responsiveness to societal demand will enter these negotiations in a stronger position than their more traditional counterparts. They are more likely to be successful in defending their autonomy. Ironically, by becoming more adaptive, universities and colleges will best be able to defend their intellectual values.

---

50. "A Transatlantic Dialogue," 9A.
51. Ibid.

CHAPTER 3

Productivity Issues in Higher Education

William F. Massy

Higher education can be described as a "black box" that moves forward in serving students when money is inserted. When money is withdrawn, the box moves in reverse, reducing educational opportunity. Perhaps it is time to open the box, examine the components and see if they can be arranged in a way that will induce more efficient and effective operations than in the past—for example, through more streamlined curriculum, administrative organization, greater use of technology, more relevant priorities.[1]

While the "black box" has represented the traditional model of higher education since World War II, new accountability demands and increased competition are challenging the tradition. Therefore, colleges and universities must "unpack" the black box. They will have to learn how components designed for an era of growth might be rearranged to function better in an era of limits and accountability.

Crafting an effective understanding of productivity requires deep knowledge about—and not a little sympathy with—how things actually work in colleges and universities. First, we consider definitions of productivity and gross productivity and examine two justifications that colleges and universities frequently cite for declines in gross productivity: the cost disease and the growth force. Then we look at improving productivity through growth-by-substitution, which offers a potential mitigant for cost-rise. Second, we begin to unpack the black box by examining its inputs and outputs. Third, we present theories of how those inputs and outputs fit together: the workings of the box itself. From the economic model of productivity that we have presented, we analyze how current

---

1. Patrick M. Callan, "The California Higher Education Policy Vacuum: the Example of Student Fees," policy report, The California Higher Education Policy Center, 1993.

resource allocation systems perform. Finally, we look at two particular phenomena that have strong implications for productivity: the administrative lattice and the academic ratchet.

The Productivity Paradigm

Productivity is essentially an economic concept, and building a proper set of economic models is a necessary condition for diagnosing productivity problems and prescribing antidotes. Unlike business firms, colleges and universities operate on a nonprofit basis and for altruistic goals. The economic models must take this difference into account lest they lead to false or misleading conclusions.

Productivity and Gross Productivity

Economists define productivity as "the ratio of output to input in an organization."[2] This definition works well with a single output and a single input such as students and faculty. To extend the productivity definition to allow for multiple inputs and outputs, we note that inputs incur costs and outputs produce benefits. Suppose the benefits of the various outputs can be compared—that is, measured on a common scale. Then one can add up the benefits and the input costs to calculate a composite productivity ratio:

$$\text{productivity} = \frac{\text{total benefits}}{\text{total cost}}$$

In the case of higher education, inputs and outputs are usually qualitative and multidimensional rather than reducible to countable measures such as tons or units. The inputs and outputs of higher education are also less tangible than those of the standard firm, making them much more difficult to define and measure. Costs are attached to inputs and value to outputs, so the study of productivity, in higher education and elsewhere, attempts to answer the question, "Are you getting what you

---

2. James L. Price and Charles W. Mueller, *Handbook of Organizational Measurement* (Marshfield, MA: Pitman, 1986), 26; Salvatore Corallo, Jeffrey L. Gilmore, and Duc-Le To, "The Productivity of American Higher Education: Issues, Problems, and Approaches to the Problem," working paper, Series on Productivity, Issue No. 1, Higher Education and Adult Learning Division, Office of Educational Research and Improvement, U.S. Dept. of Education, 1988, 12.

pay for?"[3] That, of course, is the salient question behind unpacking the black box.

Although many other, less precise ideas about productivity abound, the relevant questions are as follows: What is valued? How is the value assessed? By whom? Quality represents an underlying concern. If, for example, the quality of a college education had demonstrably improved while costs increased, state legislatures and parents might not be as critical of rising tuition costs. On the other hand, "a gain in the number of outputs per unit of input would not represent an increase in productivity if, at the same time, the quality of outputs declined."[4] In addition to the conceptualization of inputs and outputs, therefore, the quality dimension must be considered when measuring productivity. Yet, for higher education, the quality of its outputs is even more difficult to assess than the quantity of its outputs. Quality is an elusive term that consists of intangible factors,[5] possesses different meanings according to the evaluating audience,[6] and is usually assessed subjectively. These properties of quality make productivity a less-than-precise concept, and go far in accounting for the lack of agreement about productivity's conceptualization and measurement.[7]

Achieving precise quality definitions and measures for higher education's outputs is difficult, perhaps impossible. Achieving consensus about proxies also is difficult, because educational quality has so many nuances that judgments about it are subject to conflicts of interest. One answer is to avoid using such definitions or proxies. Following Baumol, Blackman, and Wolff,[8] one can define *gross productivity* as "the number of units of output produced per unit of input, *with no attempt to adjust for any accompanying changes in product quality*" [emphasis in the original]. They demonstrate that gross productivity can "be extremely important in explaining the behavior over time of relative prices of different

---

3. Corallo, et al., "Productivity of American Higher Education," 12.

4. Ibid., 212.

5. David S. P. Hopkins and William F. Massy, *Planning Models for Colleges and Universities* (Stanford, CA: Stanford University Press, 1981).

6. Robert Birnbaum, "Why Productivity Doesn't Improve: The View from the Campus" (paper presented at the Symposium on Productivity in Higher Education, sponsored by the Forum for College Financing, Annapolis, MD, October 26–27, 1989); Richard J. Meisinger, Ralph A. Purves, and Frank A. Schmidtlein, "Productivity from an Interorganizational Perspective," *New Directions for Institutional Research* 8 (winter 1975): 91–115.

7. Yehouda A. Shenhav and Yitchak Haberfeld, "The Various Faces of Scientific Productivity: A Contingency Analysis," *Quality and Quantity* 22 (1988): 365.

8. William J. Baumol, Sue Anne Batey Blackman, and Edward N. Wolff, *Productivity and American Leadership* (Cambridge, MA: M.I.T. Press, 1989), 235.

goods and services, in budgetary planning for various public sector activities [including public and private higher education], and in planning to
meet future manpower requirements." The rise in unit costs of higher
education that critics continually cite is, in fact, a gross productivity
indicator.

Policymakers can accept gross productivity as the relevant definition, look at the evidence, and then evaluate the causes of the observed
changes. Doing so will provide insight about quality changes. Inflation-
adjusted expenditures per full-time student, for example, increased at a
median rate of 4 percent per year for all institutions between 1985 and
1990 (the range was 5.5 percent for private research institutions to only 2
percent for state colleges and universities).[9] In the end, the policymakers will have to answer the binary questions, "Are the remaining unex-
plained cost increases indeed due to quality changes and, if so, are they
worth it?" While this strategy doesn't dispose of the quality problem, it
is far more satisfying than simply accepting or rejecting assertions that
observed cost-rise reflects desirable quality improvements.

The Cost Disease and the Growth Force

Colleges and universities offer two justifications for why gross productivity has declined. The so-called cost disease is said to require continuous
real cost-rise in order to maintain quality. The growth force represents
the collection of built-in drivers that push institutions to improve quality
at ever higher cost.

The Cost Disease. The cost disease depicts the problem labor-
intensive organizations like colleges and universities face when they try
improve their productivity.[10] The most well-known example, from economist William Baumol, is that of the string quartet. As labor-intensive
enterprises, string quartets are resistant to productivity increases. For
example, the performance of a thirty-minute piece requires two person-
hours, and two centuries ago that person-hour requirement was exactly
the same. Any effort to reduce the time would be disastrous. Playing

---

9. Scott W. Blasdell, Michael S. McPherson, and Morton Owen Schapiro, "Trends
in Revenues and Expenditures in U.S. Higher Education: Where Does the Money Come
From? Where Does it Go?" in Michael S. McPherson, Morton Owen Schapiro, and
Gordon C. Winston, *Paying the Piper* (Ann Arbor, MI: University of Michigan Press
1993), 15–34.

10. William J. Baumol and Sue Anne Batey Blackman, "Electronics, the Cost
Disease, and the Operation of Libraries," *Journal of the American Society for Informa-
tion Sciences* 34, no. 3 (1983): 181–91; and Baumol et al., *Productivity and American
Leadership*.

faster would cut the person-hour requirement, but who would enjoy the result? The second violin might seem redundant, but those who appreciate string quartets will attest to its essential role. So the two person-hours persist from generation to generation. Economists call this "stagnant productivity."

In the meantime, the labor requirements for other goods and services produced in the economy have been decreasing. The fruits of these gains are shared with workers in the form of increased real (inflation-adjusted) wages. Because the musical industry competes in the general labor market, the industry must match these real wage increases if it is to recruit new players. Other things being equal, this means that ticket prices must rise in real terms. Over time, tickets will cost more and more relative to prices for other goods and services that have, on average, been enjoying the productivity increases denied to the string quartet. This upward creep of real price, and the underlying unit cost, is what we mean by the cost disease.

On its face, the cost disease seems to provide a strong justification for higher education's price and unit cost escalation. Colleges and universities are undeniably labor intensive: between 70 and 80 percent of operating expenditures go to wages and benefits according to most estimates. Moreover, academic production is sticky in the sense that student-faculty ratios are often perceived as surrogates for academic quality.[11] No wonder, then, that unit costs keep spiraling upward: one might say that "as long as quality is maintained, nothing can stop them."

We disagree. First, the numbers don't add up. The cost disease can account for one percent or so of cost-rise at most, whereas under normal conditions institutional costs tend to grow at two or three times that rate. Productivity increases in the United States rarely exceed $1\frac{1}{2}$ to 2 percent on a sustained basis, and faculty compensation rarely exceeds 50 to 70 percent of educational and general expense. Assuming the rest of an institution's activities are subject to average productivity gains, the productivity-stagnant part should not drive costs faster than the product of these two figures: 1 percent in round numbers.

Even stronger reasons exist for refusing to accept the cost-disease argument uncritically. We saw that traditional budgeting projects the maintenance level of expense and, absent budget adjustments, treats it as a floor for subsequent allocation decisions. This includes the cost disease as an element of policy because deans and department chairs are

---

11. Robert Zemsky and William F. Massy, "Expanding Perimeters, Melting Cores, and Sticky Functions: Toward an Understanding of Current Predicaments" (paper written for The Cost of Undergraduate Education Project), May 1995.

unlikely to examine critically a budget base that already has been vetted for funding. The policy reinforces sticky production rather than encouraging a search for more cost-effective educational methods. Hence the cost disease becomes a self-fulfilling prophecy. Only by challenging the cost-disease assertion can one test its underlying assumption of stagnant productivity.

Such tests may be successful in today's environment. Though the process is slow, information technology promises to transform higher education's productivity. We believe that it is only a matter of time before the traditional lockstep between student-faculty ratio and educational quality comes to be seen as outdated. Faculty will not become irrelevant, but their roles and responsibilities will change. A new mix of capital and labor, and of faculty and nonfaculty labor, will improve value for money without diminishing quality. Consider how information technology has diminished the cost disease for the string quartet. Those two person-hours can now bring musical benefits to countless thousands via compact discs at ever-lower unit costs. Despite higher musician wages, the attendant financial returns can lower ticket prices for those who wish to enjoy the greater ambience of the concert chamber. The quartet's productivity is no longer stagnant. The same benefits will accrue to higher education.

The Growth Force. Many a university president has pointed out that the opportunities for education and research—and, indeed, knowledge itself—grow without limit.[12] They say that, because their universe is expanding, universities and colleges must grow continually in order to maintain their excellence and their place in the academic pecking order. The traditional view of library acquisitions was to collect a "constant share of world book production," which is expanding at an exponential rate.[13] A continuous stream of new academic programs is required for an institution to maintain its vitality: each decade brings new scientific discoveries and literatures, with little diminution of the old. Departments desire new faculty to bring in fresh ideas and cover new specialties, thus increasing the total number of faculty required to cover a given field.

Regulation is often cited as the second driver of growth. Undoubtedly, colleges and universities are subject to much more regulation than they were two or three decades ago. Institutions are no longer exempt

---

12. See, for example, Donald Kennedy, "How Can We Look So Rich, Yet Feel So Poor?" (paper presented at the Stanford University Alumni Conference, Los Angeles, CA, 1986).

13. An increasing number of institutions are using information technology to substitute "just in time" for "just in case" library service.

from the National Labor Relations Act and have never been exempt from the growing body of health and safety, affirmative action, and environmental rules. Institutions receiving federal research funds now are expected to field accounting systems that meet the highest standards of integrity and detail. While decreased state line-item budget control has brought some relief for public institutions, the assessment movement and similar initiatives have added substantial information-generating burdens. As these requirements increase unit costs, they drag down gross productivity.

While these growth forces are undoubtedly real, citing them falls short of explaining why gross productivity has declined. Why, one may ask, hasn't the productivity of other activities increased enough to offset these cost increases? We asserted in chapter 2 that traditional budgeting systems provide little incentive for productivity improvement. Now it is time to examine that question in more detail.

Improving Productivity

The productivity improvement idea does not come naturally to faculty, but it is not foreign to them either.[14] When faculty think about improving their own productivity they talk of:

> increasing benefits while holding costs constant or, better, increasing resource utilization while increasing benefits faster.

In other words, for faculty, improving productivity means increasing the level and quality of output: hopefully, "doing more with more." This view of productivity is closely related to the growth force.

External stakeholders hold a different view. For them, productivity improvement is more likely to mean:

> reducing cost while holding benefits constant, or, in tight financial times, reducing cost faster than any erosion of benefits; or
> increasing benefits while reducing costs ("doing more with less").

For people who hold this view, increasing productivity means finding more cost-effective ways to do things. Productivity is linked with the ideas of efficiency and reengineering.

---

14. William F. Massy and Andrea K. Wilger, "Improving Productivity," *Change* 27, no. 4 (July/August 1995): 10–20.

The two views might seem incompatible, but reconciling their differences is possible through a third view of productivity. The economic theory of nonprofit enterprises holds that institutional decision makers maximize total benefits subject to a limit on total expenditures. Because of the expenditure limit, the model implies "growth by substitution" rather than any requirement for reducing total cost.

To practice growth by substitution, decision makers look for ways to shift resources toward areas where the return per extra dollar is highest. Formally, growth by substitution implies that changes in benefits divided by the associated change in cost ("marginal cost-effectiveness") should be equal across all activities and programs. If the ratios are not all equal, resources should be moved from activities with lower marginal cost-effectiveness to those with higher marginal cost-effectiveness. In other words, decision makers adopt the faculty view of productivity for the growth element of growth by substitution. They try to find programs and areas where extra resources can be invested to good effect. So far so good.

Growth by substitution also requires, however, that resources be taken away from present "owners," thus violating the principle of property rights. By focusing on *relative* cost-effectiveness, growth by substitution requires that resources be shifted from programs with lower to higher marginal cost-effectiveness even when the former produce good results in absolute terms. For example, a dean might tell a program director:

> I have good news and bad news. The good news is that you're doing a great job, the money you're spending produces real benefits. The bad news is that I'm closing you down because your colleague down the hall produces even greater value for money.

Such a scenario would seem arbitrary and unfair to most faculty. They would object that the judgments about marginal cost-effectiveness are flawed and that budget allocators have no right to make them in the first place. These concerns merit consideration. Such judgments are extraordinarily difficult to make, and one can never be sure that they are free from error. More important, the definition of *benefits* lies to some extent in the eye of the beholder. Literature will be more important to an English professor than to a chemistry professor, for example. Building an area of excellence in chemistry at the expense of English probably would seem arbitrary and unfair to humanists, no matter how careful the judgments and how extensive the consultations. These are some of the reasons that the assumption of property rights arose in the first place: to protect good work, and those doing good work, from others' judgments about benefits.

Unfortunately, the principle of property rights does more than protect good work. The principle also locks in past definitions of excellence and relevance, thus preventing an institution from adapting to changing conditions. Even worse, property rights can protect programs that have declined in quality and blunt incentives for improvement. A program has to be of demonstrably unacceptable quality before it can be reduced or eliminated. This represents a difficult burden of proof, so that another principle, "live and let live," often enters by default.

Institutions must add new programs in order to retain their vitality. As long as the principle of property rights remains paramount, the growth force will press institutions to increase resources wherever and however they can. Self-imposed efforts to moderate price escalation can be effective when other revenue sources are growing, but these efforts do not last long when finances become scarce. External funders may respond to the academy's exhortations for greater largesse, but what happens when those funders suffer financial difficulties?

Will colleges and universities simply "freeze up" when revenues cease to expand, or will they find ways to grow by substitution despite the strength of internal property rights? This book is about how to "unfreeze" resource allocation and grow by substitution. To search for clues about how to do this, we shall now proceed to unpack the black box.

Unpacking the Black Box

Unpacking the black box requires that we examine in detail the principles of resource allocation decision making in colleges and universities. This section begins by looking at higher education's inputs and outputs, then moves to the relation between objectives and productivity, and ends with consideration of the production, market, and financial constraints that all institutions face. The next section integrates these components into a unified theory of resource allocation decision making.

Inputs and Outputs

The characteristics of higher education's inputs and outputs that make them difficult to measure are the following: they are very numerous, some are highly intangible, and many of their values accrue over time. Table 1 presents the list developed by David Hopkins and me in the mid-1970s and refined by Hopkins ten years later.[15] Other authors offer

---

15. Hopkins and Massy, *Planning Models*.

TABLE 1. Inputs and Outputs of Higher Education

		Tangible	Less Tangible
Inputs		New students matriculating	Quality and diversity of matriculating students
		Faculty time and effort	Quality of effort put forth by faculty
		Student time and effort	Quality of effort put forth by students
		Staff time and effort	Quality of effort put forth by staff
		Buildings and equipment	Quality, age, and style of buildings; age and quality of equipment
Outputs		Library holdings	Quality of library holdings
		Supplies, travel, etc.	
		Student enrollment in courses	Quality of education obtained
		Degrees awarded	Quality of education obtained
		Research quantity: awards	Quality of research performed articles, and citations
		Services to the general public	Quality of services rendered

Sources: Adapted from table 1 in David S. P. Hopkins, "The Higher Education Production Function: Theoretical Foundations and Empirical Findings," in Hoenack and Collins, eds., *The Economics of American Universities* (Albany, NY: SUNY Press, 1990), 11–32 and from table 3 in Hopkins and Massy, *Planning Models for Colleges and Universities* (Stanford, CA: Stanford University Press, 1981).

variations that are important for quantitative modeling,[16] but the list in table 1 is sufficient for present purposes.[17]

The basic inputs of colleges and universities are faculty, student, and staff effort plus supplies, travel, etc., as well as capital stocks like buildings and library materials. The basic outputs consist of education, research, and public service. Within education, one can distinguish between the teaching function itself and the certification value associated with the attainment of a degree. The quality dimension is important for all items in the list, but higher education especially focuses on the quality of educa-

16. See, for example, June O'Neill, "Productivity Trends in Higher Education," in Joseph Froomkin, Dean Jamison, and Roy Radner, eds., *Education as an Industry* (Cambridge, MA: Ballinger, 1976), 349–65; G.C. Archibald, "On the Measurement of Inputs and Outputs in Higher Education," in Keith G. Lumsden, ed., *Efficiency in Universities: the La Paz Papers* (New York: Elsevier Scientific Publishing Co., 1974), 113–30; Elchanan Cohn and Michael J. Morgan, "Improving Resource Allocation Within School Districts: A Goal-Programming Approach," *Journal of Education Finance* 4 (summer 1978): 89–104; Jeffrey Ernest Olson, "Values Implicit in Resource Allocations of Universities," Ph.D. dissertation, Stanford University School of Education, 1989; Howard P. Tuckman and Cyril F. Chang, "Participant Goals, Institutional Goals, and University Resource Allocation Decisions," in Stephen A. Hoenack and Eileen L. Collins, eds., *The Economics of American Universities* (Albany, NY: SUNY Press, 1990), 53–72.

17. See also the bibliography compiled by Klaus Hufner, Thomas R. Hummel, and Einhard Rau, *Efficiency in Higher Education: An Annotated Bibliography* (Frankfurt am Main: P. Lang, 1987).

tion and research outputs and of the faculty and student inputs. Finally, the value of research and education does not accrue immediately. It may be spread out over a whole lifetime or even multiple generations.

The inputs and outputs listed in table 1 are far from homogeneous. Take "degrees awarded," for instance. These include undergraduate degrees, professional degrees of various types (from masters of business administration to doctors of medicine), terminal masters degrees, and research doctorates (the Ph.D.). Certificates from continuing education and two-year undergraduate programs also should be counted in any "degrees awarded" output measure. "Student enrollment in courses" and "student time and effort" also vary significantly, even for students in the same degree program. Students have different majors, and sometimes even students in the same major approach the subject with different aspirations, aptitudes, and levels of preparation.

Though an improvement over looking at simple per-student costs, analyzing productivity at the level of aggregation depicted in table 1 will obscure many interesting and important relationships. A more considered analysis of productivity requires that the outputs be segmented by type of program and type of student. We cannot specify all the segmentation criteria here, but some broad desiderata can be laid down. First, education almost always should be segmented according to level: two-year undergraduate, four-year undergraduate, professional, graduate (disciplinary-based, usually oriented toward research), and continuing. Further segmentation is required for the analysis of productivity within individual institutions. Both education and research should be segmented at least according to subject matter domain—that is, by broad groupings of disciplines. The following breakdown represents a good combination of refinement and parsimony for many purposes: humanities, languages, natural sciences, mathematics, and social sciences.[18] In addition, institution-level analysis requires differentiation of full- and part-time modes of attendance, of traditional and nontraditional students and, in many cases, whether the student is "at risk" or not.

Objectives and Productivity

With such a range of choices, how do colleges and universities determine their input and output mix? How *should* they choose their input and output mix? These two different questions frame any analysis of institutional productivity, because a university may well be productive but not

---

18. This breakdown is being used by Robert Zemsky and me in our empirical models of academic departments.

in the ways deemed useful by those who pay for higher education. For this reason, we will briefly consider the goals of higher education, both from the point of view of society at large and of those who work within institutions, before moving on to how those inputs and outputs are actually chosen.

From the standpoint of social policy, colleges and universities should strive to enhance welfare by producing an educated citizenry, a qualified and motivated workforce, and a continuing stream of creative ideas and conceptual breakthroughs— including, but not limited to, scientific research. Furthermore, higher education is supposed to improve equity by offering opportunities for the disadvantaged to better themselves, both socially and economically. Viewed from a private perspective, schools should deliver on their promise to provide the basis for a meaningful life, and, in most cases, a premium in lifetime income.

Few would quarrel with these goals, but a number of factors limit the degree to which they are operationally meaningful. First, the intangible character of higher education's outputs makes the goal definitions hard to pin down. Second, even if precise definitions could be developed, the task of measuring results would still be daunting. Finally, it is by no means clear that—lip service aside—the factors motivating institutional decision makers coincide very closely with the list of overarching social and private goals.

For those within the institutions, the goals of higher education can in fact seem quite different. Many authors argue that institutional prestige is the overriding operational goal of college and university decision makers.[19] Prestige provides professional fulfillment for faculty and administrators; it enhances the value of the degree, thus improving application and acceptance rates; and, it improves the prospects for obtaining gifts and sponsored research support. At some level, prestige probably correlates with achievement of the aforementioned social and private goals, but the relationship does not appear to be as strong as one might hope. Since prestige appears to correlate with high-visibility research, universities and colleges that strive for prestige may emphasize research at the expense of teaching. Although teaching and research are often complements, our later analysis of the academic ratchet suggests that

---

19. David W. Breneman, "An Economic Theory of Ph.D. Production," Office of the Vice President—Planning and Analysis, University of California (Berkeley), Research Program in University Administration, 1970; David Garvin, *The Economics of University Behavior* (New York: Academic Press, 1980); Estelle James, "Decisions Processes and Priorities in Higher Education," in Hoenack and Collins, eds., *The Economics of American Universities*, 77–106.

many schools carry research beyond the point of diminishing returns to teaching quality.

The heterogeneity of goals within higher education institutions represents another source of concern: groups within the institution may work toward different and sometimes conflicting goals. In particular, faculty heavily influence decisions in many colleges and universities. They tend to be oriented toward their discipline and be somewhat more distant from the schools' external constituencies than are the trustees and officers. Faculty wish to emphasize prestige, but they care more about increasing the prestige of their particular department than general institutional prestige.[20] Where different departments compete for funds in a zero-sum game, departments with highly visible and productive faculty have greater bargaining power. Not only can those departments offer promises of increased prestige, but individual faculty may also threaten to leave if their demands are not met. Discrepancies in bargaining power thus reinforce the polarities between strong departments and weak departments: as Estelle James writes, strong departments are likely to stay strong, while weak departments may become even weaker.[21] These trends have increased in recent years, to the point where my colleague Robert Zemsky and I have come to believe that faculty behave more as independent entrepreneurs than as institutional "officers of instruction."[22]

The following list of college and university goals is based on James's recent literature review.[23] These goals confirm the observations that faculty heavily influence decisions and that maximizing prestige is a major goal for many institutions.

Goal 1. *Research and low teaching loads:* faculty tend to enjoy research more than teaching, and research contributes to the discipline and to individual visibility as well as institutional prestige.

Goal 2. *Quantity of undergraduate and graduate students:* graduate students are valued because of their contributions to research and propagation of the discipline; undergraduates probably are positively valued in colleges that specialize in teaching but may be negatively valued (at the margin) in research universities.

---

20. Estelle James, "Decision Processes and Priorities in Higher Education," in Hoenack and Collins, eds., *The Economics of American Universities*, 98–100.

21. Ibid., 99.

22. "Testimony from the Belly of the Whale," *Policy Perspectives* 4, no. 3 (Sept. 1992).

23. James, "Decision Processes and Priorities," 80–87.

Goal 3. *Quality of students:* better students are more fun to teach and do better at teaching each other; good students also show better in public announcements of admissions statistics and tend to do better after graduation, thus contributing more to institutional prestige.

Goal 4. *Class size and teaching support services:* since independent assessments of educational outcomes are difficult, class size and teaching support services may be viewed as proxies for quality. Cost reductions are resisted on grounds of quality erosion. As in Williamson's "expense-preference firm," expenses may also be viewed as goals in and of themselves.[24]

Goal 5. *Teaching quality:* anecdotal evidence suggests that teaching quality may be important for colleges, but that it is much less important than research in the case of universities; none of the models (of research universities) James surveyed includes any direct measure of teaching quality or outcomes from learning in its lists of objectives.

Professor Zemsky and I have modeled the faculty's trade-offs between teaching load and class size, the determinants of their discretionary time and, therefore, of their capacity for research.[25] Not surprisingly, we demonstrated that faculty generally prefer lower teaching loads even when loads are already low. Preferences for class sizes reflect monitoring by the central administration: classes smaller than the departmental norm for a given type of pedagogy (e.g., a seminar or a lecture) are not always favored for fear that underenrolled courses may be cut. Our results also imply, however, that over the years, lower class sizes have come to be accepted as the new norms, thus increasing faculty discretionary time. The results reinforce James's notion that research and publication tend to overtake teaching in the competition for faculty time and attention, and that the imbalance has been increasing.[26]

Zemsky and I also believe that institutions value faculty intrinsically, like monks in the medieval monastery. In a 1988 survey of more than 200 department chairs asking how they would spend their department's money if given a free choice, only one chair suggested that he could function with fewer tenure track faculty in return for more depart-

---

24. Oliver Williamson, *The Economics of Discretionary Behavior: Managerial Objectives in a Theory of the Firm* (Englewood Cliffs: Prentice Hall, 1964).

25. William F. Massy and Robert Zemsky, "Faculty Discretionary Time: Departments and the 'Academic Ratchet'," *Journal of Higher Education* 65, no. 1 (January/February 1994): 1–22.

26. "The Lattice and the Ratchet," *Policy Perspectives* 2, no. 4 (June 1990).

mental research money and secretarial support.[27] Despite the economic benefits of leveraging faculty through a pyramid of secretaries, graduate students, and others, most chairs and deans nevertheless want more faculty. This leads us to add a sixth goal to James's list:

Goal 6. *Quantity of tenure-line faculty:* faculty are valued because they represent the "community of scholars" upon which the traditional college or university is modeled. Adding faculty extends the community and often expands the department's range of subdisciplines while diffusing the pedagogical load.

These goals help explain the growth force discussed earlier in this chapter. Unlike the for-profit firm, where the fruits of gross productivity improvements "drop to the bottom line," colleges and universities strive to *increase* expenditures per unit of output. This is not necessarily an unreasonable objective, since such expenditure increases may indeed improve quality. Institutions, however, should assure themselves that the quality increases will be forthcoming, that they can be financed, and that they represent incremental value for money for those who will pay the bills. These questions move us from consideration of values alone to consideration of values in the context of production, market, and financial constraints.

Production, Market, and Financial Constraints

Like other enterprises, colleges and universities must abide by certain realities of economic life. Production constraints limit what can be accomplished using any mix of inputs and activities. Market constraints, the familiar "demand functions" of economic parlance, represent what people outside the enterprise are willing to pay institutions to produce. Financial constraints reflect the obvious fact that institutions cannot continually spend more money than they receive, lest they go bankrupt and cease to exist. How the three types of constraints interact with the aforementioned objectives to determine institutional activities will be discussed in the next section.

Production constraints stem from technical, legal, and behavioral factors. Technical constraints indicate factors beyond human control. For example, there are only so many hours in a day, a certain computer only runs so fast, a given classroom can seat only so many people, and reading or listening can produce only so much learning per unit of time

---

27. "Double Trouble," *Policy Perspectives* 2, no. 1 (Sept. 1989).

even under optimal conditions. Legal constraints are determined by people but are beyond the institution's control. These include health and safety regulations, record-keeping requirements, and the need to safeguard the rights of employees and students. Behavioral factors include teaching-load and class-size norms, views about the proper style of pedagogy, and similar considerations that, though changeable in principle, may be deeply embedded in the institutional culture.

Market constraints stem from the decisions of independent actors with whom the institution engages in economic transactions.[28] We shall refer to such actors as the institution's "clients," which implies a closer relationship than "customer" but a degree of independence nevertheless. Clients usually do not share the institution's full set of objectives but instead offer money in exchange for benefits. The benefits may be tangible or intangible, and they may or may not be costly for the institution to provide. The key issue is whether the benefits are worth their cost to both institution and client. If so, a transaction ensues and money changes hands. If not, the university does not receive the funds: no matter how strongly it feels about *its* objectives, it can do nothing except change the terms of the offer to better accommodate the objectives of the potential client.

Students, research sponsors, donors, and some state funding agencies can be fruitfully viewed as clients. Students seek educational benefits and in return pay tuition and fees while suffering the opportunity loss of forgone earnings. Research sponsors seek research results, either

---

28. There have been many studies of enrollment demand for higher education. Cf.: Joseph E. Hight, "The Demand for Higher Education in the U.S., 1927–72: The Public and Private Institutions," *Journal of Human Resources* 10 (1975): 512–20; John M. Abowd, *An Econometric Model of the U.S. Market for Higher Education* (New York: Garland, 1984); Elmore R. Alexander and Donald E. Frey, "An Econometric Estimate of the Demand for MBA Enrollment," *Economics of Education Review* 3 (1984): 97–103; Salim Chishti, "International Demand for American Higher Education," *Research in Higher Education* 20 (1984): 329–44; William C. Weiler, "Using Enrollment Demand Models in Institutional Pricing Decisions," *New Directions for Institutional Research* 42 (June 1984): 19–34; George A. Chressanthis, "The Impacts of Tuition Rate Changes on College Undergraduate Headcounts and Credit Hours Over Time—a Case Study," *Economics of Education Review* 5, no. 2 (1986): 205–17; David J. Berg and Stephen A. Hoenack, "The Concept of Cost-Related Tuition and Its Implementation at the University of Minnesota," *Journal of Higher Education* 58 (1987): 276–305; Julia A. Heath and Howard P. Tuckman, "Effects of Tuition Level and Financial Aid on the Demand of Undergraduate and Advanced Terminal Degrees," *Economics of Education Review* 6 (1987): 227–38; Larry L. Leslie and Paul T. Brinkman, "Student Price Response in Higher Education: The Student Demand Studies," *Journal of Higher Education* 58 (1987): 181–204; William E. Becker, "The Demand for Higher Education," in Hoenack and Collins, eds., *The Economics of American Universities*, 155–88.

for themselves or for society in general. Donors seek the satisfaction of furthering some (but usually not all) of the institution's objectives, and donors sometimes seek recognition or perquisites as well. Increasingly, state funding agencies view themselves as procuring educational services at reasonable prices in relation to quality rather than simply funding institutions and buying into the institutions' full set of objectives.[29] In the new model, state agencies negotiate a match between costs and benefits.

The financial constraint holds that an institution's expenses cannot exceed its revenues, on average over time, or else the institution will eventually deplete its reserves and go out of business. Given the pressure to spend, however, the inequality constraint is transmuted as a practical matter to an equality between long-run revenues and long-run expenses. Defining "long-run revenues" and "long-run expenses" is beyond the scope of this chapter, but one might consult Gordon Winston's work on global accounting in chapter 11 and mine on endowment and capital management in chapters 4 and 5. For present purposes, we will consider revenues as consisting of:

1. *transaction income,* from transactions like those described in the previous paragraph; that is, prices determined in part by the institution's demand functions, times an appropriate measure of quantity as determined by its activities; and
2. *fixed income,* such as from endowments, which does not depend on the institution's current activities.

Expense consists of:

1. *variable cost,* the element of cost that changes with the institution's activities; and
2. *fixed cost,* the element of cost that does not change as activities are varied over ranges that are likely to be observed in practice.

The cost definitions are identical to those used in business. Because businesses rarely receive fixed revenue, however, that definition tends to be unique to the nonprofit sector and to colleges and universities in particular. In the next section we will refer to *marginal revenue (MR)* and *marginal cost (MC);* that is, the change in transaction revenue and variable cost in response to output changes. While the technical defini-

---

29. "A Transatlantic Dialogue," *Policy Perspectives* 5, no. 1 (June 1993): 2A.

tions are complicated, one usually can regard *MR* and *MC* as *prices* and *unit costs*, respectively.[30]

Resource Allocation Theories: How the Black Box Works

Now that we have considered piece-by-piece the various inputs, outputs, objectives, and constraints of higher education institutions, let us bring all this information together and examine how resource allocation works. In his illustration of the black box, Patrick Callan noted that higher education moves forward when money is inserted and moves backward when money is withdrawn. In recent years, critics of higher education also claim that, because per-student expenditures have increased, gross productivity has remained the same or even declined. The so-called *revenue theory of budgeting* attempts to explain these circumstances. Propagated by Howard Bowen, the theory maintains that "Universities will raise all the money they can and spend all the money they raise."[31]

Supporters of this theory maintain that quality improvement requires increased expenditure and thus depends on a growing resource base. That per-student revenue grew for so many years demonstrates higher education's success in selling the expenditure-quality linkage. One of the strong lessons from service-industry quality improvement programs, however, is that such a linkage is by no means necessary: that is, quality improvement and cost reduction *can* be achieved simultaneously (see chap. 6 for more information).

Recent research challenges the expenditure-quality linkage in higher education and provides an alternative to the revenue theory of budgeting. We call this theory, based on the microeconomic theory of the not-for-profit entity, the *value theory of budgeting*. While a regular for-profit firm seeks to maximize profit, a nonprofit firm seeks to maximize utility. The theory reflects how colleges and universities serve altruistic purposes rather than profit-maximizing ones.

Readers familiar with the basic economic theory of the business firm will recall that a for-profit firm:

---

30. See chapter 12 for an approach to estimating variable cost; also the excellent discussion by Richard Allen and Paul Brinkman, *Marginal Costing Techniques for Higher Education* (Boulder, CO: NCHEMS, 1983).

31. Howard Bowen, *The Cost of Higher Education: How Much Do Colleges and Universities Spend Per Student and How Much Should They Spend?* (San Francisco: Jossey-Bass, 1980).

1. seeks to maximize the difference between revenue and cost (*profit*);
2. takes account of applicable technology, human factors, and regulations (*production possibilities*);
3. abides by the discipline of its input and output markets (*demand and supply curves*); and
4. uses its profits to provide reserves or finance expansion, or distributes them to company stakeholders as dividend and debt-service payments or stock buybacks.

On the other hand, the nonprofit enterprise:

1. seeks to maximize the amount of value it contributes to society as provided for in its charter (*utility*);
2. takes account of applicable technology, human factors, and regulations (*production possibilities*);
3. abides by the discipline of its input and output markets (*demand and supply curves*);
4. maintains a balance between revenues and expenditures, on average over time in real terms (*financial limits*); and
5. forbids private distribution of surplus to stakeholders.[32]

The nonprofit firm, therefore, seeks to maximize *subjectively* determined utility instead of *objectively* determined profit. The difference

---

32. I derived the general mathematical theory in working papers beginning in 1987, which were published as chapter 3 of Hopkins and Massy, *Planning Models* (1991). The work was motivated in part by Mark V. Pauly and Michael Redisch, "The Not-for-Profit Hospital as a Physicians' Cooperative," *American Economic Review* 63 (1973): 87–99; and William E. Becker, Jr., "The University Professor as a Utility Maximizer and Producer of Learning, Research, and Income," *Journal of Human Resources* 10 (1975): 107–15. For other lines of development see Estelle James, "Product Mix and Cost Disaggregation: A Reinterpretation of the Economics of Higher Education," *Journal of Human Resources* 13 (1978): 157–86; William E. Becker, Jr., "Perspectives from Economics: The Economic Consequences of Changing Faculty Reward Structures" in Darrell R. Lewis and William E. Becker, Jr., eds., *Academic Rewards in Higher Education* (Cambridge, MA: Ballinger, 1979), 21–39; Estelle James and Egon Neuberger, "The University Department as a Non-Profit Labor Cooperative," *Public Choice* 36 (1981): 585–612; Estelle James, "How Nonprofits Grow: A Model," *Journal of Policy Analysis* 2 (1982): 350–66; James A. Yunker and James W. Martin, Jr., "Performance Evaluation of College and University Faculty: An Economic Perspective," *Educational Administration Quarterly* 20, no. 1 (Winter 1984): 9–37; Estelle James, "The Private Nonprofit Provision of Education: A Theoretical Model and Application to Japan," *Journal of Comparative Economics* 10 (1986): 255–76; and Estelle James, "Decision Processes and Priorities in Higher Education" in Hoenack and Collins, eds., *The Economics of American Universities*, 77–106.

between revenue and cost is set out as a limitation or constraint, something to be lived with rather than maximized. The financial limit requires that costs not exceed revenues over the long run. If they did, the enterprise eventually would cease to exist. Finally, a nonprofit firm is forbidden by law from paying out any profits to stakeholders.

Value Budgeting

The *value theory of budgeting* postulates that institutions will expand program size and quality as long as the extra value plus the extra revenue obtained exceeds the extra cost incurred. Value stands for what matters intrinsically to the institution and its constituents. *Revenue* embodies the consequences of market forces, and *cost* arises from the technical characteristics of production and the prices of inputs to production. For example, a liberal arts college might invest in a literature program because the college intrinsically values literary studies and can obtain extra tuition revenue by doing so. Once the cost of additional faculty time exceeds the benefits obtained, however, the college will cease investing.

Value budgeting follows the spirit of the classic business decision rule, "expand output as long as the extra revenue exceeds the extra cost" (marginal cost versus marginal revenue), but the rule has been extended to reflect the social responsibility mission of the nonprofit enterprise. In equation form, the nonprofit rule would appear as follows:

$$EMU + MR = MC,$$

which must hold for each of the institution's many outputs. *EMU* represents "effective marginal utility"; *MR*, "marginal revenue"; and *MC*, "marginal cost." The latter two terms, as defined in elementary economics courses, are the extra revenue or cost resulting from small changes in output. In many cases, one can think of *MR* and *MC* as per-unit revenue and cost, respectively.

The equation balances two kinds of value on the left with the cost of producing that value on the right. Effective marginal utility (*EMU*) represents "intrinsic value," or value for the output's own sake. Marginal revenue (*MR*), on the other hand, represents "instrumental value," reflecting the sales revenue generated—which can be used for any institutional purpose. One might say that "love" and "money," on the left side of the equation, are balanced with cost on the right.

Why do we describe the intrinsic-value term as *effective* marginal utility (*EMU*) rather than just the marginal utility (*MU*) of the output itself? The answer is that *EMU* represents the extra utility obtained from a change in output *divided by the marginal utility of money*. The marginal utility of money represents the extra utility obtainable from an extra dollar of discretionary revenue—for example, the utility of whatever outputs the institution would add after receiving an increase in unrestricted endowment. *EMU* normalizes *MU* to make it commensurate with *MR* and *MC*, which are measured in dollar terms. This normalization is derived from the theory and not given as an assumption—and becomes quite important for predicting the behavior of nonprofit firms under financial duress.

The nonprofit decision rule can be recast into this algebraically equivalent form:

$$EMU = -(MR - MC)$$

or, in words, the effective marginal utility of an output equals minus the output's *contribution margin*. Contribution margin represents the difference between the extra revenue garnered by increasing the quantity of a certain output and the cost of supplying the extra output. While some might view a focus on the contribution margins of education and research outputs as crass, we see from the theory that, for a well-managed institution, the contribution margins provide important information about effective marginal utility.

The following example illustrates the linkage between utilities and contribution margins:

> Suppose a liberal arts college wishes to expand its highly valued literature program, even though the marginal cost of expanding that program exceed its marginal revenue. A summer music appreciation program that the college values less but which has a high contribution margin can help fund the literature program.

In this example, the institution and its faculty would prefer less emphasis on music appreciation, so *EMU* for music appreciation is negative. The contribution margin is positive (i.e., *MR* exceeds *MC*), as required by the theory. On the other hand, the institution wants to expand its literature program, and hence literature's *EMU* is positive and the contribution margin is negative. Notice that only the *incremental* utility of music appreciation is negative; the program might still be highly valued in absolute terms.

Suppose for a moment that the college has only the two outputs, music appreciation and literature, and no fixed costs or fixed revenues such as endowment. Now the loss incurred in literature must equal the surplus accrued in music appreciation; in other words, music cross-subsidizes literature. For multiple outputs, the algebraic sum of all the contribution margins must equal zero if there are no fixed costs or fixed revenues. In the two-output case, the college cannot expand literature without also expanding music appreciation. However, if we assume the college is already maximizing its utility, the extra *EMU* obtained by expanding literature will be less than the loss in *EMU* due to concomitant expansion of music appreciation.

The example reveals how knowledge about contribution margins, which can be measured fairly accurately by proper use of accounting data, can provide insight about hard-to-measure utilities— providing, of course, that the institution has been doing a good job of maximizing its utility subject to the requisite production, demand, and financial constraints. Economists call this kind of information "revealed preference." Alternatively, an institution can calculate the contribution margins of its programs, array them from most negative to most positive, and then ask whether this correlates with its sense of relative subjective value. We know of an institution doing this quite explicitly. Discrepancies would lead to changes in budget allocations.

Some of the angst faculty currently experience may arise because financial stringency is forcing them to pursue activities for which marginal value is negative. Most professors grew up under conditions where their institutions did not have to push activities with positive contribution margins simply to gain revenue. Funds limitations have always been present, so faculty are used to curtailing their activities when time or money runs out—while they still want to do more because marginal value remains positive. Now, however, they are being asked to pursue activities with negative marginal value so their institution can make financial ends meet.

Implications of the Value Budgeting Theory

Value budgeting theory allows us to predict the behavior of higher education institutions. From the nonprofit decision rule described above, we can deduce certain implications strongly relevant to higher education productivity:

> *Value knows no bounds.* The value an institution can create is limited only by its resources. Hence the revenue theory of budgeting follows as an implication of value theory—institutions will raise all the money they can and spend all the money they raise. The

college referred to above will improve its literature program to the extent permitted by revenue availability. No natural stopping point exists where the institution says, "We are as good as we want to be, so let's stop looking for new revenue." Market forces and productivity issues do not enter this calculation.

Cross-subsidies among programs reflect an institution's preferences. As illustrated in the above example, some contribution margins will be positive and others negative. Activities with a positive contribution margin provide cross-subsidies for other, less profitable activities and are analogous to the business world's profit contribution—except that higher education institution surpluses must be plowed back into the enterprise rather than distributed to shareholders. Without cross-subsidies (or fixed revenues), the institution would have no discretion, no way to further its own values—its sense of social responsibility—as opposed to simply following the market.

The choice of spending targets depends on market forces in addition to values. Market forces determine the extra revenue, if any, that will accrue from program expansion. The extra revenue determines the program's *contribution margin* (i.e., the difference between per-unit revenue and per-unit cost), which in turn affects program affordability. Higher education spokespersons who claim that market forces should not influence the allocation of resources within an institution are not being realistic. The forces of value and those of the market work in dynamic tension: in the well-run and financially sound nonprofit enterprise, both will influence decisions but neither will dominate them.

Efficiency matters. Delivering a desired program size and quality at lower cost means a smaller draw on the institution's cross-subsidy pool or a larger contribution to the pool. Improving production efficiency (taking account of output quality as well as quantity) reduces incremental cost and improves contribution margin, thus increasing institutional discretion and allowing it to generate more value overall.

Value budgeting theory can also help us predict the behavior of colleges and universities in different economic circumstances. Let us consider three different instances, keeping in mind the nonprofit rule above.

Absent fixed revenue, cross-subsidies will be the rule rather than the exception. In systems that have no fixed income source, positively valued outputs receive cross-subsidies at the expense of at least one other output, which must be negatively valued at the margin. This is the two-output scenario described above, which requires a music program if the literature program is to exist. Institutional outputs that have both positive marginal intrinsic value and positive contribution margin do not remain that way for long. Identifying such a worthwhile output, an institution quickly would begin pouring more resources into it until marginal costs started rising faster than marginal revenue and contribution margins went negative, or alternatively, the institution would end up with so much of the output that its marginal intrinsic value eventually would flatten or decline.

Fixed revenue makes cross-subsidies less than inevitable but does not preclude them. Many universities have fixed revenues, such as income generated from endowment. Regardless of the current quality, quantity, or price of outputs, fixed income allows an institution to improve the quality of its outputs, or alternatively, to hold down price in much the same way that a government subsidy permits a business to produce goods even when price is set below cost. In terms of our example, a liberal arts college with a fixed revenue source could fund its literature program—creating positively valued output—without having to enlarge its summer music appreciation course and create additional negatively valued output.

Thus, if an institution has a source of fixed revenue, then all its outputs can have positive marginal intrinsic value; no output must be negatively valued at the margin. Contribution margins, in fact, could all be negative. The fixed revenue source, such as endowment income, acts to subsidize the programs. Cross-subsidies no longer are needed (although nothing prevents them from existing alongside the fixed revenue subsidy).

When the financial constraints become bad enough, the nonprofit institution's behavior approaches that of a for-profit firm. Suppose an institution falls on financial hard times. Money is scarce and consequently its marginal utility increases. Because *EMU* represents the value of an output divided by the marginal utility of money, the larger the marginal utility of money the smaller the impact of value. If the liberal arts college is barely breaking even, it will put aside expanding the literature program in favor of raising revenues simply to remain afloat. These actions do not mean that the college values literature less but rather that the college has been forced to value money more. Now consider the extreme situation in which conditions are so bad and the marginal utility of money is so high that *EMU* approaches zero. In this case, all the marginal revenues must equal their marginal costs, and the nonprofit institution effectively becomes a for-profit!

Substitution and Income Effects

Cross-subsidies are influenced not only by value or utility but also by market demand and production cost. Price and cost changes produce *substitution effects* and *income effects*, which one should evaluate separately when designing resource allocation systems and other policy interventions. Cyril Chang and Howard Tuckman of Michigan State University provide an example of substitution effects in action. Despite the tendency, mentioned earlier, for academic units to view costs as fixed, Chang and Tuckman demonstrated that "college faculty were substitutable and that differences in faculty salaries influenced the distribution of faculty by rank and sex," and that institutions with different missions have slightly different substitution patterns and price elasticities.[33]

Substitution effects may be either revenue based or cost based. Revenue-based substitution effects represent shifts in output due to price changes. These effects can cause college and university decision makers to behave in ways that might seem contrary to their underlying value or utility structure. If a lower-valued output increases in price, for example, production of that output will generally increase. For example, an increase in the market price of the summer music appreciation program would lead to an increase in the size of that program even though its marginal utility is negative. Cost-based substitution effects represent shifts in output due to changes in the cost of inputs. If, for example, faculty salaries double in relation to staff salaries, then products dependent on staff will increase (student services, counseling) while products dependent exclusively on faculty will decrease (teaching, research). Income effects, on the other hand, are more difficult to predict. Most schools, for example, will increase the output of research, publication, and professional services faster than educational services when discretionary income rises; therefore, the income effects of the former are greater than those of the latter. Programs that "only make money" (and hence have low value) will shrink when discretionary income rises, so their income effects are negative.

---

33. Howard P. Tuckman and Cyril F. Chang, "Own Price and Cross Elasticities of Demand for College Faculty," *Southern Economic Journal* 52 (1986): 735–44; and Cyril F. Chang and Howard P. Tuckman, "Price Induced Substitution of Faculty in Academe: Does Mission Make a Difference?" *Economics of Education Review* 5 (1986): 197–204. The quotation is from the abstract of the second reference.

Cross-subsidies are particularly important in analyzing productivity, for they demand that we ask the question "for whom?" For example, much of what appears to be a productivity problem in higher education— namely, the increase in tuition without a corresponding educational quality increase—is due to the growth of cross-subsidies. The cross-subsidies in higher education now generally run from undergraduate teaching, especially in the lower division, toward graduate study and research.[34] Schools' efforts to enhance their prestige, coupled with the professional drive of modern faculty to achieve visibility through research and publication, are shifting the output mix toward research. Extramural research sponsors are not increasing their allocations fast enough to meet the demand for research funding, so institutions are redirecting their own funds. In some schools, moreover, the focus of faculty attention toward research may be reducing the quality of undergraduate teaching. This shift of resources and outputs is given the name *output creep,* inasmuch as it represents a slow (and from the point of view of many who pay for higher education, undesirable) change in the mix of outputs at many colleges and universities. We will consider the consequences of this particular type of cross-subsidy and its consequences in much greater detail in our section on the academic ratchet. Thus, an analysis of cross-subsidies leads to the conclusion that while internal productivity may have been maintained or even increased during the period of cost-rise, productivity as viewed by those who pay for U.S. higher education may well have declined.

Externalities and Agency Theory

Budget-system designers must take two complicating factors into account: (1) economic and value externalities, and (2) value incongruity leading to principle-agent problems.

Externalities arise when one entity reaps the benefits of an action while another pays the price. Polluting the atmosphere provides a classic example; the pollution blows downwind and affects not the polluter but his neighbor. In academia, value externalities might inhibit a math department from redesigning calculus curricula to meet the particular

---

34. See, for example, James, "Product Mix and Cost Disaggregation," 157–86; Donald Verry and Bleddyn Davies, *University Costs and Outputs* (New York: Elsevier Scientific Publishing, 1976); Estelle James and Egon Neuberger, "The University Department as a Non-Profit Labor Cooperative," *Public Choice* 36 (1981): 585–612; Estelle James, "Decision Processes and Priorities in Higher Education," and Stephen A. Hoenack, "An Economist: Perspective on Costs Within Higher Education Institutions," in Hoenack and Collins, eds., *The Economics of American Universities.*

needs of nontraditional engineering students. Conversely, economic motives might drive an engineering school to teach its own calculus course if funding varies with enrollments and the marginal revenue from such teaching exceeds marginal cost. Economic externalities also can arise when one department's actions raise another's cost or reduce its revenue—for instance, when one unit dumps a certain administrative task on another.

Economic *agency theory* was designed to analyze situations in which, for example, an entity's employees have a different utility function than its managers or owners.[35] Agency theory generalizes the assumption, implicit in the value budgeting theory described earlier, that all the institution's decision makers have the same values—in technical terms, a *team utility function*. We know, however, that this is far too simple: faculty values often differ from those of the administration, and the administration may differ in its views on important issues with the trustees and state governing boards.[36]

Agency theory addresses the problem: "How does a principal prevent the agent from diverting resources to his or her own ends?" Although the resource diversions contemplated in agency theory usually accrue to the agent's private benefit, most diversions in higher education result from good-faith differences of opinion about what is important. The quintessential example of this is the increased diversion of funds to research, which leads to output creep as described above. Institutions as well as faculty tend to value research over teaching; the pursuit of prestige is seen to benefit the entire institution even when education is explicitly chartered as the primary mission.

Agency problems can be mitigated by one of three methods adapted from Hoenack.[37]

1. Assigning *specific responsibilities* (SpR). In SpR systems, the principal tells the agent exactly what to spend money for and then follows up to make sure there are no deviations. Line-item budgeting represents the most familiar example in higher education. In other words, SpR represents a priori control over the

35. Stephen A. Hoenack, "Direct and Incentive Planning within a University," *Socio-Economic Planning Sciences* 11 (1977): 191–204; *Economic Behavior within Organizations* (New York: Cambridge University Press, 1983); "An Economist's Perspective on Costs within Higher Education Institutions," in Hoenack and Collins, eds., *The Economics of American Universities*.

36. James, "Decision Processes and Priorities."

37. Hoenack, "Direct and Incentive Planning."

agent's activities; no action can be taken without the principle's prior approval. SpR systems can be effective when scope and complexity are small, but the costs of information, regulation, and employee disempowerment grow geometrically as scale and complexity increase. Line-item budgeting degrades decision-making performance and increases cost in large institutions.

2. Using *price as a regulator* (PriR). PriR systems mitigate agency problems through arms-length adjustments to marginal revenues and costs. For example, an institution might tax research revenues or subsidize educational expenditures if it fears that departments are shortchanging instruction. PriR's main problem is that a principal must predict how adjustments to MR and MC will affect agents' behavior and then assess the resulting impact on his or her own values. This task requires detailed knowledge about the agents' values—which self-interest suggests cannot be obtained simply by asking—and also about any value or economic externalities.

3. Assigning *responsibility for the overall value of outcomes* (OVR). In OVR systems, principal and agent agree on the kinds of outcomes to be achieved, the resource levels needed to achieve them, and the measures that will be applied to determine the agent's performance. The agent takes responsibility for achieving the outcomes, and the principal provides rewards based on the level of success achieved. The performance measures may be quantitative or qualitative, and they may or may not include revenue- and cost-generation elements. OVR's distinguishing features are: (*a*) the principal holds the agent accountable for outcomes, and (*b*) the principal does not regulate how the agent achieves the outcomes. OVR systems often include outcome assessments and a program where the agent "buys into the vision" of the institution, thus aligning his utility function with that of the larger organization.

The three methods focus on three distinct aspects of the agent's utility maximization process: SpR on the variables over which the agent has discretion and their ranges of admissibility; PriR on prices, the marginal revenues and marginal costs faced by the agent; and OVR on the agent's utility function itself. The costs of the detailed regulation required for SpR usually preclude complete reliance on this strategy, though some limits usually must be set even in PriR and OVR in order to keep resource diversion within acceptable bounds. Likewise, pure PriR strategies generally are too complex to be manageable. In a two-stage utility maximization model constructed by David Hopkins and me,[38] we found, like Hoenack,[39] that the amount of data required for implementation exceeds what institutions could likely supply. The model we constructed, however, does provide guidance about implementing a combination of PriR and OVR in the design of resource allocation, a topic we reserve for later chapters.

Summary of Budgeting System Characteristics

As shown in table 2, the higher education budgeting systems introduced in chapter 2 can now be analyzed in terms of income and substitution effects, externalities, and the methods of agency theory. The column labeled "agency method" indicates which method is the motivating approach, but none of the budgeting systems is a pure form of the agency theory methods described above. In general, LIB systems allow little delegation; they rely on SpR methods (specifically, line-item control) to reserve all decisions for the central authority. PRB and RRB systems, on the other hand, delegate a great deal of responsibility. They use combinations of price and nonprice methods to motivate the operating units to perform in the ways the central authorities desire. By using OVR methods, PRB systems ultimately seek to align the operating units' utility functions with the central authorities' utility function. RRB systems seek to motivate operating units with PriR methods.

Table 2 also shows how performance responsibility budgeting and revenue responsibility budgeting use income and substitution effects to influence behavior, and how these effects are further differentiated according to whether they are revenue based or cost based.

In PRB systems, the central authority negotiates plans with each center and then allocates funding in an unrestricted block, thus controlling income effects through the size of the block grants. No revenue-based substitution effects can occur, since each center is free to spend its grant as it wishes. Cost-based substitution effects occur internally through surcharge differentials and exogenously through changes in input price. If centers agree to implement a new software technology the administration wishes to encourage, for example, the central authority could offer a waiver of indirect costs as a surcharge differential.

In RRB, each center receives credit for the income it generates and is responsible for the full cost of its operation, but centers must also pay a subvention, or "tax," for centrally provided support services. The central authority controls the operating units' income effects through these subventions. The subventions also represent cross-subsidies by the

---

38. Hopkins and Massy, *Planning Models*, 102, 484.
39. Hoenack, *Economic Behavior*.

TABLE 2. Income and Substitution Effects for Alternative Budgeting Systems

			Substitution Effects	
	Agency Method	Income Effects	Revenue-Based	Cost-Based
Line item budgeting (LIB)	SpR	none	none	none
Performance responsibility budgeting (PRB)	OVR	size of blocks	none	input market prices; surcharge differentials
Revenue responsibility budgeting (RRB)	PriR (but vulnerable to externalities)	size of subventions	output market prices; surcharge differentials	input market prices; surcharge differentials

central authority of programs it deems valuable, such as the cross-subsidy from the music program to the literature program described earlier; the result at the operating unit level is to produce income effects. Revenue-based substitution effects in RRB result from output prices and thus are mostly exogenous, although the central authority can use differential surcharges to alter the prices as seen by the operating unit.

Cost-based substitution effects are the same for RRB and PRB systems. Both systems can limit total resource use and control income and cost-based substitution; however, they differ in complexity and the ability to induce revenue-based substitution. PRB is by far the simplest system, since the budget allocations are done in lump sums. RRB involves revenue attribution accounting, which will be especially complex if there are cross-enrollments and joint research projects.

The most significant difference among the budgeting systems lies in their delegation of revenue responsibility. RRB does this by assigning revenue to the operating unit that generates it. For example, departments that shortchange their teaching may eventually lose enrollments, which in turn will reduce their tuition revenue. (Even the threat of demand-side discipline may be enough to motivate desired behavior.) Departments may be able to increase their enrollments by putting their best teachers in the elementary courses. However, RRB makes the institution vulnerable to cost-based substitution bias stemming from economic externalities. PRB systems avoid such bias, but at the cost of diluted focus on output-market trade-offs. PRB systems offer no direct price-based inhibitions or incentives, since the operating units' marginal revenues are strictly zero and thus do not depend on quality.

The budgeting systems listed in table 2 provide colleges with many useful tools but not a single, effective system. LIB fails because most institutions are too complicated for detailed central control. Substantial authority should be delegated to the subunits, which have the information necessary to make good decisions. Furthermore, the principle of empowerment, discussed in chapter 6, requires that local entities be free to shift resources as needed to achieve goals and solve problems. Budget delegations must be done in a way that preserves the central authority's influence and places limits on the subunits' ability to divert resources, but line-item budgeting violates the empowerment principle and also overloads the central authorities.

RRB relies almost exclusively on price-based effects, but, while powerful, these effects may not be precise enough to motivate operating units to achieve important institutional goals. PRB limits total resource usage, but relies mainly on nonprice considerations for determining the units' program priorities. The subjective judgments and negotiations can be finely honed, but, unfortunately, presidents and provosts find it difficult to sustain significant variations in budget allocations across schools. The burden of proof on why schools should receive different planning allocations becomes unworkably high, so the allocations tend to vary only within a narrow range. Institutional leaders face overwhelming burdens when financial dislocations force negative allocations and all too often resort to across-the-board cuts. We have designed a resource allocation system, which will be discussed in the last chapter, that embodies the methods of agency theory while mitigating these problems.

The Lattice and the Ratchet

Although by this point we have covered many ideas helpful in understanding productivity and resource allocation in higher education, we have yet to offer specific causes for the cost rise and apparent loss of gross productivity that characterized the 1970s and the 1980s. Ideas such as the revenue theory of budgeting are useful, but they do not explain in particular what happened. On the other hand, we could not address the root causes of cost rise with the analytical tools just presented. We shall conclude our discussion, therefore, with two specific theories of why costs have risen so much. Perhaps these two ideas, the lattice and the ratchet, can also help us answer the questions, "Has productivity really decreased in higher education?" and "Are faculty less productive than they were in past decades?"

Unlike the increased government regulation and the cost disease described earlier in this chapter, both the lattice and the ratchet reflect institutional choices.[40] The lattice applies to the administrative realm, while the ratchet applies to faculty. In a 1990 study of data from the U.S. Equal Employment Opportunity Commission, journalist Karen Grassmuck noted that administrative staffs of colleges and universities had grown an average of 60 percent between 1975 and 1985, while faculty had increased an average of less than 6 percent in the same time period.[41] She had detected the presence of the administrative lattice: the proliferation and entrenchment of administrative staff at American colleges and universities. The term *lattice* refers not only to this increase in staff but also to its effects on an institution's operations and costs.

---

40. William F. Massy and Andrea K. Wilger, "Productivity in Postsecondary Education: A New Approach," *Educational Evaluation and Policy Analysis* 14, no. 4. (Winter 1992): 361–76.

41. Karen Grassmuck, "Colleges Feel Effects of Economic Downturn in Student Aid, Endowment, Job Hunting," *Chronicle of Higher Education* 37, no. 14 (1990): A1, A27.

Among those effects are the transfer of tasks formerly accorded to the faculty (such as career counseling), the growth of consensus management, which effectively diffuses risk and responsibility for decisions, and the increase of costs and decline of efficiency as administrative bureaucracy extends and solidifies its ties within an institution.[42] Like a healthy vine, the growth of support staff often leads to more growth as professionals seek to expand their areas; yet another possible result is that professionals may perform tasks to a better degree—and consequently, at a higher cost—than an institution requires. Named *function lust*, an example of this latter phenomenon might be a landscape architect who urges millions of dollars of landscaping when the university's value trade-offs suggest that $500,000 worth would be sufficient. The architect may be working from pure motives, but he is in no position to gauge how important landscaping is in relation to the university's other needs.

While the lattice's effects on productivity are easily visible, as anyone who has had to deal with a huge university bureaucracy can attest, the effects of the academic ratchet are more subtle. The *ratchet* denotes the specific process that causes the output creep discussed earlier and describes the steady, irreversible shift of faculty allegiance away from the goals of a given institution, toward those of an academic specialty. In pursuit of prestige, some faculty have developed an independent, entrepreneurial spirit leading to increased emphasis on research and publication and on teaching their own specialty instead of general introduction courses, often at the expense of coherence in an academic curriculum. The increasing outputs or primary gainers from the ratchet are research, publications, professional services (consulting), and curriculum specialization. Diminishing outputs or the primary losers include teaching quality, advising, mentoring, tutoring, and curriculum structure.

Not all institutions suffer from the ratchet to the same extent. Many colleges and universities continue to offer excellent undergraduate education and to emphasize the role of professor as teacher. The phenomenon of output creep occurs most dramatically at research institutions, where competition for admission allows institutions to dictate the "output mix" that students buy. Since these prestigious institutions receive most of the publicity, however, their behavior influences higher education as a whole. The influence is felt throughout the research and doctoral-granting sector, which trains future faculty for all institutions. Indeed, output creep has progressed to the point that even a few liberal arts institutions have begun referring to themselves as research colleges.

---

42. Robert Zemsky and William F. Massy, "Cost Containment: Committing to a New Economic Reality," *Change* 22, no. 6 (November/December 1990): 22.

Research need not necessarily draw resources away from teaching; the two can be complements, as illustrated in Nerlov's conceptual model (fig. 1).[43] When research is first introduced, teaching benefits, as shown in the production possibility curve's positive slope (1). At this point, faculty transfer some of the excitement of research to their teaching. As Nerlov's model indicates, however, if pursued too strongly, research will eventually diminish educational quality due to time and attention constraints. The model indicates that the most efficient point is an equilibrium (2) where teaching and research serve as substitutes, not complements. This equilibrium point would be reached in a classical business firm when $MR = MC$; however, since higher education institutions operate on the $EMU + MR = MC$ condition, they choose their own equilibrium anywhere on the curve. All too often, the institution chooses to pursue research until it is constrained by the demands of teaching (3). The process called the academic ratchet begins operating when research and teaching become substitutes (2), but soon overshoots irreversibly into the far right region of the curve (3).

Teaching is not unimportant, even in those institutions operating well inside the region of substitution. Indeed, teaching may indeed place the first call on faculty time and energy up to the point where classroom competence has been achieved. Faculty cannot maximize both sides of a substitution trade-off simultaneously, so they reach an accommodation called "satisficing."[44] Here is how Andrea Wilger and I described the concept as it emerged in our interviews with faculty about their roles and responsibilities:

> Faculty *satisfice* their teaching, whereas they *maximize* their research efforts. By "satisfice" we mean doing enough to meet a quality standard—but once the threshold has been achieved, one turns one's attention elsewhere. The threshold may be quite high, and for many of our respondents, we believe it is. Nevertheless, many professors' teaching effort is distinctly finite. They are anxious to return to their research, and they will do so once convinced that teaching duties are safely under control.[45]

43. Marc Nerlov, "On Tuition and the Costs of Higher Education: Prolegomena to a Conceptual Framework," *Journal of Political Economy* 80, no. 3 (May–June 1992): S178–S218.

44. The satisficing concept was introduced into microeconomic theory by Richard M. Cyert and James G. March in *A Behavioral Theory of the Firm* (Englewood Cliffs, NJ: Prentice-Hall, 1963).

45. Massy and Wilger, "Improving Productivity."

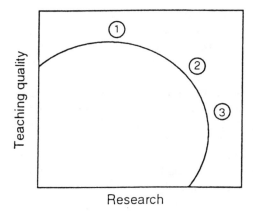

Fig. 1. Production possibility frontier for teaching quality and research

While faculty in research-intensive institutions do not usually neglect their teaching, it does not represent their prime objective, and this has profound implications for educational quality. Hence the academic ratchet represents an agency-theory problem when viewed from the vantage point of funders concerned with undergraduate education.

The ratchet can be traced to several processes, in combination, that operate at the departmental level. The processes are (1) the pursuit of faculty lines, (2) leveraging faculty time, (3) destructuring the curriculum, and (4) enactment of group norms and propagation of perceived property rights. Together, these four processes form the potent force that drives output creep; a clear understanding of the dynamics of these processes is crucial to cost containment efforts. The pursuit of faculty lines reflects the desire of chairs and faculty to add more faculty, regardless of enrollment level. The push to hire more faculty is strong whether they are wanted for their ability to enhance department prestige, teach introductory courses, or just increase the intellectual climate of the department. Leveraging faculty time refers to the use of graduate assistants, research assistants, secretaries and administrative assistants, and others to free up faculty time for research and professional activities. In most cases, such leveraging drives up the cost of education while students have less direct contact with faculty. Destructuring the curriculum, initiated in response to student demand in the 1960s, has placed the burden of coordination of courses on individual faculty. Negotiation and coordination of curriculum is costly in terms of time; faculty may opt to devote that time for research and professional interests, leaving students with a highly unstructured curriculum. These first three processes describe the tension between faculty desire for increased leverage of their time and the financial realities of the department.

Enactment of group norms and propagation of perceived property rights is perhaps the most powerful process at work in the ratchet, a process that solidifies and magnifies the effects of the other three. Faculty members in all academic departments possess enacted norms, which are strongly held, shared beliefs about their relationship to their environment. Examples of such norms, which are usually rooted in particular disciplines, include "introductory science is best taught in large lecture courses" or "academic programs should be maintained as long as enrollments are reasonable, regardless of how well they relate to the goals and missions of the institution." On the basis of these norms, faculty develop certain property rights that they believe are inherent to their faculty position and that they use to govern their activities. A senior faculty member, for example, may believe he has a right not to teach any large introductory courses, for those courses are traditionally assigned to junior faculty. Other perceived property rights include number of courses taught per term, student-teacher ratio, and ideal class sizes. Desirable circumstances and working conditions are seen as entitlements once they are achieved. As we saw earlier, these norms and property rights can obstruct change, even if change could bring about improved productivity and efficiency during financially stringent times.

In figure 2, we illustrate how the combined effects of these four processes interact over time to produce the ratchet. Each phase is described as follows.

> Phase 1. Enrollment rises for reasons not connected to output creep: the number of faculty is fixed in the short run so faculty are forced to teach more. This causes the departmental research to fall below the level generally considered to be normal.
>
> Phase 2. Lower departmental research represents a violation of perceived property rights, which triggers a demand for more faculty. When these are acceded to, which usually happens if the problem lasts long enough, teaching loads and departmental research return to their normal levels.
>
> Phase 3. Enrollment drops back to its original level (again for reasons unrelated to output creep), and a combination of perceived property rights and faculty employment contracts (e.g., tenure) prevents immediate downsizing; faculty members teach less, so departmental research rises above its normal level.
>
> Phase 4. The stickiness in faculty size persists long enough for the

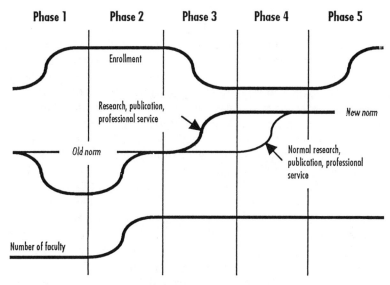

Fig. 2. The academic "ratchet"

new departmental research level to become embedded in the department's sense of social reality, that is, to become a perceived property right.

Phase 5. There is a new enrollment surge: the process starts over again, but now from a higher base. The ratchet has operated.

The academic ratchet requires several conditions that exist more strongly in some institutions than in others. These conditions are (1) strongly held beliefs about the intrinsic worth of teaching and research programs, (2) a collegial approach to decision making that places consensus at the center and allows little room for alternative points of view, (3) powerful beliefs about academic freedom that are sometimes interpreted as forbidding interference in faculty activities, and (4) the influence of students and alumni who do not want to see the reputation of their program or department negatively impacted. The power of these property rights, discussed in chapter 2, comes from the ultimate threat of losing unhappy faculty to competing institutions. The academic ratchet is thus reinforced both internally, by faculty members who prefer research to teaching and administrators who see the benefits of sponsored research, and externally, by students, alumni, and donors who want their programs and departments to be of the highest caliber.

Conclusion

We can now offer some answers to the two questions we posed at the beginning of this section: "Has productivity really decreased in higher education?" and "Are faculty less productive than they were in past decades?" If we consider productivity as strongly linked to the quality of undergraduate education, then prestigious research institutions and many of the institutions seeking the prestige associated with research have indeed shown decreased productivity over the past two decades. If we consider research production as the primary measure of productivity, however, then the U.S. higher education system has been remarkably productive. The question of productivity would be better served if each institution could determine an optimal balance between research and teaching based on its mission. As far as faculty is concerned—the question is not "are they less productive," for faculty seem for the most part to be competent and hard working, but, rather, "are they productive in desirable ways?" Output creep and the academic ratchet indicate that while faculty may not be working less, they may be pursuing goals divergent from those who pay for higher education. How to remedy that situation will be addressed in later chapters.

Part 2
Capital

CHAPTER 4

Endowment

William F. Massy

"Spend now or spend later" is a classic economic problem, but for many higher education institutions it has become an all too familiar quandary. Enrollment shortfalls and other revenue erosion trigger demands to spend capital in order to lessen the pain. While the tension between the need to maintain or add to capital and the desire to spend for current purposes is difficult enough to manage even in normal times, the problem is exacerbated when an institution faces financial difficulties. This chapter develops principles and procedures for use by institutions that wish to put endowment spending on a rational basis.

The endowment spending-saving trade-off takes on even greater importance because higher education itself represents an investment in human and intellectual capital that eventually benefits the greater society. While few would question the importance of such benefits, many who argue about spending-saving decisions have vested interests in the outcomes. Current spending benefits today's students and faculty, whereas investments in institutional capital may well benefit those whose voices cannot be heard now but who will be with us in future years.

The capital in question may be financial in character, as in the case of operating reserves and endowment, or tangible, as in facilities and equipment. Even an institution's debt capacity represents a kind of capital, "virtual capital," which needs to be balanced between current and future usage. It is the job of college and university trustees, above all others, to balance the urgency of today's needs and the self-interest of current stakeholders conspire against the interests of the underrepresented future beneficiaries of an institution's capital.

According to Yale economist James Tobin, "trustees are supposed to have a zero subjective rate of time preference,"[1] which means that they

---

Based on Massy 1990, no. 967, with the permission of the Association of Governing Boards of Universities and Colleges.

1. Tobin 1974; as quoted in Hansmann 1990, 14.

should value spending in the present no more than spending in the future. He cites as evidence the typical trustee's propensity to place "discretionary funds" (e.g., gifts and bequests not already committed to current operations or facilities) into the endowment, thus accumulating endowment balances for the benefit of future students and faculty. On the other hand, law professor Henry Hansmann argues that such thinking is misguided. He argues that current spending usually should dominate deferred spending, and that trustees can find many valid reasons for favoring the present.[2]

In this chapter, we address the principles by which institutions can be as responsive as possible to current needs without shortchanging the future. First we examine how trustees should set the endowment spending rate to maintain the purchasing power of individual endowment funds. In other words, how much of the current endowment can be spent while meeting commitments, often required by donors, to maintain the endowed program in perpetuity? In the following chapter, we address the broader question of whether discretionary funds (e.g., large unrestricted gifts not already committed to current operations) should be spent or added to capital, and, if the latter, to which form of capital. We conclude the section by analyzing the use of debt and presenting a set of financial ratios that can be used to guide policy and to track institutional strategic financial performance.

Maintaining Endowment's Purchasing Power

In an older and simpler time, the question of how much to spend and how much to save was essentially self-answering. The amount of savings was limited mostly to true endowment funds supplied by donors, and because today's activist fund-raising techniques had yet to be invented, the choice of whether a gift should be endowment or expendable generally was left to the donor. (*True endowments* are those for which donors have prohibited spending principal; no such restrictions apply to *quasi endowments*, which are simply expendable funds committed by trustees to function as endowments.) The rule for spending investment return from true endowments was simple: only current yield (dividends, interest, and rents) was available for spending. Laws governing investment and spending limited trustees' discretion.

The legal constraints on both investment diversification and the spending of capital appreciation were liberalized in the 1960s. This raised the option—some would say the specter—of basing spending on something other than interest, dividends, and rents.

---

2. Hansmann 1990, 14–19.

The Ford Foundation focused the spending issue in 1969[3] by pointing out that most college and university (and foundation) endowments were being managed too conservatively and that spending only investment yield made little sense in a world where the average dividend rate on corporate stocks was only a few percent. Those were the days of heady market advances and stratospheric price-earnings ratios for the "nifty fifty" most high-flying stocks, yet higher education was in a period of retrenchment. Interest rates had been low through most of the 1960s, and institutions that invested their endowments mainly in bonds had lost money in real terms. Those that shifted to stocks had enjoyed high total returns but were unable to take full advantage of them because of low dividend rates. The shortage of funds for higher education meant the conventional wisdom should be reformed, said the reports to the Ford Foundation, and many institutions were quick to agree.

Here were the essential points of the new wisdom:

1. Investment decisions should be based on portfolio total return. This requires that individual endowment funds to be pooled for purposes of investment to simplify asset allocations and diversify risk.
2. Investment returns should be calculated on a "unitized" basis, with the unit value based on the market rather than on cost, just like a mutual fund. In this system, interest, dividends, and rent receipts are credited to the pool rather than to individual endowment funds. The pool's unit value is "marked to market" on a regular basis, and funds buying into or cashing out of the pool do so at market value.
3. Each year the governing board should declare a "spending rate" (also called a "payout rate") that appropriates a fraction of the then-current unit value for expenditure. For example, a unit value of ten dollars and a declared spending rate of 5 percent would make fifty cents available for expenditure by share owners. The appropriated funds should be promptly removed from the pool, thus reducing share value.

These concepts were well established by 1972, when NACUBO surveyed 1,059 institutions on the subject. Of the 189 responses (which includes most of the schools with significant endowments), more than half reported that they operated one or more investment pools on a

---

3. See, for example, Ford Foundation 1969; Cary and Bright 1969. A good account of this period can be found in Ennis and Williamson 1976, chapter 1.

unitized market-value basis. Of these, 26 were investing for total return—without regard to the distinction between portfolio yield and gain.[4] The concepts also were incorporated into the Uniform Management of Institutional Funds Act (UMIFA), which was introduced in 1972.

Not well established, however, were the criteria for deciding exactly how much to spend each year. The idea of spending all total return seemed imprudent. Indeed, William Cary and Craig Bright qualified the argument for spending appreciation in their pioneering report to the Ford Foundation, as follows, by suggesting:

> a sort of "prudent man" standard to govern the spending of income where the definition of income included realized appreciation. The first element of this prudent man standard called for addition to principal of enough of the realized appreciation to offset inflation and bring about a steady flow of real spendable income. A second element would be appropriate provision for probable losses before appreciation were spent.[5]

This dictum was consistent with the "support in perpetuity" concept as memorialized in donor contracts. Unfortunately, however, ways to comply with the dictum were not worked out until some years later.

Support in Perpetuity

The rise of inflation in the 1970s triggered some rethinking about what it means to *support in perpetuity*. The interpretation that drives most modern spending policies is that the entire function for which endowed support originally was provided should be supported indefinitely, regardless of increases in cost. For example, if an endowed professor's salary of $100,000 is supported by the endowment fund today, the $200,000 salary a decade or so hence also should be fully supported. That, of course, requires sufficient endowment earnings to be reinvested to cause the principal balance to double over the decade.

Calibrating the growth of individual endowment funds to inflationary forces on their associated cost bundles is impractical. One never has sufficient lead time to affect the necessary reinvestment. Moreover, the different cost bundles will grow at different rates, and trying to match the growth rates of each would lead to an accounting morass. As a

---

4. Adams 1972.
5. Ennis and Williamson 1976, 9. Their reference is to Cary and Bright 1969.

practical matter, the best a school can do is match the growth of the average endowment fund—which turns out to be the endowment pool's share value—to some broadly based cost-rise average. This is now the working definition of support in perpetuity.

Some commentators do not agree that donor obligations call for maintaining endowment purchasing power. They point out that donative instruments focus on preserving the book value of the corpus, not its real value. There are advantages to this, given the need for approximation discussed in the previous paragraph. One also can argue that the institution has discharged its commitment to the donor if it simply maintains the dollar value of the fund and continues to honor the namesake by attribution to the whole of the original activity. The school meets its obligation by continuing the "XYZ Endowed Chair" even though most of the salary eventually comes to be paid for by other funds. Seen in this light, maintaining real endowment value results from the institution's desire to avoid making up shortfalls in endowment income rather than its efforts to meet donor obligations.

Maintaining the book value of endowment funds should be viewed as a necessary but not sufficient condition for meeting donor obligations. Suppose a donor is concerned as much about the supported activity as honoring a namesake. He or she will want that activity to flourish regardless of cost-rise or changes in institutional priorities. If the school must supplement endowment-income shortfalls with infusions of general funds, the program will be, in time, at the mercy of institutional priorities. Corners can be cut and the program effectively downsized in scope or quality if that is the institution's preference; presumably, however, the donor wants to avoid such outcomes. The cure is to maintain the purchasing power of the endowment fund, so that covering shortfalls is not an issue.

Intergenerational Equity

Preserving equity among generations is another reason for preserving the purchasing power of endowment funds. Tobin offers this eloquent argument:

> The trustees of an endowed institution are the guardians of the future against the claims of the present. Their task is to preserve equity among generations. The trustees of an endowed university like my own assume the institution to be immortal. They want to know, therefore, the rate of consumption from endowment that can

be sustained indefinitely. . . . In formal terms, the trustees are supposed to have a zero rate of time preference.

Consuming endowment income so defined means in principle that the existing endowment can continue to support the same set of activities that it is now supporting. This rule says that current consumption should not benefit from the prospects of future gifts to endowment. Sustainable consumption rises to encompass an enlarged scope of activities when, but not before, capital gifts enlarge the endowment.[6]

Intergenerational equity means that future students should enjoy the same benefits as present ones. Likewise, today's students should not have differential access to specific endowed activities compared with students of future generations who are not yet able to plead their case. Nor should today's faculty (or staff or alumni) be granted differential access to resources derived from endowments.

According to the intergenerational-equity argument, trustees should resist efforts to spend now at the expense of future stakeholders. The urgency of today's claims and the intensity with which they are pressed make this no easy task. Today's students and their parents want immediate program enrichment and relief from high tuition rates. Today's faculty have more good ideas for teaching, research, and scholarship than can be funded from currently available resources. The disadvantaged want greater access to special programs and facilities now.

Many in higher education support the intergenerational-equity argument, but it is not self-evident. According to Hansmann, in fact, "Under close scrutiny, concerns for intergenerational equity provide very doubtful support for current endowment policies."[7]

One line of argument against intergenerational equity holds that today's needs are so demanding that concerns about the future should take a back seat by comparison. Reinforcing such opinions are the stringent financial constraints that have come to dominate budgeting at many endowed colleges and universities and, indeed, social-purpose spending in America generally. That urgent needs exist—minority access and attainment, for instance—gives calls for spending rather than saving a certain credibility. Furthermore, it is argued, future generations gener-

---

6. Tobin 1974; as quoted in Hansmann 1990, 14.

7. Hansmann, 1990, 14. He also points out in a footnote that Tobin, "Is offering an interpretation of the view of university trustees and does not clearly commit himself to an endorsement of the policy he described."

ally will be better off, and they may not require the same endowment subsidy enjoyed by today's student.

A second criticism of the intergenerational-equity rationale is that current investments in higher education will pay dividends in the future, through the good works of graduates and the fruits of research. The sooner the investments are made, the sooner the returns will begin to accrue. Furthermore, the tendency for college and university costs to rise in real terms—for their productivity to lag, in other words—means that future investments will cost more than today's investments.[8] Therefore, the critics say, it is better to invest now than invest later.

The final argument is that colleges and universities simply should not be in the business of making decisions about intergenerational equity. The institutions were not created to further intergenerational equity, and making it an overriding concern seems presumptuous to the critics. The argument goes on to say that the uncertainty connected with intergenerational-equity decisions dooms the entire effort anyway, so it is better simply to go ahead and take advantage of today's opportunities.

The arguments against intergenerational equity are suspect for a number of reasons. The overriding objection is that those who make the arguments generally either have a personal stake in the matter (they are students, faculty, or staff who would benefit from more current spending) or are trying to pry resources from endowments to aid favored social programs. Theirs are advocacy arguments that should be evaluated as such, recognizing that potential future beneficiaries are not present to defend their interests. The uncertainty inherent in making trade-offs between present and future means that self-interested arguments for immediate spending should be discounted.

Some specific counterarguments exist as well. First, an increasingly competitive world means that the lifetime income of successive student generations is not assured of growing in real terms. Current graduates are finding it harder than their parents to afford a home, for instance. America's debtor status and lagging productivity, coupled with the work force's increasing burden of carrying retirement incomes, makes some erosion of living standards likely, if not inevitable. Second, the information revolution actually might increase academic productivity in quality-adjusted terms, and the greater consciousness of the need for productivity enhancement may bear fruit. Hence, future expenditures may arguably be more productive than current ones.

---

8. College and universities are labor intensive and thus tend to lag economy-wide productivity increases, at least in simple quantity terms. See Massy 1990.

Whether one is prepared to accept this thesis, ample basis exists for rejecting the critics' assertions on the subject.

Finally, trustees cannot ignore the question of intergenerational equity. The decisions they make about endowment spending and accumulation affect it, regardless of whether or not they set out to do so. In other words, colleges and universities are in the "intergenerational-equity business" just as they are in the "investment responsibility business" (with respect to tobacco companies, for instance), simply because they have endowments. Every generation has needs it considers urgent, and the trustees must swim against the tide to balance those needs against the claims of those not yet present. Deliberate allocation of resources from the future to the present certainly is possible, but this is a slippery slope, and governing boards should demand a high burden of proof of those who propose—possibly from a self-serving point of view—to do so.

Setting the Target Spending Rate

The end of the great bull market in 1974 not only brought financial hardship to many institutions but also underscored the need for a disciplined approach to setting the endowment-spending appropriation. However seriously one takes the foregoing philosophical issues, an account of the crash of '74 brings home the practical consequences of spending too much and saving too little. Stanford's experience, summarized in a passage I wrote in 1977, illustrates what happened:

> The payout rate had been in the 4 to 5 percent range until the 1960s, when Stanford, like many other institutions, embraced the total return concept of endowment management; that is, evaluating investment performance on yield plus capital appreciation rather than on yield alone. The change resulted in an increase of payout to a projected 5.5 percent for 1974–75, a rate that, although based on the idea of spending some capital appreciation, remained conservative by many other schools' standards. However, a declining stock market raised the effective payout rate for 1974–75 to 6.5 percent, and the amount of appreciation available for distribution was declining rapidly. By April 1974, it was exhausted. The payout rate was immediately reduced to the level of current yield—a necessary but disruptive procedure.[9]

---

9. Hopkins and Massy 1981, 44–45.

The next five years saw Stanford adjust its operating budget downward by about 10 percent in real terms. As part of this plan, we reduced the spending rate to 4.75 percent, a policy target that has remained in place ever since. Other institutions have had similar experiences.

In retrospect, the problem was not that the principles enumerated by the Ford Foundation were wrong but that they were incomplete. Experience and theory have combined to demonstrate that a properly diversified portfolio that includes risky assets will outperform a conservative portfolio over most time periods longer than a business cycle. Moreover, the distinction between yield and gain breaks down when assets are highly liquid and portfolios turn over rapidly. (I shall return to this point in a moment.) What was missed, however, was that the requirement to spend only yield provided an important, though ad hoc, discipline on the spending-saving relation. The needed discipline can be restored by hewing to a proper spending rule, but that requires the governing board to make a conscious decision of exercising its will.

What kind of spending rule should be adopted? John Kemeny, former president of Dartmouth College, wrote the following in an article published in *AGB Reports*:

> In summary, a utilization strategy must have the following components: (1) a good long-term estimate of total return and gifts to endowment; (2) a strategy for allocation, dividing the total between current use and additions to principal; (3) a means of smoothing out year-to-year oscillations; and (4) a self-corrective formula that adjusts slowly to changing conditions. Other approaches, such as a "magic" 5 percent, will lead to catastrophic cuts during an extended unfavorable period and so to overspending after a period of good years.[10]

Kemeny's position is based on the long-run financial equilibrium concepts described later in this chapter.[11] These concepts are powerful, but from the outset we should acknowledge that not everyone agrees

---

10. Kemeny 1983, no. 1, 19.

11. Kemeny builds on the financial equilibrium equation described by Hopkins and Massy 1981, chapter 6. The material in this chapter is based on the same concepts, modified to take in account of Kemeny's work and Anthony's criticism. The main modification consists of separating "Policy I" and "Policy II," as presented at the end of the chapter. Previously, the "fundamental question" (that discussed by Kemeny) balanced the sum of total return and the rate of gifts and other endowment addition, on the one hand, and endowment total return and utilization on the other. Stanford adopted the revised approach circa 1986.

with Kemeny's four criteria. Professor Robert Anthony of the Harvard Business School offered this rebuttal, "Defending 5 percent":

[Kemeny's] criticism of the use of an "arbitrary" 5 percent spending rate overlooks one important point. . . .

His alternative requires that in preparing a budget, estimates be made of the total endowment return and of gift revenue and that a judgment be made as to how this total should be divided between revenue and capital. I am skittish about permitting the budget to be influenced by these estimates and judgment. The great advantage of an arbitrary 5 percent (applied to a three- or five-year moving average market value) is that the only estimate required is the market value of the final year. Using an average reduces year-to-year fluctuations to a relatively small amount.[12]

The greater the leeway for estimates and judgment, the greater the temptation to provide for increased spending requests by manipulating the endowment revenue number, rather than by the painful alternatives of curbing expenses or raising tuition. The institution is less likely to resist such temptations when there is an easy way out.

Anthony continues to say that, although 5 percent sounds arbitrary, it approximates the long-run real total return for an investment portfolio, "with risk characteristics appropriate for a college."

The procedure for determining spending presented in this chapter is based on Kemeny's four criteria, but the approach has been modified to take account of Anthony's concern about lack of precision ("leeway," in his words). Before describing the procedure, however, yet another excursion into the realm of college and university economics may be helpful. Consider the following example:

Mrs. X gave an endowed professorship in 1955. The spending appropriation was expected to cover the professor's compensation and a modest amount of research support. She intended that this be done "in perpetuity" so now, 40 years later, the endowment should cover the same expenses, inflated by salary increases and other cost-rise factors. The original endowment gift was sufficient to fund $20,000 of annual expense in 1955.

Suppose that, over the years, the university's internal inflation rate has been 5 percent compounded—say 3.5 percent due to economy-wide inflation and 1.5 percent due to real salary increases and simi-

---

12. Kemeny 1983, no. 2, sidebar on p. 15.

lar internal cost-rise factors. Suppose, also, that the long-run expected real rate of return on the endowment is 5.5 percent, which, when added to the inflation rate, comes to 9 percent nominal. The university determines its spending rate at the beginning of the year, but manages its cash so as to leave the funds in the endowment pool as long as possible; usually that amounts to most of the year.

What rate of endowment spending is consistent with Mrs. X's wishes? How much would she have had to give to fully fund the chair in 1955, given the school's chosen spending rate?

One way to answer these questions is to do some trial-and-error arithmetic. Suppose the spending rate was 6 percent, for instance. That means Mrs. X's gift would have had to be $20,000 + 0.06 = $333,333, to cover the chair's expenses in 1955 dollars. The difference between the 9 percent total return from investments and the 6 percent spending rate is reinvested in the "Mrs. X Endowment Fund." If the actual total return was equal to its expected value, the fund balance would grow by 9 percent − 6 percent = 3 percent per year. In 1956, the balance would be $343,333, and in 1990, forty years after the gift, it would be $1,087,345. Applying the 6 percent spending rate yields $20,600 of budget support in 1956 and $65,241 in 1995. Unfortunately, however, the applicable expenses grow at 5 percent: to $21,000 in 1956 and to nearly $140,800 in 1995. By 1995, the gap between the endowment spending appropriation and the chair's expense level is $75,559. In only forty years the endowment fund has shrunk in real terms to the point where it pays less than half of the applicable expenses! So much for support in perpetuity.

The calculations for 1995 are summarized in table 1 (rounded to the nearest thousand), along with those based on a number of other potential spending rates.

A spending rate of 4 percent keeps the growth of budget support from Mrs. X's endowment just equal to the growth of applicable expense. The state of affairs in which the growth rates of income and expense are equal is called *long-run financial equilibrium*. The spending rate that produces this result is called the *equilibrium spending rate*.

TABLE 1.   Sensitivity of Endowment Growth to the Spending Rate

Spending Rate	Initial Expense	Initial Balance	Endowment Growth	1995 Balance	1995 Spending	1995 Expense	1995 Gap
6%	$20	$333	3%	$1,087	$65	$141	$76
5	20	400	4	1,920	96	141	45
4	20	500	5	3,520	141	141	0
3	20	667	6	6,857	206	141	(65)

One does not have to find the equilibrium spending rate by trial and error. Table 2 illustrates a simple but powerful relationship between the growth rates of the sources and uses of endowment funds.

Long-run financial equilibrium requires the growth rates of total sources and uses of funds to be equal. Real total return is determined by the investment mix. Real cost-rise is a function of many factors, such as salaries and supplies. Therefore, the spending rate is the only variable over which the institution has discretion. The procedure is to solve for the spending rate given the other variables. Notice, however, that inflation appears on both sides of the table and thus cancels out. Hence the formula for computing the equilibrium spending rate:[13]

equilibrium spending rate = real total return − real cost-rise.

This formula assumes that the spending appropriation stays in the endowment and earns a return for the full year. The endowment growth implied by the formula is:

ending endowment = (1 + total return − spending rate)

× (beginning endowment).

If, on the other hand, the institution were to withdraw the spending appropriation at the beginning of the year, the endowment growth would be:

ending endowment = (1 + total return)(1 − spending rate)

× (beginning endowment).

That is, in the example, only 96 percent of the beginning-of-year endowment would earn a return. The spending rate must be adjusted downward to take this into account. The result is the following revised equilibrium spending formula:

$$\text{equilibrium spending rate} = 1 - \frac{1 + \text{cost rise}}{1 + \text{total return}},$$

---

13. See Hopkins and Massy 1981, chapter 5, for extensive discussion of long-run financial equilibrium and the role of the equilibrium spending rate. The concepts were first described in Massy 1973. See also Massy 1975; Massy 1976. Some of the same ideas can be found in Ennis and Williamson 1976, chapter 4.

TABLE 2. Calculation of the Equilibrium Spending Rate

Source of Funds	Growth Rate	Use of Funds	Growth Rate
Inflation	3.5%	Inflation	3.5%
Real total return	5.5	Real cost-rise	1.5
		Spending appropriation	4.0
Total	9.0	Total	9.0

which holds when the spending appropriation is withdrawn at the beginning of the year.[14] This formula produces an equilibrium spending rate of 3.7 percent rather than 4 percent.

The equilibrium spending rate is zero when cost-rise equals total return and goes negative when it exceeds total return.[15] What is the interpretation of this anomaly? First, efforts to maintain the endowment's real purchasing power are bound to fail when costs escalate faster than investment return. If this state of affairs persists long enough, the idea of support in perpetuity would be meaningless. Long-run studies of investment return show, however, that the chance that long-run total return will be less than long-run cost-rise is remote if the institution follows a reasonable investment strategy.

All the equilibrium formulas are based on long-run growth rates. That actual total return is less than cost-rise for a few years produces a "smoothing problem" (which will be considered later), but this difference does not affect the equilibrium calculations. Smoothing the payout helps answer Anthony's concern about leeway. The figure for long-run expected total return should be calculated from market data developed by professional investment analysts. Although total-return estimates require a good degree of judgment, the investment professionals can distance themselves from the spending needs of the institution. Once the total-return estimates have been made, the calculation of long-run expected total return follows objectively.

The problem with the move to total-return investing in the early 1970s was that spending rates moved up from levels that were too low to utilize endowment assets properly to levels that were too high to compensate for institutions' internal cost-rise. Exacerbating the problem was a rise in inflation and a decrease in investment returns during the remainder of the 1970s.

---

14. The formula is obtained by setting the ratio of this year's to last year's endowment to the nominal rate of cost-rise and solving for the payout. Notice that both cost-rise and total return are measured in nominal, not real terms. See Ennis and Williamson 1976, 27, for a different way of getting the adjustment.

15. The phenomenon was discussed by Kemeny 1983, no. 2, 13–14.

In contrast, the conventional method of spending only yield provided for the automatic reinvestment of capital gains and thus an approximation to the foregoing calculation. This is most easily seen in the case of real estate investments, though the principle applies to all investments. Suppose one owns a shopping center that produces an annual rent of $1 million, calculated as a percentage of sales. Inflation drives up prices, which translates quickly into increased rents. The value of the shopping center goes up too, as long as the "capitalization rate" (the analogy to the price-earning rate for stocks) remains constant. The total return from the shopping center is the sum of the year's rents plus the appreciation, divided by the center's beginning market value. Spending all or most total return amounts to dipping into capital, whereas spending only yield keeps the real value of capital intact by allowing the appreciation—the portion of total return due to inflation—to remain in the business.

Reinvestment is automatic under a spend only yield policy, whereas under the total-return approach it must be the subject of careful decision making and disciplined follow-through. Therefore, one might ask, would it not be better to call the total-return approach a failure and revert to the conventional wisdom? The answer is "no" for two reasons:

1. The amount of reinvestment delivered by a spend only yield policy bears no relation to the amount needed by colleges and universities to offset their internal cost-rise. This is illustrated by the shopping center example. If all rents are based on a percentage of sales, and capitalization rates are constant, the automatic reinvestment rate will be exactly the inflation rate, which is too low by an amount equal to the institution's real cost-rise. (In the Mrs. X example, the reinvestment rate would be only 3.5 percent compared with the 5 percent needed to sustain the academic program.) In general, the amount of reinvestment under the spend only yield policy may be either too low or too high, depending on the investment vehicle and economic conditions.

2. Even more important is the fact that a spend only yield policy binds investment strategy closely to the institution's need for current funds. Some investment vehicles have fine prospects for long-run total return but limited or even negative current yield. Real estate investments with low or negative initial cash flows fall into this category, as do venture capital investments. The difficulty of justifying such investments in the face of an immediate "hit" on the budget should not be underestimated, yet they may be highly desirable from a long-run point of view. Marking

all investments to market and then determining spending on the basis of total return goes a long way toward mitigating these difficulties.

Constructing a spending rule to meet the criterion for long-run financial equilibrium is preferable to relying on the "natural" linkages between yield, total return, and cost-rise. Though better than nothing, those linkages are too uncertain to be relied upon unequivocally. Two additional considerations must be addressed, however: (1) the problem of total-return volatility and (2) legal and accounting problems associated with blurring the distinction between yield and gain.

Smoothing the Spending Level

A well-run modern portfolio consisting of, say, 70 percent stocks and 30 percent bonds has an expected volatility (as measured by the standard deviation of total return) of about twelve percentage points. The expected return for this portfolio is about 5.5 percent over inflation. Translated into English and ignoring some statistical niceties, the actual total return for a given year has about a one in three chance of falling outside the range 5.5 ± 12 percent (that is, less than −6.5 percent or more than 17.5 percent). The effect of such volatility is apparent in the following example.

> Imagine an institution with: (1) $300 million of endowment, 70 percent invested in stock and 30 percent in bonds; and (2) an operating budget of $120 million that grows 1.5 percent faster than an inflation rate of 3.5 percent. (The last two figures are the same as in our earlier example.) The equilibrium spending rate is 4 percent, so the endowment covers $12 million of expense, which is 10 percent of the budget. Expected endowment growth is 5 percent per year, which would produce $600,000 of extra spending. This is just what is needed to cover cost-rise on the 10 percent of the budget supported by endowment.
>
> But what if real total return turns out to be −6.5 percent, one standard deviation less than expected? Then the endowment market value drops by 6 percent.[16] Available spending from the endowment decreases by $720,000 instead of increasing by $600,000 as

---

16. The calculation is 6 percent = 3.5 percent − 6.5 percent − 4 percent, where the first figure is inflation, the second is the actual total return, and the third is the spending rate.

expected in long-run financial equilibrium. On the other hand, if total return exceeds its expectation by one standard deviation, the endowment grows by 17.5 percent. These results are summarized in table 3.

The swing in spending is $1.32 million, which amounts to 11 percent of the budget. An 11 percent budget "hole" is very difficult to handle, yet losses of this or greater magnitude would be expected to occur in about one year out of six! Unexpected gains are always welcome, of course, but they can be destabilizing just the same. No higher education institution can tolerate such boom-bust cycles without disadvantaging its academic program.

The example shows that applying a constant spending rate—even the equilibrium rate—to a fluctuating endowment market value produces unacceptable swings in budget support. Fortunately, a better way to set the spending level exists.

Most institutions that use a total return-based spending strategy have developed a procedure for smoothing year-to-year spending fluctuations. Such a procedure permits the actual spending rate to diverge from the equilibrium spending rate in a controlled way. Ideally, this procedure also builds in a feedback mechanism to continually pull back the actual rate toward an equilibrium or target value.[17] Although many smoothing approaches exist, they tend to fall into one of the following categories: (1) methods based on escalating the level of spending by a preset amount over that of the previous year, (2) methods based on a moving average of past endowment market values, (3) hybrid methods, and (4) methods based on judging the "need for spending," usually as part of the budget process.[18] Any of the methods can be constrained by preset minimum or maximum spending rates or levels, as described later.

1. *Preset increment over last year.* The first step is to calculate the expected growth rate in the spending level based on the expected total return and the chosen spending rate:

---

17. If the institution hasn't calculated its equilibrium-payout rate, then some other target rate can be used instead. In general, though, the feedback mechanisms don't work well unless the target rate is close to the equilibrium rate.

18. An entirely different approach, based on the dynamic programming, can be found in Grinold, Hopkins, and Massy 1978. To the best of my knowledge, this model has never been used in practice, though.

expected growth rate of spending = expected total return

$$- \text{ spending rate.}$$

The calculation can operate either in real or nominal terms, but using real total return has some advantages. That way, inflation is added back in at the next stage of the calculation, thus indexing the spending increment.

The second step is to apply the escalation factor to the previous year's spending level, regardless of what has happened to the endowment market value in the meantime. In foregoing example, this would produce a spending increment of $600,000 regardless of the actual total return. In practice, the escalator usually is applied to the per-share spending rather than to spending in the aggregate. Using the aggregate amount would not take into account new gifts and similar additions to the endowment.

Taken by itself, this procedure is "open loop," in that it contains no feedback mechanism to compensate for deviations of total return from its expectation. Continuing with the example used earlier, suppose total return was −6.5 percent but now a "5 percent escalation rule" is in effect. The preset escalator guarantees that there is no budget hole. On the other hand, the actual spending rate has deviated sharply from the target rate, as shown in the following calculation:

$$\frac{\text{actual spending}}{\text{rate [year 2]}} = \frac{\text{spending [year 2]}}{\text{beginning endowment}} = \frac{\$12.6\,\text{million}}{\$282\,\text{million}} = 4.5\%.$$
$$\text{[year 2]}$$

The equilibrium spending rate was 4 percent, so the disappointing total-return figure has opened up a spending rate gap of 0.5 percent.

TABLE 3.   **Sensitivity of Unsmoothed Spending to Investment Return**

Total Return	Endowment Year 1	Spending Year 1	Endowment Year 2	Spending Year 2	Real % Change in Spending
5.5%	$300	$12.00	$315	$12.60	−5%
−6.5	300	12.00	282	11.28	−6
17.5	300	12.00	353	14.10	17.5

Research shows that markets cannot be counted upon to retrace their steps, so we cannot be sure that market actions will restore the equilibrium spending rate. Indeed, the gap may well get larger unless there is an intervention to move the system back toward equilibrium. One can intervene in two ways:

By monitoring the spending rate over time and making ad hoc adjustments when the deviation from the equilibrium rate becomes too large for comfort. The problem with this approach is that it begs the question of "how much divergence is too much," which in turn throws the matter back into the institution's budgeting arena. There never is a good time to reduce spending below the amount previously scheduled under the percentage-increment rule, and pressures always will exist to increase spending when the actual spending rate is below the equilibrium rate. (Recall Anthony's concern about leeway.) The pressures to spend bias the average rate upward as compared to the equilibrium rate.

By using ceilings and floors to constrain spending within acceptable limits. The procedure is to override the percent-increase rule when it would take spending outside the preset limits. The problem with ceilings and floors is that they can be jerky when the spending rate is near a limit. Suppose, in our example, that the school had decided it would not allow the actual spending rate go above 4.5 percent and that the total return in year one turned out to be -6.5 percent. Applying this rule in its simplest form would mean that a disappointing total return the following year would be transmitted to the budget without smoothing.

2. *Moving average.* The most common smoothing method is to apply the target spending rate to an average of the last n years of endowment-share market values. Larger values of n produce more smoothing, but this comes at the price of greater divergence between actual and target spending rates. Another problem with the moving-average method is that the effect of a large total-return deviation will stay in the moving average with undiminished weight until it is dropped at the end of the nth year. Such "start-stop" averaging, which represents another kind of jerkiness, can undermine the discipline of the smoothing procedure. This occurs when people responsible for the budget say things like, "The market crash of '87 will be out of the moving average in another two years, so why not anticipate that and give us some extra income now?"

3. *A hybrid approach.* Currently used by Stanford and Yale, the hybrid approach combines the best of the moving-average and percentage-increment methods.[19] The procedure is applied this way:

> Calculate per-share spending under the preset-increment method, setting the escalator equal to the expected budget growth.
>
> Calculate target per-share spending, which is the product of the target spending rate and the beginning (unsmoothed) per-share market value.
>
> Set next year's per-share spending equal to a weighted average of the preset-increment and target values.

The weight usually runs between 0.25 and 0.4. (It is applied to the target spending level.) My research suggests that one-third is about right, though the exact value is a matter of institutional choice.

Suppose last year's spending appropriation is 50¢ a share, this year's beginning market value is $10 per share, cost-rise is 5 percent, the target spending rate is 4 percent, and the weight 0.33. Then next year's spending appropriation is:

$$(0.33)(0.04)(\$10.00) + (0.67)(1.05)(\$0.50) = \$0.483.$$

Notice that, in this example, per-share spending declined from 50¢ to 48.3¢ instead of increasing by the desired 5 percent. This is because the current per-share market value of $10 will sustain a target spending level of only 40¢. The smoothing rule phases in the lower spending level a little at a time. On the other hand, if the total return on the endowment had been higher—so that the market value had been $13, for instance—the formula would yield 52.3¢. This compares favorably with the desired value of 52.5¢.

The hybrid procedure simultaneously takes account of the target spending rate and the desired spending increment, and the actual spending appropriation always tends to converge to its equilibrium value. The formula is called an "exponentially weighted moving average" because the influence of each prior year's total

---

19. See Hopkins and Massy 1981, chapter 7. A detailed mathematical representation of the model and the procedures used to test it can be found in Massy, Grinold, Hopkins, and Gerson 1981.

return declines exponentially. For example, the weight applied to the current year's market value is 0.33, that for last year's is 0.33^2, the one for the previous year's is 0.33^3, and so on. This avoids the problem, mentioned earlier, that a given data point may vanish abruptly from the conventional moving average.[20] Spending growth is continuously adjusted in response to market results, so jerkiness is avoided.

The degree to which the formula tracks the target spending rate can be adjusted by changing the weight. At the extreme, a weight of 1.0 means there is no smoothing at all (perfect tracking, but also maximal variation in spending). Conversely, when the weight is zero, there is no smoothing and we have the preset-increment method.

Figure 1 gives an example of how the choice of weight affects the degree of smoothing.[21] With no smoothing, the line tracks the values of pE (the payout rate times the endowment market value, shown as dots). Moving the weight to 0.541 introduces a considerable amount of smoothing—the same amount, in fact, as a three-year moving average, though without the jerkiness.[22] Going to 0.398, the equivalent of a five-year moving average, adds more smoothing. Even smaller weights (0.2 and 0.1) increase the smoothing still further. A zero weight (not shown) would be a horizontal line.[23]

4. *Judgment.* Certain institutions still rely on judgment for smoothing the level of spending. Some spend all or a portion of current income (yield), while others decide during the budget pro-

---

20. Ennis and Williamson 1976, conclude (p. 47) that the exponentially weighted moving average spending rule is unnecessarily complicated and that the complication serves no purpose. I disagree.

21. The figure assumes that total return follows a log-normal distribution with mean 1.055 and standard deviation 0.12. (The 20 points shown have been selected to have a geometric mean very close to 1.055.) The other parameters are as described in the text example: cost-rise of 5 percent, target payout rate of 4.75 percent, and spending level of 1.00. The system was started at a random position within a longer time series of endowment market values and spending appropriations.

22. The value 0.541 is obtained by setting the expression for the variance of the exponentially weighted moving average equal to that for the variance of a five-year moving average, and solving for the weight. The value 0.398 is obtained by doing the same for a three-year moving average.

23. Per-share spending is expressed in real terms, based on the school's internal rate of cost-rise. Therefore, the preset increment method (the equivalent of no smoothing) maintains spending at 1.0 which is a horizontal line.

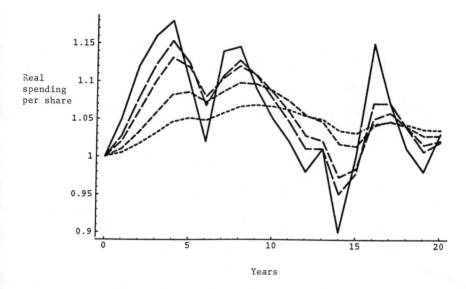

Line   = 1.0   (no smoothing).
Long dash   = 0.541 (three-year moving average)
Medium dash = 0.398 (five-year moving average)
Short dash   = 0.2
Dotted   = 0.1

Fig. 1. Simulation of exponentially weighted moving average smoothing rule

cess. The latter institutions have abandoned the strict spend only yield policy but have not replaced it with another formula. The flexibility so gained can be a great advantage, especially for a small college where decisions can be made by a compact and cohesive group of people representing all constituencies. On the other hand, only time will tell if the benefits outweigh the costs, cited by Anthony, of operating without a firm spending discipline.

The basic smoothing procedures I have described can be augmented with ceilings and floors, as shown in the following examples.

Increase spending by 4 percent each year, up to a ceiling of 5.5 percent of market value.

Increase spending by 6 percent each year. Spending must range between 4.5 percent and 5.5 percent of a twelve-quarter moving average of market values.

Spend 4.5 percent of a three-year moving average of market values, but not less than the prior year's spending expressed in nominal dollars.

The last example avoids the problem of reducing spending in nominal dollars, which would be politically difficult on many campuses.

The popularity of ceilings and floors seems to be increasing. They have a certain grounding in common sense, and they can avoid what might seem to the layperson to be anomalous results. On the other hand, they also have an ad hoc flavor, being less grounded in principle than one might like. The spending rule will lose credibility, undermining the entire endowment-spending discipline if additional ad hoc limits are added whenever some new problem arises. The advantage of the exponentially weighted moving-average method is that it largely eliminates the need for ad hoc limits. Though more complicated to explain, it can handle a broader array of circumstances and is less prone to second-guessing than the three-year or five-year moving-average or preset-increment methods.

Statistics on College and University Spending Rates

Institutions have a well-founded interest in the policies of their peers. This arises both from the need to establish benchmarks and because the courts tend to look to the precedent of common practice in assessing whether an institution has met its fiduciary responsibilities.

Data on endowment spending rates for 1994 are presented in table 4. (The data are for actual spending rates, as distinguished from the target rates written into the spending rule.) Weighting institutions equally produces a mean of 6 percent, whereas the median was 5.1. The dollar-weighted mean is 5 percent, which indicates that the larger schools tend to have lower spending rates. This is confirmed by the distribution of rates by size categories. In fact, only the schools in the smallest endowment category have the larger spending rates. Perhaps they are more likely to base spending strictly on yield, which was fairly high during the period in question.

One should not confuse actual spending rates with target or equilibrium rates. Assuming an institution uses some kind of smoothing rule, the actual spending rate will lag below the target during periods when markets are rising and exceed it when markets are falling. Information on target spending rates is difficult to collect because of the variety of spending and smoothing rules. However, analysis of the spending rules for the clients of Cambridge Associates, the consulting firm that provides data services and advice to college and university financial managers, provides a useful database on a small group of relatively well-endowed schools.

Table 5 shows that the moving average method is used by 56

TABLE 4.   Endowment Spending Rates (in percentage), Fiscal Year 1994

Responding Institutions	Endowment Spending Rate
In Aggregate	
Equal-weighted mean	6.0
Dollar-weighted mean	5.0
Median	5.1
By Endowment Size (equal-weighted mean)	
$25 million and under	7.2
Over $25 million to $100 million	6.1
Over $100 million to $400 million	5.2
Over $400 million	4.5
By Type (equal-weighted mean)	
Public	6.6
Private	5.7

Source: 1994 NACUBO Endowment Study (Washington, DC: Cambridge Assoc., 1995) 46. Reprinted by permission.

Note: The endowment spending rates represents endowment payout, investment management and custody expenses, and other distributions and transfers from the endowment expressed as a percentage of the average of fiscal year beginning and ending endowment market values. For this analysis, 83% of respondents provided data.

TABLE 5.   Endowment Spending Rules

Spending Rule	Number of Institutions	Percentage of Total
Spend all current income	33	7.4%
Spend a prespecified percentage of current income	14	3.1
Spend a prespecified percentage of beginning market value	29	6.5
Spend a prespecified percentage of a moving average of market values	252	56.4
Increase prior year's spending by a prespecified percentage	26	5.8
Decide on an appropriate rule each year	35	7.8
Other rule	50	11.2
No established policy	2	0.4
No response	6	1.3
Total	447	100

Source: 1994 NACUBO Endowment Study (Washington, DC: Cambridge Associates, 1995), 4. Reprinted by permission.

percent of the schools responding to the 1994 NACUBO endowment study, up from 40 percent in 1991. Ad hoc arrangements and spending all current income (yield) come next at 7.8 percent and 7.4 percent respectively. (The aggregate for "other rules" is 11 percent, but no single rule comes close to this figure.) About 6.5 percent of schools spend a prespecified percentage of market value, presumably without smoothing, and 5.8 percent increase prior year's spending by a prespecified amount. The prespecified increment method, which is flawed in our opinion, has dropped substantially since 1991 when it represented some 10 percent of the sample. Only two schools report no established policy, compared to thirty-five schools in 1991's smaller sample.

An ever-increasing number of American colleges and universities are concerned with endowment management. In 1989, 315 schools reported on their endowment to NACUBO; in 1991, 390 schools; and by 1994, that number had risen to 447. The amount of endowment American colleges and universities has accumulated is substantial. As shown in table 6, the total sum involved is almost $89 billion, up from a reported $65 billion in 1991. The endowment holdings are quite concentrated, with about 9 percent of the institutions possessing over half the total dollars. Yet substantial sums remain in the smaller size categories, and these endowments are of great importance to the institutions that hold them.

Like other major institutional investors, large endowments have been the beneficiaries of proven, systematic investment strategies made possible by extraordinary analytical and technological advances. Discussion of these methods lies beyond the scope of this chapter, but it will suffice to say that they involve diversification of asset classes and management styles, and the rigorous control of investment risk. That these benefits have to some extent eluded the small endowment is demonstrated by table 7, which shows investment total returns (interest, dividends, and capital appreciation) by endowment size and type for the three years ending in 1994. The average small endowment earns about 2.2 percent less each year than the average large endowment. Moreover, the small endowment pays 15 basis points (0.15 percent) more in manager and custodial costs (not shown in the table), and it spends some 2.7 percent more (see table 4). In other words, the small endowment gets less, pays more, and spends more. Hopefully the ideas in this chapter will provide impetus for small and medium-sized endowments to take advantage of the modern techniques proved out by their larger cousins.

TABLE 6. Endowment Assets Aggregate Market Values as of Fiscal 1994 Year End

Responding Institutions	Number of Institutions	Percentage of Institutions	Endowment Assets ($000s)	Percentage of Aggregate Endowment Assets	Life Income Fund Assets ($000s)
In Aggregate	446	100.0	88,940,849	100.0	3,081,654
By Endowment Size					
$25 million and under	96	21.5	1,429,209	1.6	91,448
Over $25 million to					
$100 million	187	41.9	10,021,488	11.3	528,776
Over $100 million					
to $400 million	122	27.4	24,999,602	28.1	1,225,865
Over $400 million	41	9.2	52,490,550	59.0	1,235,565
By type					
Public	138	30.9	23,041,174	25.9	655,040
Private	308	69.1	65,899,675	74.1	2,426,614

Source: 1994 NACUBO Endowment Study (Washington, DC: Cambridge Assoc., 1995), 21. Reprinted by permission.

TABLE 7. Endowment Total Returns: 1992–94

Responding Institutions	Average Annual Compound Nominal Return 1992–94
In Aggregate	
Equal-weighted mean	9.7
Dollar-weighted mean	10.8
Median	9.7
By Investment Pool Size (equal-weighted mean)	
$25 million and under	8.6
Over $25 million to $100 million	9.4
Over $100 million to $400 million	10.5
Over $400 million	10.8
By Type (equal-weighted mean)	
Public	9.4
Private	9.8
Market Indexes	
Wilshire 5000	10.2
S&P 500	9.3
LB Aggregate	8.0
CPI (W)	2.7

Source: 1994 NACUBO Endowment Study (Washington, DC: Cambridge Assoc., 1995), 96. Reprinted by permission.

REFERENCES

Adams, Rodney H. 1972. "Current Trends in College and University Investment Policies and Practices." *NACUBO Studies in Management* 1, no. 3.

Cary, William L., and Craig B. Bright. 1969. *The Law and Lore of Endowment Funds*. New York: Ford Foundation.

Ennis, Richard M., and Peter Williamson. 1976. *Spending Policy for Educational Endowments: A Research and Publication Project of The Common Fund*. New York: The Common Fund.

Ford Foundation Advisory Committee on Endowment Management. 1969. "Managing Educational Endowments: Report to the Ford Foundation." New York: Ford Foundation.

Grinold, Richard C., David S. P. Hopkins, and William F. Massy. 1978. "A Model for Long-Range University Budget Planning under Uncertainty." *Bell Journal of Economics and Management Science* 9:396–420.

Hansmann, Henry. 1990. "Why Do Universities Have Endowments?" *Journal of Legal Studies* 19, no. 1:3–42.

Hopkins, David S. P., and William F. Massy. 1981. *Planning Models for Colleges and Universities*. Stanford, CA: Stanford University Press.

Kemeny, John G. 1983. "The Mystique of University Endowments." *AGB Reports* 25, no. 1:13–19, and no. 2:11–15.

Massy, William F. 1973. "The Economics of Endowed Universities." Academic Planning Office Report. Stanford, CA: Academic Planning Office, Stanford University.

———. 1975. "Resource Management for Financial Equilibrium." *NACUBO Professional File* 7, no. 7:1–7.

———. 1976. "A Dynamic Equilibrium Model for University Budget Planning." *Management Science* 23:248–56.

———. 1990. "A Paradigm for Research on Higher Education." In John C. Smart, ed., *Handbook of Higher Education Theory and Research,* 6:1–34. New York: Agathon Press.

Massy, William F., Richard C. Grinold, David S. P. Hopkins, and Alejandro Gerson. 1981. "Optimal Smoothing Rules for University Financial Planning." *Operations Research* 29:1121–36.

National Association of College and University Business Officers. 1995. *1994 NACUBO Endowment Study*. Prepared by Cambridge Associates (Washington, DC).

Tobin, James. 1974. "What Is Permanent Endowment Income?" *American Economic Review* 64.

CHAPTER 5

Optimizing Capital Decisions

William F. Massy

Having examined the principles by which spending from existing endowments should be determined, we now turn to the broader question of whether trustees should put new money into the endowment when given the opportunity to do so, invest in physical capital (facilities and equipment), or spend for current purposes. While the disposition of discretionary funds might sound like a narrow question, it in fact opens the broad issue of integrated, strategic financial planning.

Suppose, by way of example, that an institution has just received a large and unexpected unrestricted bequest. The nature of the gift implies that the funds have not already been "spoken for" by those responsible for balancing the operating budget, or by a particular school or department. Therefore, the institution's central administration and board have a relatively free hand in determining how the money will be used. We shall imagine that they have identified five choices. The first two are generic in the sense that they are always available. The last two are specific to this particular institution, but they represent a broad class of similar opportunities.

> *Use the money to increase the operating budget.* This choice would permit additions to faculty or staff, boosting salaries, or adding to supplies and travel budgets.
>
> *Use the money to fund current expenditures of a one-time nature.* This will produce a burst of current spending, but for purposes with finite time horizons commensurate with the funding capacity of the gift. Examples include paying the expenses of a fund-raising campaign or financing a burst of faculty early retirements.
>
> *Put the money in quasi endowment.* This will produce a constant stream of incremental spending, pX, where p is the endowment

Based on Massy 1990, no. 967, with the permission of the Association of Governing Boards of Universities and Colleges.

payout rate. The incremental spending will permit the addition of certain program options or provide relief from existing budget pressures, but to a lesser degree than if the whole gift had been used for operations.

Construct a new science building. This will meet an urgent current program need. It also may increase the flow of research grants and contracts, adding to the school's stature and allowing the institution to spread its fixed costs over a larger operating base. On the negative side, it will add requirements for operations and maintenance, not all of which will be reimbursed as part of research overhead. The useful life of the building is likely to be short (say thirty years) compared with the school's other facilities because of the rapid pace of scientific obsolescence. Furthermore, the expected scientific breakthroughs and extra research funds are far from certain, which adds another element of subjective discounting to the equation. The construction and maintenance costs for high-tech buildings are uncertain, too.

Renovate the undergraduate dormitories. This will mitigate student complaints and possibly increase the number of applicants and acceptances. Furthermore, because the dormitories are decaying at an accelerating rate, and the renovation will have to be done sooner or later if the dorms are to remain usable, renovating now instead of later will cost less in constant dollars. The renovation is expected to last a long time, much longer than the science building. (Of course, the useful life of dormitories is not infinitely long, as is the time horizon for endowment.)

This example illustrates several major complications that make choosing among investments more difficult than the analogous problem of choosing among current spending alternatives. Expanding the operating budget would be popular and would generate immediate utility. However, committing the money to the operating budget might well produce an expenditure level that cannot be sustained. Whereas tuition, state appropriations, endowment payout, overhead from grants and contracts, and the on-going flow of annual giving are likely to persist from year to year, and thus are appropriate for funding ongoing operations, experience shows that using one-time income from individual gifts to balance the operating budget invites future financial problems.

None of the other alternatives can be dismissed so easily. Complications include:

1. The judgments not only are subjective, but they involve indirect as well as direct effects, and they operate over disparate conceptual domains.
2. The investments can increase operating costs as well as produce benefits.
3. The investments can increase operating income, either directly or indirectly.
4. The benefits, costs, and income changes can be uncertain.
5. Endowment investments are reversible; investments in facilities are not.
6. The benefits, costs, and income changes can occur over long time periods, and the time profiles can differ markedly from investment to investment.

Points 1 through 4 are self-evident, but 5 and 6 require additional discussion.

Reversibility

Endowment investments are liquid, and thus reversible, because the securities that comprise the bulk of the portfolio can be sold quickly. Investments in college and university physical plant are highly illiquid, because the facilities usually are specialized, and in any case, no institution wants to rent or sell campus buildings to an outsider. This means that trustees can reverse decisions to invest in the endowment, but they rarely can do so for plant investments.

Reversibility is important because unrestricted quasi endowment is a school's ultimate liquid reserve. It is a fund that can be used to handle deficits, to rebuild after a catastrophe, to take advantage of some momentous opportunity, or even to act as dowry in a merger. While facilities sometimes can serve these purposes (especially the last), their ability to do so is limited. Unrestricted quasi endowment can be liquidated in a matter of days, if necessary, and then spent for any legitimate purpose.

Restricted quasi endowment plays a similar role, though to a lesser degree. Although spending is limited to donor-specified purposes, in a financial crisis the general funds that jointly support those purposes can be withdrawn from the budget and the restricted quasi endowment liquidated to take up the slack. Therefore, disclosing restricted as well as unrestricted quasi endowment on the balance sheet is important.

The smaller the unrestricted and restricted expendable-funds balances and the funded self-insurance reserves, the more important quasi endowment is for liquidity. The governing board should review the totality of these *available funds* in light of its assessment of the school's risk profile. (Available funds comprise the restricted and unrestricted expendable and quasi endowment funds.) These funds represent money that can be obtained on short notice to cover debt or other needs. In general, this is the sum of unrestricted expendable-funds balances and unrestricted quasi endowment.

If the available funds are too small, the trustees must choose between increasing expendable balances (operating reserves, for instance), self-insurance reserves, or the quasi endowment. The choice is difficult. Accounting principles may suggest segregating the funds in specific insurance reserves, but the need for flexibility encourages keeping the funds together in a general operating reserve. Being invested in the endowment pool, quasi endowment has a much larger total-return expectation than the current funds pool, where reserves are usually invested. On the other hand, the extra return is bought at the expense of market value fluctuations that may reduce the fund's value just when it is most needed.

Discounting

Colleges and universities discount future utility the same way business firms discount profits. The relation between utility and financial discounting, however, may not be clear. The following model addresses this question by examining the conditions under which funds should be spent now or put into the quasi endowment.[1] (Readers who are not comfortable with utility functions and present-value analysis can skip this section without loss of continuity.)

Let X represent the amount of discretionary funds under consideration. Spending X now will produce a certain amount of immediate extra utility, which we will denote by $DU(X)$. Putting X into the endowment would produce a stream of payments equal to pX, where p is the equilibrium endowment spending rate. (Using the equilibrium spending rate ensures that pX maintains its purchasing power over time.) We will denote the resulting annual utility gain by $DU(pX)$.

Let d be the trustees' subjective time-discount rate for utility, the factor by which a given amount of utility obtained next year will be

---

1. A more comprehensive, though also more abstract, model can be found in Hopkins and Massy 1981, 96–100.

discounted compared with the same amount obtained right away. Then the present value of the time stream of utilities $U(pX)$ is the sum of the infinite series:

$$DU(pX) + d^{-1}D(pX) + d^{-2}DU(pX) + \ldots = \frac{DU(pX)}{d}.$$

According to this analysis, it will be best to put the money into the endowment if the discounted time stream of $DU(pX)$ is greater than the one-time benefit $DU(X)$. That is,

$$\frac{DU(pX)}{d} > DU(X).$$

It will be best to spend now if the inequality points the other way.

Suppose, now, that utility is proportional to the change in spending over the range of levels being considered (i.e., that the utility function is linear, which may well be approximately true for small changes). Then (and only then) $DU(pX) = pDU(X)$, in which case the decision criterion becomes:

$$\frac{pDU(X)}{d} > DU(X), \text{ which reduces to } \frac{p}{d} > 1.$$

In other words, providing utility varies linearly with expenditures, *the board should put discretionary funds into the endowment whenever the spending rate is greater than their subjective time-discount rate for utility.*

A correction factor must be added to the right-hand side of the formula when utility does not vary linearly with spending. For decreasing marginal utility—that is, where equal spending increments produce diminishing increments to utility—the factor is positive. This has the effect of biasing the result away from immediate spending, though the effect is small. The correction factor is likely to be less than 0.1—in which case the right-hand side won't exceed 1.1— and this difference is not material.[2]

---

2. Given a logarithmic utility function and a 5 percent spending rate, for example, the additive factor will be 0.0004 when X is 1 percent of total spending and 0.046 when X is 10 percent of total spending.

The subjective time-discount rate is neither the same as a financial discount rate nor equal to the opportunity cost of capital. The time-discount rate is expressed in terms of real outcomes and so does not include inflation, and the formula already takes into account the expected return on capital.

While the foregoing may seem esoteric, it does demonstrate that a zero rate of time preference is not a necessary condition for putting discretionary funds into quasi endowment. That is, investment in quasi endowment represents the optimal strategy as long as the discount rate is less than the endowment spending rate. Equilibrium spending rates tend to run in the vicinity of 4 percent to 5 percent. Trustees do in fact put discretionary income into quasi endowment, which suggests that their subjective time preference rates are less that 4 or 5 percent in some circumstances.

The same logic carries over to decisions about whether to seek gifts for endowment or plant as opposed to expendable gifts. A higher time-discount rate generates pressures to obtain expendable gifts for current purposes. A lower rate musters capital campaigns and efforts to steer individual donors toward gifts for capital.

Generally speaking, one would expect trustees to have a lower subjective time-discount rate than most other college and university constituencies. Students generally have the highest rate because of their youthful impatience and the rational conclusion that, as individuals, they have more to gain from spending now than spending later. Faculty, too, generally have a higher discount rate than trustees. They see the school's teaching and research up close and are acutely aware of the opportunity costs of saving. Moreover, they have more at stake in terms of their personal careers, because extra spending can mean more research output, more visibility, and higher salaries. Trustees truly are "the guardians of the future against the claims of the present" (to repeat Tobin's words), even though their subjective rate of time preference need not be zero.

Benefits to be achieved in the future are of greater consequence for colleges and universities than they are for the typical business firm. The fact that trustees put discretionary funds into quasi endowment suggests that their subjective time-discount rate is in the order of 4 percent or less. Table 1 shows how much faster a future benefit is discounted to insignificance at a 10 percent rate compared with a 4 percent rate. (Hurdle rates of 15 percent or more are not uncommon in the business world. When discounted for inflation, this produces the 10 percent standard we use for comparison.)

Governing boards are able to exercise relatively low time-discount

TABLE 1.   Typical Discount Factors in Higher Education and Business

Number of Years Out	Colleges and Universities (4%)	Business Firms (10%)
1	0.96	0.91
5	0.82	0.62
10	0.68	0.39
25	0.37	0.09
50	0.14	0.01
100	0.02	0.00

rates for many reasons. The boards need not worry about financial stakeholders with voting rights or the need to raise equity capital in competitive financial markets. Moreover, colleges and universities usually face a more certain environment than business firms. Uncertainty boosts rates because of the need to discount for risk as well as time preference, and this correction is likely to be larger for businesses than for colleges and universities. Finally, trustees tend to believe that they are in fact guardians of the future and that their institutions are (or should be) immortal. This, too, exerts a downward pressure on discount rates.

Increasing the trustees' time-discount rate would shift capital allocations away from endowment and toward investments in plant and equipment. (This follows from the fact that endowment investments continue to produce benefits beyond the time horizon of even the longest lived tangible investments.) An increase in the discount rate would also reduce the overall level of capital investment, because the current program would be valued more highly relative to the benefits from such investments.

The evidence on whether boards should invest more in plant and equipment relative to endowment is mixed. A recent National Science Foundation survey of university science facilities identified a shortfall but also reported that institutions have made substantial investments in recent years and that the level of investment is continuing.[3] Although some noteworthy cases show that overriding physical capital needs have been sacrificed to endowment building, many counter examples exist as well. The best defense against biased decision-making in either direction is for trustees to ponder the trade-offs carefully and articulate the reasons for their choices.

---

3. National Science Foundation 1988.

Optimizing Liabilities

Colleges and universities have added massive amounts of debt to their balance sheets during the last two decades. The creation of tax-exempt bond authorities in many states has stimulated the trend, which has been further driven by growing facilities needs and the difficulty of raising gifts to improve the physical plant. The facilities needs resulted from the development of capital-intensive science and technology and the over-hang of deferred maintenance and modernization from the retrench-ment years. Like the rush to total return-based spending a decade ear-lier, debt's new acceptability raises the possibility of abuse and therefore demands the development of guiding principles and limits. This leads us to consider the reasons for leverage, debt capacity, and the relation of debt to endowment.

Leverage

The prima facie reason for borrowing is that it permits one to build now and pay later. Although this can be a valid reason for taking on debt, the logic behind a strategy that emphasizes financial leverage is more subtle. For business firms, debt increases the expected rate of return on equity, albeit at the expense of additional risk. That is the origin of the term *leverage*. We need to articulate the concept of leverage as it applies to nonprofit entities in general and higher education in particular.

Colleges and universities maximize utility instead of profits. Lever-age allows the entity to generate extra utility from the pool of available assets. Leverage also has financial effects, however. This requires that we distinguish between two kinds of borrowing:

1. *Borrowing for projects or purposes that will generate an incremen-tal income stream at least equal to debt service.* The classic exam-ple is the dormitory project where incremental room revenue pays the debt service. Scientific research facilities that will be fully utilized for sponsored research will fall into this category if the institution fully recovers its indirect costs and matches debt repayments to depreciation recovery.[4]
2. *Borrowing for projects that do not directly result in additions to the revenue stream.* General-purpose academic buildings and li-braries represent cases in point. They further the institution's

---

4. Interest is fully recoverable, and the depreciation can be used to fund retirement of principal. See Massy 1989.

mission and thus, arguably, increase its revenue-generating capacity over the long run, but the links are not explicit. On the other hand, debt service is a direct drain on operating funds.

Both kinds of borrowing further the institution's mission by leveraging its available assets. The difference is that, in the first case, debt service requires no sacrifice in current utility. Indeed, a utility gain could arise if the new activity generates excess cash flows. The second case is roughly analogous to business investments with substantial and prolonged initial negative cash flows. The analogy isn't precise, however, because even after the fact, determining whether the project generated the anticipated incremental revenues is difficult.[5] For many years, borrowing by colleges and universities was limited mostly to auxiliary activities, which tend to fall under case 1. That has changed in recent years, however, and now a great deal of borrowing for academic facilities occurs.

Why do endowed schools borrow when it might seem easier simply to use the endowment to finance needed facilities? First, prohibitions exist against spending the principal of true endowment funds. The purpose of expenditures is also restricted; one can't use the income from an endowed chair in history to build a science facility, for instance.

What about borrowing from an endowment fund, or the endowment pools for that matter, and then paying back the loan from future operating income? This strategy may be attractive if the purpose of the fund matches the purpose of the capital expenditure. If the purposes do not match, however, the internal loan must pay a market interest rate. Anything less would violate the trustees' fiduciary obligation to maximize the income available for the fund's donor-specified purpose consistent with risk. But if a market rate of interest has to be paid anyway, why not simply borrow externally and avoid all questions of self-dealing? External borrowing has the added advantage of providing an automatic market discipline on the school's cost of capital and debt capacity.

Consequences of Borrowing from Endowment

Yet another argument exists against borrowing from endowment. This argument is best understood by modeling an endowed school's *net total return*—the total return on endowment investments minus the cost of

---

5. The linkage between investments in general academic facilities and revenue is closer for institutions that have to worry about student demand than it is for highly selective schools. There are no marginal revenue effects with respect to students as long as a school remains selective, though marginal revenues in terms of gifts still might exist.

borrowing. (Once again, some readers may wish to skip the technical material in this section.)

Consider the following variable definitions:

NTR Net total return, which is the net of total return on endowment investments and interest paid on the debt

E Amount of endowment

D Amount of debt

f_S Desired holdings of stocks, expressed as a fraction of the endowment portfolio

f_B Desired holdings of bonds, expressed as a fraction of the endowment portfolio

r_S Expected total return on the stocks in the endowment portfolio

r_B Expected interest rate on the bonds in the endowment portfolio, also called the *lending rate*, because it is the rate the school receives when it lends to external or internal borrowers

i_T Interest rate on external taxable borrowing

i_E Interest rate on external tax-exempt borrowing

The expected total return on stocks will always be greater than the interest rate for bonds. The school's external borrowing rate will be less than the bond rate if the school has access to tax-exempt debt. Otherwise, the borrowing rate generally will be greater than the lending rate, though special circumstances relating to maturities and credit ratings could reverse the relationship.

External borrowing. The net total return under this scenario is:

$$NTR = (r_S f_S + r_B f_B) E - i_E D, \quad \text{or} \quad NTR = (r_S f_S + r_B f_B) E - i_T D$$

depending on whether the school can issue tax-exempt bonds.

Internal borrowing: "off the top." Here, the borrowing is from the endowment pool, with the stipulation that it comes off the top, before the allocation of investments among asset classes. The internal borrowing must be at taxable rates; otherwise, the restricted funds would suffer an opportunity loss, which would open the trustees to a charge of self-dealing. Therefore, the net total return is:

$$NTR = (r_S f_S + r_B f_B) (E - D).$$

We didn't need a model to tell us that internal borrowing is costly when the alternative is tax-exempt bonds. An additional loss is incurred as well, due to the distortion of the asset mix. Taking internal borrowing off the top of endowment investment, in effect, causes the fixed-income investment component of the portfolio to grow from f_B to $f_B + D \div E$, which reduces the pool's total return even when $i_T = r_B$. Whether a court would construe this as a violation of the trustees' fiduciary responsibility to the restricted-fund stakeholders is not clear, but it definitely would disadvantage the restricted funds.

The following example demonstrates that the loss can be significant. Assume, conservatively, that in real terms, $r_S = 5.5$ percent and $r_B = i_T = 2$ percent and that the college normally employs a 70-30 stock-bond mix. The net total return for external and internal borrowing off the top are as follows:

External: $NTR = (0.055 \times 0.7 + 0.02 \times 0.3)\ (\$80)$
$\qquad\qquad -0.02\ (\$26) = \$3.04;$
Internal: $NTR = (0.055 \times 0.7 + 0.02 \times 0.3)\ (\$80 - \$26)$
$\qquad\qquad = \$2.40.$

The loss is $0.64 million, some 21 percent of the net total return for external borrowing.

Internal borrowing: offset portfolio bonds. This scenario mitigates the asset-mix distortion problem by limiting the amount of internal borrowing to less than the amount of endowment that would have been held in fixed income vehicles anyway. Now the net total return is:

$$NTR = r_S f_S E + r_B (f_B E - D).$$

This still may disadvantage the restricted-fund stakeholders, but only if $i_T < r_B$. The discrepancy is likely to be small, however, so there probably is little to worry about on that score.

The biggest problem with this approach, other than the loss of market discipline to which we referred earlier, is that if carried very far it degrades the diversification of the school's bond portfolio. For now, though, imagine a scenario in which bonds are intended to carry the institution through times of economic distress. In such times, the returns from other assets are down, gifts have dried up, and the school's main operating income sources are under pressure. Heavy internal borrowing means the institution must rely on its own debt-service payments to meet its obligations, which amounts to devouring one's own tail.

Debt Capacity

An institution's ability to borrow externally depends on the market's willingness to buy the debt securities. Schools judged by the market to be in sound financial shape will pay less than those facing financial difficulties. The difference can be as much as one percentage point or even much more if a school is in trouble. The two major bond-rating agencies in the United States, Moodys and Standard and Poors, continually research the financial strength and prospects of college and universities that have bonds outstanding. The research is updated whenever a new issue is in the offing. The agencies' ratings have a strong influence on bond prices.

One factor that sets endowed colleges and universities apart from other creditors is that they often have financial assets in excess—sometimes well in excess—of total borrowings. This is seldom the case for business firms or governmental units, for example.

The most direct way to use the endowment to improve an institution's credit rating and hence lower its borrowing cost is to "collateralize" the bond issue. Endowment-pool investment securities are deposited with a bond trustee, who is authorized to sell them if the institution defaults. The securities in question must be readily marketable, and the amount of collateralization is adjusted from time to time to take account of changing market values. Because the securities are in the custody of an independent entity (usually a bank), the bondholders are assured that the payments to them will be on schedule. Naturally, the rating agencies take this into account.

Collateralization is relatively easy but not a free ride. Putting the securities in the hands of a bond trustee limits the school's investment flexibility. Depending on the bond indenture, the collateral may have to be in the form of fixed-income securities. All income, gains, and losses are passed through, but the school's investment managers may not be free to substitute other kinds of investment vehicles. Even where the indenture contains no such restriction, or the total borrowing is small relative to the institution's desired level of fixed-income investment, the separation of custodial arrangements can add costs and slow down the investment process. These costs must be balanced against the gains stemming from the improved credit rating.

What about the obligations to the restricted-endowment stakeholders, who "own" the collateral, in case of default? The answer is that the trustees must find a way to make good on their obligations. This might mean selling plant and equipment or borrowing at a much higher interest rate. Neither would be easy, but an institution would have difficulty taking a default in its endowment pool while continuing as a going concern. (What would happen in the case of bankruptcy is a matter for lawyers and beyond the scope of this chapter.) In other words, collateralization provides the liquidity needed to protect bondholders but does not underwrite the debt from the institution's long-term point of view.

Absent collateralization, debt capacity depends on projections of the institution's ability to pay interest and principal during the entire term of the debt. Though I have participated in many meetings dealing with Stanford's ratings, I am hardly an expert on the subject of how the agencies make their judgments. Endowment, however, can clearly make a significant difference even without collateralization.[6] The reasons were offered earlier in this chapter in the discussion of liquidity. The effect of unrestricted quasi endowment on a school's credit rating is obvious. Restricted quasi endowment helps too, because substituting restricted for unrestricted operating funds is usually possible, thus making the latter available for debt service. True endowment (as well as quasi endowment) helps the institution avoid difficulties in the first place by strengthening its program and relieving pressure on tuition rates.

In summary, debt capacity provides yet another reason for an institution to value endowment and to maintain or increase the fraction of the budget supported by endowment. By increasing unused debt capacity, a larger endowment reduces the cost of borrowing and provides "latent liquidity." In other words, endowment's favorable effect on debt capacity amplifies the liquidity benefits discussed earlier in this chapter. Boards hope never to use all of this capacity, but its presence is a comfort.

How Much Endowment? How Much Debt?

The concept of *net total return* (investment return minus debt service) arose in our discussion of internal vs. external borrowing. Now we consider the closely related concept of *net fixed revenue*, which is defined as appropriated spending from endowment minus debt service. Spending from existing endowment funds and debt service are the only two income items that are completely invariant, even in the long run, to decisions about academic program. The debt is, of course, contractually committed. Spending from endowment depends on the school's success

---

6. In addition to financial factors, the raters examine the health of the institution's programs (such as admissions yields and sponsored research awards), trends in giving and—perhaps above all—the quality and financial discipline of the institution's management.

as an investment manager and on the capital markets but not on teaching, research, or public service.[7]

Some schools have adopted limits on debt service as a fraction of the operating budget. At Stanford, for instance, board policy requires that we hold that fraction to less than 5 percent.[8] This limit is a good deal more stringent than anything the credit markets are likely to impose. It is an internal policy parameter, analogous to the endowment-support ratio, whose purpose is to avoid over-mortgaging the future. This limit also preserves our remaining debt capacity to deal with a true emergency should that be necessary. On October 17, 1989, the Bay Area had an earthshaking reminder that such an emergency is not just a hypothetical possibility.

A single policy parameter should cover both support from the endowment and debt service. Therefore, we define net fixed revenue as a fraction of the budget. The larger this fraction, the more the endowment provides net subsidy and freedom from economic and political influence. The fraction goes negative when debt service exceeds endowment spending. This means that the institution has crossed over into the zone of "net leverage" rather than "net subsidy," a zone quite familiar to corporate executives but mostly uncharted territory for the endowed college or university. Trustees should ponder long and hard before sanctioning such a move.

Ideally, the trustees should consider the net fixed-revenue ratio for their institution in relation to that of other schools with which they compete. This helps answer questions such as, "How good is 10 percent?" That number will be fine if most peer institutions operate with 5 percent, for instance. A 10 percent ratio means that the school will enjoy a 5 percent price or quality advantage. The trend in the net fixed-revenue ratio relative to that of other schools also carries important information about how the institution positions itself for the future. The data needed to make precise comparisons are not easily available, but rough approximations are possible. Developing good comparable measures for the net fixed-revenue ratio should be a strong priority for higher education data-sharing organizations.

Controlling the net fixed-revenue ratio requires that targets be set with respect to each available policy tool. These targets are long-run in

---

7. I ignore the situation, which does happen occasionally, in which a faculty member invents a new method that improves investment return. Faculty entrepreneurship that results in venture capital opportunities may be another exception.

8. Strictly speaking, the policy is that debt service covered by general funds be no larger than 5 percent of the operating budget, which is primarily made up of general funds. The policy has been in place for the better part of a decade, and the fraction now stands at about 3 percent.

nature, and management cannot be expected to meet them every year. The endowment spending rate illustrates the point: any reasonable smoothing rule will cause the actual rate to diverge from the target rate given unavoidable variations in total return. Targets for gifts and other additions to the endowment work the same way. The targets should be achieved cumulatively over a period of years, though not necessarily in any particular year. Long-term fixed-rate debt is more precisely controllable, though short-term and variable-rate debt service have some of the same characteristics as endowment total return.

Both the targets themselves and the track record on achieving them will affect current decision making. The board will find it easier to make exceptions to policy if finances are healthy, whereas redoubled efforts are needed if the net fixed-revenue ratio is lagging its target. The process cannot work unless the responsible decision makers pay attention and take variances between actual and target seriously. The governing board must ensure this happens.

Integrated Financial Planning

Integrated financial planning is the best way to demonstrate that an institution's capital-allocation decisions are wise. Few schools perform integrated financial planning, although increasing numbers are developing facilities plans, which is an essential first step. The facilities plan should describe the need for buildings and equipment and the potential sources of funds for each project. Ideally, the plan should provide explicit guidance for funding the projects needed over the next three to five years and offer a context for considering the out-years.

Integrated capital planning can begin once the facilities plan has been presented. College and university officers and boards should consider the following steps.

1. *Sensitivity analysis on the facilities plan.* Examine the benefits, costs, and income implications of facilities projects just above and just below the capital budgeting cutoff line for the immediate future and the out-years. (I use *capital budget* to mean the institutional general funds—both equity and debt—available for facilities. These funds come into use after all restricted fund sources for a given project have been utilized.) Ask whether priorities would be changed if the amount of capital funding were to be increased or decreased by a given percentage. Agree on a strategy for responding to such changes, suspending disbelief at this stage about whether they are desirable.

2. *Comparison with the endowment-support ratio projections*. Calculate the effects on the endowment-support ratio if the capital budget adjustments analyzed in step 1 were achieved by diverting funds to or from additions to endowment. Ask whether, at the margin, facilities needs are more or less important than improving the endowment-support ratio. Which way the debate comes out will depend on the school's particular circumstances. Presumably, though, the less healthy the endowment-support ratio projection, the more likely the board will want to maintain or enhance the flow of funds to quasi endowment. Conversely, urgent facilities needs and a robust endowment-support ratio will tip the scales the other way.

3. *Comparisons with "available funds" projections*. Determine the adequacy of the "available funds" level as projected on the basis of the decisions tentatively taken in step 2. A pressing need for such funds should shift the emphasis toward increasing the endowment support ratio, as opposed to investing in facilities.

4. *Consideration of current spending rate adjustments*. Current spending is the last element in the equation. Other things being equal, a reduction in the spending growth rate will reduce the denominator of the endowment-support ratio and make more funds available for capital. Acute pain in steps 2 or 3 signals the need to push hard for relief here in step 4. The amount of capital also can be increased by pushing long-term borrowing above the level projected in the facilities plan. This will satisfy some of the demand for facilities capital, thus freeing more money for quasi endowment. Unfortunately, as we have just shown, increasing debt has the same effect on institutional finances as reducing the endowment support ratio.

Some people believe that flows of unrestricted funds to quasi endowment should be handled quietly, outside either the operating or capital budget process. (This is done at many institutions.) They argue that attempts at integrated financial planning will make flows to endowment vulnerable to shrill demands for more current spending and that the present will be more likely to hold the future hostage. To this, I offer the rejoinder that if secrecy is required to do the right thing, then the president and governing board aren't doing their jobs. Opening the process to sunshine and making the decisions explicitly in the light of available facts will give the best results over the long haul.

The spending rate question focuses mainly on whether individual endowment funds maintain their purchasing power. The broader issue, however, is what happens to the institution's endowment as a whole? Is the endowment's share of operating-budget income being maintained? How about endowment per faculty member? Per student? These are the measures of endowment purchasing power at the institution-wide level. Whether purchasing power is maintained will depend on the rate of gifts and other additions to the endowment as well as the spending rate and total return.

Managing the Endowment-Support Ratio

The fraction of the budget supported by endowment is the key strategic variable for tracking and managing endowment's contribution to institutional finance. The endowment-support ratio is defined as follows:

$$\text{endowment-support ratio} = \frac{\text{spending rate} \times \text{endowment (\$)}}{\text{budget (\$)}}.$$

Viewing the endowment-support ratio as a strategic variable implies it should be managed consciously rather than be allowed to evolve as an unintended consequence of other policies. The responsibility for managing this strategic variable rests with the institution's senior planners and governing board.

Increasing the spending rate increases the endowment-support ratio, other things being equal. One must be careful, however, because more spending means less reinvestment and thus a smaller endowment growth rate. Here is the formula for the endowment growth rate:

$$\text{endowment growth rate} = \frac{\text{total return}}{\text{spending rate}} + \frac{\text{gifts} + \text{other additions}}{\text{beginning endowment}}.$$

Holding the endowment-support ratio constant over time (with a fixed spending rate) requires (1) the endowment growth rate to equal the budget growth rate and (2) the spending rate to be consistent with the endowment growth rate, given the expected total return, gifts, and other additions to endowment.[9]

The foregoing suggests three policy levers are available for managing the endowment-support ratio.

---

9. These are the conditions for stationary long run financial equilibrium, where *stationary* means that the endowment support fraction is constant over time. See Hopkins and Massy 1981, chapter 6, for a detailed mathematical treatment.

1. *The real budget growth rate.* The greater the budget growth rate the more upward pressure there is on the endowment-support ratio. Using the equilibrium-spending rate described earlier is a sufficient condition for maintaining the endowment-support ratio only when the budget is not growing faster than the rate of cost-rise. (Growth at cost-rise simply sustains current activities, whereas faster growth adds to them.) Expansion, such as increasing faculty numbers, tends to reduce the endowment-support ratio.

2. *The spending rule and total return.* The amount of income reinvested (total return minus spending) affects the numerator of the endowment-support ratio. Therefore, reinvested income can offset the effect of budget growth. Adjusting the asset mix to increase expected total return is an effective strategy, provided it can be done without unduly increasing risk. Reducing the spending rate also increases reinvestment but at the expense of the initial endowment-support ratio. This represents a difficult trade-off but, as Stanford found in 1974, it is sometimes the best action to take.

3. *Gifts and other additions to endowment.* A capital campaign is the most visible method of increasing the flow of gifts to endowment. Trustees may decide on a campaign because of concerns about the endowment-support ratio, though the reasons are rarely couched in that language. Funding a deficit from quasi endowment is the most common cause of sharp declines in the endowment-support ratio, the deficit amounting to a negative value for "other additions." In between, a host of small decisions must be made about whether to save expendable gifts or operating surpluses as quasi endowment, rather than spending them or putting them into capital facilities, equipment, or operating reserves.

How Much Endowment Is Enough?

Posed literally, this question has an easy answer: "No imaginable amount of endowment is sufficient to subsidize every program the institution would like to support and to give it all desired independence from economic and political forces." Posed pragmatically: an institution has enough endowment when its governing board says so, by setting accumulation and spending priorities so that the endowment-support ratio does not increase over time. Today, no systematic procedure exists for determining the optimum endowment-support ratio given the totality of circumstances an institution faces. The approach must allow policymakers to consider the consequences of actions that would increase or decrease the ratio, imagine life in the future with the larger or smaller level of endowment support, and then judge the utility of the alternatives subjectively.

The board is responsible for overseeing financial planning and, where necessary, setting priorities. Setting targets for the endowment-support ratio is an important element of financial planning. The default position should be to maintain the existing ratio, because reductions can occur easily and are difficult to recoup. Alternatively, the board might set a target for increasing the endowment-support ratio over time. This should lead budget and development officers to take a series of small actions to increase the flow of gifts and other additions to endowment. In adverse circumstances, the board might authorize a reduction in the endowment-support ratio to accomplish other pressing institutional goals.

Some critics hold that trustees put undue weight on endowment accumulation and not enough on other institutional needs. Trustees may certainly take particular satisfaction in augmenting the endowment. Conversely, no trustee likes the idea of seeing endowment support decline in real terms. "Not on my watch" is the understandable outcry. Nevertheless, endowment-support ratios decrease—and not infrequently. Making any general statements about whether this is good or bad is impossible, because so much depends on the specific circumstances.

The important point is that the endowment-support ratio should not be allowed to change by default. Governing boards should focus attention on it, ensuring that decisions are made in a considered manner. They should require an especially high burden of proof for decisions that would erode this strategically important element.

A Comprehensive Policy for Spending and Endowment Accumulation

The complex body of material covered in this chapter is summarized in the following comprehensive policy for spending and accumulation. It consists of four mutually reinforcing components.

Policy I: Follow a spending policy based on total return, not yield. Yield and realized capital gains are economically indistinguishable. To base spending on yield is to (1) eschew the concept of long-run financial equilibrium, (2) unnecessarily limit investment options, and (3) subject the budget to unnecessary volatility resulting from asset mix changes or shifts between current distributions and retained earnings by companies in which the school has invested. A total return-based policy avoids these difficulties. The board may wish to limit spending to yield and realized gains or to apply other restrictions that do not undermine the basic properties of a total return-based policy.

Policy I requires the board to use the endowment fund and to make investments on a pooled basis. This also improves investment management. The pooled shares are marked to market on a periodic basis (monthly or quarterly), and additions to and withdrawals from the endowment are accomplished by buying and selling shares. Total returns and appropriations for spending are quoted on a per-share basis.

Some pure endowment funds contain restrictions that prohibit spending capital appreciation in any form. It may be necessary to segregate these funds and give them special treatment—either in a separate pool or by capping spending. The latter procedure results in a lower spending rate for these funds in years when the institution's overall spending rule calls for appropriating gains.

Policy II: Maintain endowment spending's share of operating budget support. Sufficient total return must be reinvested and new funds added—such as through gifts—to maintain the endowment's share of total income supporting academic operations. The reinvestments and additions will have to be larger if the institution is growing than if its size is constant. This implies that capital campaigns to increase the flow of gifts for current operations also should include an endowment component aimed at maintaining the endowment-support ratio. No growth, on the other hand, means that reinvestments and additions at the rate of internal cost-rise will be sufficient.

Modifications to Policy II may be appropriate in special circumstances. If the governing board concludes that the institution needs to change its price or quality position relative to other schools in its class, raising additional endowment funds may be a feasible solution to relieving the situation. In that case, a goal would be set for increasing the endowment-support ratio over a specified period of years, with fundraising and resource-allocation priorities adjusted accordingly. Usually, however, such a strategy can be undertaken only by trading off current program objectives or raising price.

An institution in financial difficulty will have little choice but to allow the endowment-support ratio to decline. Officials should do this only after exhausting all other alternatives and after thorough consideration by the governing board, because reversing a decline in the endowment-support ratio is difficult. If approved, the strategy can be implemented by pegging the spending rate above its equilibrium level and diverting more new gifts toward current operations rather than toward the endowment.

Changes in the endowment-support ratio should be reviewed by the board on an annual basis. Short-run fluctuations due to financial market performance and the operation of the smoothing rule are inevitable, but boards should carefully watch the trend over a market cycle and longer.

Policy III: Maintain the purchasing power of each existing endowment fund. Endowments are not monolithic but instead consist of a great number of individual funds. Most funds carry restrictions as to use, and many are pure as opposed to quasi endowments. Each fund must be accounted for separately. The objective of Policy III is to maintain the purchasing power of each fund in relation to the average level of cost-rise across the institution.

Maintenance of purchasing power requires setting the target spending rate on endowment shares equal to the equilibrium spending value. The equilibrium spending rate goes up in proportion to expected total return on the endowment, so it may be desirable to consider changes in asset mix to increase total return if the spending rate initially calculated is too low. The equilibrium rate depends inversely on the rate of cost-rise, and policy interventions may be possible there too.

Policy III has a lower priority than Policy II, but success in maintaining the purchasing power of individual funds makes it easier to maintain the endowment-support ratio. (Conversely, a decision to lower the endowment-support ratio by upping the spending rate also will erode the purchasing power of individual funds.) In some circumstances, it may be better to relax Policy III in favor of improved fund-raising. An expected real total return in the 5 percent to 6 percent range may well produce an equilibrium spending rate near 4 percent, as shown in the examples presented earlier. Some experts believe a 4 percent spending rate is too low for effective fund-raising, because donors can't fund enough current program for a given amount of money and because 4 percent just sounds too low. People tend to confuse spending rates with nominal total return. "I could get more than 4 percent from a certificate of deposit," they reason, "and such a low expected return would be unconscionable in today's investment environment."

Trustees should ask for a calculation of the equilibrium spending rate and then debate the merits of implementing it. If their decision is against implementation, the board should satisfy itself that Policy I can be attained by substituting other funds—such as new endowment gifts or operating surpluses—for the reinvested income forgone.

Policy IV: Apply a smoothing rule to mitigate the effects of short-term market volatility on spending from endowment. Total investment returns can vary dramatically from year to year. Therefore, spending a constant percentage of endowment market value would disrupt the budget of most institutions. It is necessary to dampen these fluctuations by using a smoothing rule.

A good smoothing rule has these properties:

1. The rule should balance the risk transmitted to the budget and the risk absorbed within the endowment. Transmitting too much risk results in "start-stop budgeting." Absorbing too much in the endowment means that spending fails to track market fluctuations and causes the actual spending rate to diverge from the target rate by too great an amount, which invites even bigger budget problems later.
2. The rule should be clearly stated so that it can be applied each year without reopening the debate about spending versus saving. Boards should be flexible enough occasionally to allow individual judgment, but it should define clearly the permissible range of choice and set explicit criteria.
3. The rule should contain a built-in feedback mechanism that continually pulls the actual spending rate back toward the target rate.

Governing boards should determine how their institution's spending and accumulation policies and practices measure up to these properties. Material divergence should trigger a policy review and appropriate changes.

Appendix to Part 2:
Legal and Accounting Issues Brought
Forward by an Optimal Endowment
Spending Policy

Implementing a spending rule based on total return requires accounting and legal issues to be dealt with carefully. Failure to do so can lead to serious embarrassment and questions about the integrity of the institution's financial statements. In the worst case, trustees could be sued for breaching their fiduciary responsibility.

Investment yield and capital appreciation remain distinct concepts under the law, and in terms of generally accepted accounting principles, and these distinctions must be taken into account when implementing a spending rule. The same is true of the distinction between realized and unrealized capital gains. The following examples illustrate the problems these distinctions generate.

A corporate board decides to retain a portion of the company's current income instead of paying it out in dividends, and the change is fully reflected in the price of the stock. There is a lower current yield, but this is offset by the price increase, leaving total return unchanged. Yet other things being equal, an institution that keys its spending policy to yield would have to reduce its budget as a result of the corporate board's action.

A college owns 10,000 shares of IBM, bought at $44 and now worth $104 per share. There is an unrealized capital gain of $600,000. It sells the shares and uses the money to buy shares in General Electric. The gain now has been realized, but because there are no tax consequences, the college's economic asset balance shows no change. Furthermore, the college could have sold IBM shares at any time in the past and the same will be true of GE shares in the future. Market liquidity ensures that the gains, unrealized or realized, are always immediately convertible to cash, yet the college's net worth as shown on its audited financial statements has just gone up by $600,000 as a result of this "nonevent." The difference between realized and unrealized gain is not a cause for worry when deciding how much of this total return to spend.

On the other hand, the distinctions are still important for transactions in illiquid markets.

A real estate partnership experiences increased rents, which are passed along to the college as investment yield. The extra rents also may increase the value of the properties, but this cannot be calibrated precisely, and in any case, it would be difficult for the college to sell its holding. Although tracking the market value is important for purposes of measuring portfolio performance, it would not be prudent to spend appreciation in this case.

A venture capital holding has done well but has not gone public. It is not convertible to cash, and its value is uncertain. Spending the unrealized appreciation prior to a public offering would not be prudent.

The latter two situations stand in the way of changing accounting rules to conform to the realities of life in liquid markets. They also explain why trustees are reluctant to spend large amounts of unrealized appreciation. Realized appreciation, on the other hand, has by definition escaped the bounds of illiquidity.[10] No economic reason exists for not spending realized appreciation.

Let's consider the legal issues. Generally speaking (and this comes from an economist, not a lawyer), it is permissible to spend realized capital gains on endowment gifts that were made subsequent to passage of the Uniform Management of Institutional Funds Act by the state, unless the donative instrument contains a specific prohibition. This is not necessarily the case for funds given prior to the act's passage or in states without an act, however. Much depends on the language of the gift documents. Governing boards should obtain legal advice before determining policy. Capital gains on quasi-endowment funds can always be spent, because neither the corpus nor the appreciation has any prohibition against spending.

Implementing a policy that allows appreciation to be spent for some funds but not for others is difficult. The solution may be to establish two endowment pools, placing funds where appreciation can be spent in one and funds where it cannot in the other. That was the choice at Stanford when we set up our system in the early 1970s. The documentation of each fund was reviewed and the fund placed in "pool A" or "pool B," depending on whether appreciation could be spent. We wanted to be able to spend capital gain for as many funds as possible, but our lawyers made sure we did not step beyond the bounds of propriety. These determinations have been reviewed periodically over the years as case law has evolved.

Although spending capital appreciation requires careful legal review, the situation is easier when it comes to reinvesting yield in excess of monies appropriated under the institution's spending rule. There do not appear to be any restraints on implementing a reasonable reinvestment policy, though of course boards should obtain legal advice on this, too. On the other hand, accounting for reinvested yield can be complicated.

Generally accepted accounting principles call for yield to be taken onto the books as operating income. At Stanford, we handle reinvestment by a nonmandatory transfer from current funds to endowment funds, where the amounts are shown as quasi endowment. We reinvested substantial amounts of yield during the late 1970s and early 1980s, when interest rates and stock yields were high. The reinvestments buy shares in the endowment pool, which are held in separate quasi-

---

10. "Cary and Bright concluded that a court might reasonably be expected to regard realized appreciation as part of the income of a charitable corporation but that it was probably asking too much of the court to expect unrealized appreciation to be treated as part of income, at least given the existing state of the law." Ennis and Williamson 1976, 9.

endowment funds set up alongside each pure endowment fund. Their restrictions as to purpose are the same as for the associated pure endowment fund.

The process works the opposite way in years when yield is less than the approved spending level. Current yield is spent first, after which the needed sums are obtained by selling shares held by the reinvested-income funds. (Most of this the computer handles automatically.) If a reinvested-income fund is exhausted, the next step is to appropriate realized capital gains if these are available within the underlying pure endowment fund.

Each pure endowment fund owns a certain number of pool shares, which have a known market value on any given date. (The shares are revalued monthly.) The realized and unrealized gain component of the market value of each fund must be tracked. According to Stanford policy, realized gains are available for expenditure but unrealized gains are not. Therefore, once the reinvested yield for a given fund has been depleted, the computer program turns to the accumulated realized gains. Any available sums are appropriated, up to the previously authorized spending level per share. If, as occasionally happens for a new fund, the realized gains are insufficient, the spending appropriation is "shorted," and the funded activity must make do with less.

Here, by way of example, is the Stanford board's action that authorizes the foregoing series of appropriations.

> Approval is hereby granted to expend for the fiscal year 19xx from Merged Endowment Pool A [and similarly for the other merged pools], the amount of $x.xx dollars per share, first from ordinary current income (yield) earned during the year and next from prior years' ordinary income that has been reinvested by action of the Board, and, if these sources are not sufficient, from realized net appreciation in the value of assets. If, for any specific fund within Merged Pool A, the specified sources are not sufficient, then the remainder of expenditure shall come from funds functioning as endowment [i.e., quasi endowment] to the extent available within that fund.[11]

The resolution is passed in June of each year to prepare for the fiscal year that will begin the following September 1. The spending rate itself is approved the previous April as part of the board's budget

---

11. *Agenda*, Board of Trustees of the Leland Stanford Junior University (June 1989).

resolution, based on the equilibrium spending rate and smoothing formula previously described.

Our experience with this process has been very good. It was implemented in 1974 at the bottom of a market cycle. Reinvested yield accumulated for about ten years, during which yields were greater than the calculated spending rate. The flow of reinvested yield peaked at $12.4 million, about 1 percent of the endowment's market value, in 1987. Then it declined rapidly as interest and dividend rates fell and Stanford put more money into low-yielding assets such as venture capital. We began utilizing unrealized appreciation for a significant number of funds in 1988. (The crossover point depends on when the fund was established, which determines its history of income reinvestment and capital gains accumulation.) We have simulated market action with respect to yield and gains using a large-scale computer model and have concluded that the probability of running out of both reinvested yield and realized gain is low.

REFERENCES

Cary, William L., and Craig B. Bright. 1969. *The Law and Lore of Endowment Funds*. New York: Ford Foundation.
Ennis, Richard M., and Peter Williamson. 1976. *Spending Policy for Educational Endowments: A Research and Publication Project of The Common Fund*. New York: Common Fund.
Hopkins, David S. P., and William F. Massy. 1981. *Planning Models for Colleges and Universities*. Stanford, CA.: Stanford University Press.
Massy, William F. 1989. "Capital Investment for the Future of Biomedical Research." *Academic Medicine* 64:433–37.
National Science Foundation. 1988. *Scientific and Engineering Research Facilities at Universities and Colleges: 1988*. Washington, DC: National Science Foundation.

Part 3
Decentralization

CHAPTER 6

Organizing for Effectiveness: Lessons from Business

Edward Lawler III and Susan A. Mohrman

The corporate landscape around the world has changed dramatically during the last decade. Major corporations, particularly in the United States, have gone through an unprecedented period of change. Particularly visible are the changes that have occurred in the largest U.S. corporations. Some of the most revered and respected corporations have fallen on hard times and have had to restructure dramatically: IBM, Sears, and General Motors, for example, have lost a considerable amount of market share and decreased dramatically in size. The problems with these three companies are particularly noticeable, because historically they have been identified as among the best managed corporations in the United States.

The problems of many large corporations raise interesting and challenging questions about how organizations should be managed in today's environment. Perhaps the problems of IBM, Sears, and General Motors are aberrations caused by poor management, bad luck, or extraneous events that could not be anticipated. If so, then their predicaments do not indicate anything about how corporations should be managed. We believe, however, that their problems signal the need for fundamental change in both organization and management to ensure that large corporations remain effective. So many changes have occurred in the world during the last several decades that the traditional organizational structures and management approaches of many businesses are no longer effective. Indeed, often the very businesses that were best at the old management have the worst difficulties adapting to the new competitive environment. Their past success often prevents them from changing in ways that will make them successful in a very different environment.

How has the business environment of the 1990s changed? Perhaps the most significant difference is the nature of competition. Many businesses have become global. As a result, success requires much higher levels of performance in three areas: the quality of goods and services, the cost of production, and the speed of innovation and of delivering new goods to market (Lawler, 1992). In case after case, organizations have been able to improve dramatically their products and services, not just in one of these performance areas, but sometimes in two or even all three. Automobiles today, for example, are much more technologically advanced, come to market much more quickly, and have fewer defects than just a few years ago when American companies dominated the U.S. market. The computer industry has undergone a similar performance improvement. Computers come to the market in record time, are virtually defect free, and have a price performance ratio that tends to improve by 20–30 percent annually. As a result, IBM, which the U.S. government once threatened to break up for antitrust reasons, now struggles to hold itself together. The rapid changes in technology and in the marketplace during the 1980s and early 1990s caught IBM unprepared.

In business after business, the globalization of the economy has been the driving force behind much of the increase in performance standards. Organizations that operate in different countries have different competitive advantages, and thus are often able to enter the marketplace with products that are superior in a number of ways. Foreign competitors may also enter the marketplace with different management styles, which undoubtedly contribute to some of their success (Galbraith, Lawler, and Associates, 1993). Simply stated, these competitors organize work differently, deal with people differently, and in some cases, perform better because they do. As long as U.S. companies competed only with companies that had similar management styles, the importance of management and organization was not evident.

Several popular books chronicling studies of management have been instrumental in altering thinking and practice in American corporations. A book by William Ouchi, *Theory Z* (1981), provided an alternative model of management based in part on Japanese approaches to organizing. This influenced the thinking of American managers, who had witnessed the obvious successes of some Japanese companies. The well-known book by Peters and Waterman, *In Search of Excellence* (1982), although clearly oversimplified in retrospect, provided a set of revised principles about how organizations should be managed that caused many to question their existing assumptions. The book was a multimillion copy sales sensation because more than any other book published during the 1980s, it indicated that management and organization may be critical determinants of organizational performance and a source of competitive advantage. In addition, the book suggested some new approaches to organizing that could provide competitive advantage.

Although in some cases *In Search of Excellence* made inaccurate statements about organizational effectiveness, more recent books by Peters have tended to reject some of these earlier principles but continued to expand on the themes of organizational change and the importance of new approaches to organizing (Peters 1992). Peters's and Ouchi's work was merely the tip of the iceberg: the works of Deming (1986), Juran (1989), and others have promoted the need to be able to improve continually the quality of organizational processes. More recently, Hammer and Champy (1993) and others have pointed out that incremental change is inadequate and that reengineering of the organization is required. These are just a few among many frameworks that are resulting in changes to prevailing organizational approaches.

Corporation after corporation in the United States has looked at its approach to organizing to see whether changes could bring about competitive advantage. As a result, a number of management fads have become popular and an increasing number of organizations have tried to change the way they manage (Lawler, Mohrman, and Ledford 1992). Evidence indicates that the success of these changes is, at best, mixed. Although some organizations like Xerox, Harley Davidson, and Motorola have made notable progress, many others continue to struggle with the process. Nevertheless, some new principles of organizing are gradually emerging from the research.

The new thinking about organization and management has not dramatically affected American higher education. Perhaps the most important reason for this, although others certainly exist, is that until recently, higher education did not experience the same need to change that corporations did. Now, however, higher education is experiencing the same demands for performance improvement that other corporations faced a decade ago. Decreased funding from state governments, resistance to tuition increases on the part of parents and students, competition from in-house corporate professional education programs, and finally, a shrinking student base have created a new environment. Institutions of higher education have to improve their product quality, costs, and ability to respond quickly to customer needs in order to be successful. In some respects, the performance problems of American corporations have directly led to the need for improvement in universities. Due to the poor performance of U.S. corporations, they had less money to contribute to universities and demanded more return for their investment in knowledge creation and education. Poor corporate performance also caused federal, state, and local tax revenue to decrease, so that governments had less money to support all types of education.

The relevant question is whether some of the new approaches to organizing and some of the new logic of organizing that have helped companies such as Xerox and Motorola improve their performance in the face of global competition could also help colleges and universities. This very complex question has no single, simple answer. Some approaches are clearly more relevant to the situation of institutions of higher education than others. The issue is further complicated because there is no definitive picture of an ideal form of management for the increasing performance demands that corporations face. On the contrary, a new logic or new approach to organizing is still evolving. Just as Tom Peters renounced some of his points in his 1982 book, *In Search of Excellence*, in a few years, some of today's emerging principles about how corporations should be managed will be rejected. Nevertheless, we should examine the emerging principles and decide whether some of them would have relevance to the world of higher education. In the rest of this chapter, we will therefore discuss some of the major ideas that have emerged from the work on corporate restructuring and transformation and consider how applicable they are to higher education.

Dynamic Learning Organization

The traditional organizational chart with its boxes, hierarchy, and commitment to fixed positions and job descriptions in many ways symbolizes the stability that organizations have sought as a key to effectiveness. Indeed, major organizational changes in traditional organizations rarely occur, because those changes are seen as tremendously complicated and difficult. They often involve the major dislocation of people and the rewriting and reanalysis of most of the jobs and relationships in an organization. Learning new working relationships and new jobs takes time, and thus change requires an efficiency loss. Traditionally, this has meant that organizations do not make frequent major changes.

The new logic of organizing is perhaps best described in the term "learning organization" (Senge 1990). The assumptions here are very different from those of traditional organizing. The new principles involve an emphasis on the need for organizations to change not only as the external environment changes but also as they learn how to do things better and as they learn more effective ways to interface with the external environment (Mohrman and Cummings 1987).

The external environment is changing much more rapidly than it has in the past, and as a result, organizations need to change more frequently to maintain their effectiveness and their interface with that environment. A more subtle point is that organizations need to change as they learn how to deliver their services and make their products better. As new technology becomes available, organizations must learn how to use it. Powerful new computer and communication technology, for example, make it possible to perform work and organize for it quite differently.

Because organizations today must face new environments and have access to new tools that were never encountered before, how to organize best cannot be found in any textbook or in the history of the organization. Effective organizational models and principles are becoming an increasingly scarce commodity (Lawler 1992). These models and principles must be found through the experience and learning of an organization. Indeed, those organizations that are best at finding new approaches often end up with a competitive advantage over those who cannot. How organizations learn and how well they learn are, of course, critical to effectiveness of any change that is attempted. Companies such as Toyota and 3M have maintained competitive ascendancy in their industries largely through highly effective approaches to learning and motivating (Pinchot 1985; Womack, Jones, and Roos 1990).

Organizations can learn by adopting a scientific model with respect to learning: that is, they experiment with new approaches, assess those experiments, and move forward with a dynamic learning approach to organizing. In the social science literature, this "action research" approach has long been discussed (Lawler and Associates 1985). Recently, however, it has become increasingly popular with major organizations. They are realizing that this dynamic learning approach to organizing can give them a competitive advantage. Through such learning processes, many organizations are gradually redesigning themselves in fundamental ways.

Historically, universities and colleges have been the epitome of stable organizations. Department structures have existed for centuries, as have particular schools and colleges within larger universities. Similarly, staff areas like the registrar's office and athletic departments have had a tremendous amount of stability. Their stability has tended to protect the traditional core competencies of universities and has assured outstanding programs in traditional areas. On the other hand, the stability has limited the ability of universities to respond to their external environment. Departmentalized university structures have difficulty accommodating the interdisciplinary research required to address complex social problems such as race relations, poverty, and complex sociotechnical problems that require an intersection of technical and social sciences. Indeed, stability is perhaps one of the major reasons that universities are increasingly looked upon as irrelevant to the events in today's society.

Perhaps it is time to abandon some of the conservative tendencies that institutions of higher education exhibit in organizational design, particularly with respect to the nonteaching and research activities that universities perform. Resource shortages demand the development of more cost-effective ways to deliver services. Perhaps the universities should experiment with new organizational forms that align them closer to societal issues, in order to gain more public support. The rest of this chapter will use trends from the corporate world to address some of the kinds of organizational changes that universities and colleges might implement to be more effective. We will not attempt a definitive analysis of their appropriateness, nor will we go into much detail—we simply hope to suggest how universities can become more dynamic and learning oriented in their approach to organizing, managing, and delivering services.

The Global Organization

U.S. corporations have been slower than those in many smaller countries to adapt to global markets. For decades, U.S. corporations have tended to focus on the domestic market, designing products and services for that market (Porter 1990). The size and scope of the U.S. domestic market contributed to this near-sightedness. By itself, the domestic market was able to create and support such large corporations as AT&T, IBM, and General Motors, thus decreasing the need to enter global markets. In the last decade, however, this situation has changed dramatically due to the increasing costs of developing products, greater competitiveness in domestic markets, and the need to compete with foreign competitors in their own markets so that the foreign competitors cannot cross-subsidize their products, thereby gaining a competitive advantage in the United States (Galbraith, Lawler, and Associates 1993).

The drive to create more global organizations has had a number of interesting impacts on the structure of organizations. Large corporations such as IBM and Hewlett-Packard have moved headquarters for certain businesses overseas. They have located not just production facilities but also product development facilities in other countries. A few companies, such as Shell, DHL, and ABB, have essentially become stateless corporations so that they can operate easily and comfortably without a strong national identity. This gives them the ability to avoid the image and entanglements that are associated with being primarily an American company, a French company, or a Japanese company.

Higher education has always been a heavily domestic-market oriented activity. Part of the reason for this is that funding for public universities comes from local governments while research funding often comes from the federal government. Nevertheless, American institutions of higher education have developed as major positive contributors to the balance of payments of the United States because of the number of foreign students studying in the United States.

Each year, the number of foreign students studying in the United States increases. Over four hundred thousand studied in the United States during 1992. Most of these students used funds from non-U.S. sources to pay their tuition. Meanwhile, a number of American universities have developed working relationships with foreign universities to allow students to spend semesters there, and some universities even have small campuses in other countries. No American university, however, has truly developed into a global university with campuses and facilities around the globe. Universities currently lack the ability to move functions and programs to those parts of the world where particular expertise is found and where a particular type of education can best be delivered. Even in overseas markets, universities tend to offer a standard educational product, rather than tailoring themselves to the local market.

Many American universities have only begun to market their traditional education to students around the world, even though this seems an obvious first step for American institutions of higher education. Both Europe and third world countries suffer from a dramatic shortage of higher education services. In some cases, students in these countries lack the currency to purchase a U.S. education, but in others, with government subsidies, students can pay for an American higher education. This additional market could help solve the revenue problems of American universities, and at the same time, upgrade the quality of students studying in American universities. Some technical education areas have already achieved this, but universities could be more global in the marketing of all their programs.

Universities may not need to develop the kind of stateless global orientation that characterizes Shell and ABB; however, as information technology spreads across the world, universities may have the opportunity to develop global models of higher education. One possibility would be the teaching of particular disciplines and topics by individuals who have unique expertise regardless of where they are around the globe. Another possibility would be a much more active linking of universities in different parts of the world so that students can gain knowledge and expertise from a "world's leading expert," regardless of the university in which they enroll geographically. To employ a term currently popular in the business world, higher education could create a "virtual university."

Overall, the world appears to be opening up to the possibility of American universities playing a new and much greater role in global education and events. Higher education is clearly an area where the U.S. has a competitive advantage and where universities have the opportunity to help global development by providing services to less developed parts of the world—at the same time, helping themselves identify new sources of revenue.

Small Is Beautiful

The most admired corporations in the United States, IBM, Sears, General Motors, AT&T, and Exxon, are not only among the largest corporations in the United States but among the largest corporations in the world. Such terms as "economies of scale" have often led to the conclusion that being big provides a competitive advantage. Size often allows for better access to capital, the support of extensive research and development labs, the purchasing of products and services at favorable prices, and finally, a way of accessing global markets. Increasingly apparent, however, is that the advantages of size have been overstated in many businesses. Many of the biggest corporations are now experiencing severe performance problems. In some cases, size has become more of a liability than an asset because it has made corporations inflexible, difficult to change, and has created workforces that are not involved in the business and tend not to care about the business (Lawler 1992). A great deal of research in organizational literature shows that size has its dysfunctions in terms of involvement, satisfaction, and motivation. Historically, these were thought of as solvable problems that were not severe handicaps, especially in comparison to the advantages of large size.

To improve their effectiveness, organizations such as General Electric and IBM have had to downsize and change dramatically their approach to being large. With regard to IBM and General Motors, this change is especially ironic since the U.S. government at one time considered them so large they were almost monopolies. Today, those same corporations are downsizing and restructuring so that they can be competitive with smaller organizations. In essence, in order to be effective, they are doing to themselves what the justice department tried to do to them several decades ago to make them less effective. What has happened?

Obviously, the world has changed. What used to lead to effectiveness does not necessarily lead to effectiveness in today's environment. Sheer size, particularly when poorly organized, is not an advantage but a distinct disadvantage. In many industries, the optimum size is at once small and large. In some businesses, size has many clear advantages. It pays to be big when dealing in a global market, when raising capital, when supporting a research and development lab, and when developing an expensive new product. It does not pay to be big when it comes to exercising control, coordinating performance, motivating employees, getting individuals involved in the business, and making customers feel that they are an important focus of the organization's attention and efforts. One way that companies and organizations can reap the benefits of being both small and large is by breaking themselves down into small, relatively decentralized units that face particular customers or deliver particular products. These units, in order to be effective, need to have their own financial accountability, financial information systems, and reward systems (Mills 1991).

In comparison to large corporations, universities tend to be relatively small. They do not, for example, have over a quarter of a million employees as do General Electric, General Motors, and a number of other large U.S. corporations. Nonetheless, even smaller organizations can benefit from creating smaller units that are autonomous in some respects and that operate within organization-wide systems in other respects.

Some lessons about size may be applicable to universities. Often these lessons are apparent in the history of universities themselves. The most prestigious institutions in higher education are those that have created small units within larger institutional settings. Examples include the college system at Oxford and Cambridge and graduate colleges within institutions such as Harvard and Yale. This gives them the advantages of size such as central libraries and access to services while giving the customer the experience of being part of a smaller learning community.

Overall, excessive size is not a major issue confronting American higher education. Generally, American institutions of higher education have avoided creating large multi-hundred-thousand person organizations with centralized functions and controls that try to manage and control the behavior of disparate units. Perhaps one exception here is the large state university and college systems. The message to them from the private sector is clear: "avoid creating a central bureaucracy, place decision making and accountability at the campus level and below."

Product-Customer Focus

Although in general excessive size is not a problem confronting higher education, the principle of being large while acting small has definite applicability in universities because of the changing external environment. In particular, how a university structures itself to be small and create customer responsive units is critical. Universities serve organizations and environments that change and develop new needs for knowledge creation, education, and professional training services.

Corporations, public schools, and health care institutions, for example, are beginning to need interdisciplinary solutions and educational offerings to address complex issues. These organizations also require new ways of relating to universities to address the lifelong educational needs of their employees. In order to respond effectively, universities need to generate more varied modes of knowledge creation and delivery—in essence, to generate new products. Traditional practices and organization structures may no longer apply as units begin to look and act quite differently in order to adapt to the new environment in which they must secure funds and customers for their research and educational functions.

The traditional logic of organizations calls for dividing organizations into functional specialties. Sales, marketing, production, accounting, and personnel are among the many staff and line departments that typically exist. These units carry out various steps in the process of creating a product or servicing a customer. The units are typically controlled in part through a budget that is hierarchically negotiated. The many advantages of a functional organization include the ability to have high levels of expertise in each of the functions. Specialists in sales, marketing, manufacturing, and other areas are developed in the expectation that corporations will excel because the individual business functions are excellent.

The problems with this organizational approach have become increasingly apparent as competition depends more and more on speed and quality. Speed in particular tends to suffer in functional organizations because products and services have to be passed from one function to another in order to be developed and managed, and this always takes time. In addition, customers and products may be poorly managed in the hands-off process between one function and another. Finally, functional organizations require extensive amounts of hierarchy, expensive to develop and maintain, in order to coordinate their actions. Such hierarchical controls and individuals both raise costs and slow down performance because decisions involving multiple functions must pass through multiple levels of the organization to reach a high level in the hierarchy.

A number of large organizations are moving away from the functional approach to organizations that are much more product or customer focused. They thus operate as simultaneously large and small organizations. In terms of developing a product or serving a customer, they are small because a small group of cross-functionally trained and skilled employees deals with the customer or develops a product or service to be delivered. Among the companies that have moved to smaller, relatively autonomous units that are highly focused on one particular product or market segment are Xerox, Motorola, and Hewlett-Packard.

Many institutions of higher education have always been partly organized around customers and products. Business schools, law schools, and medical schools are clear examples of this. Perhaps this approach to organizing could also give more focus and accountability to faculty and staff in other schools. More specially focused units like these schools could be created, and more autonomy could be given to the new schools. In particular, units could be created as profit centers with accountability for and control over costs and revenues. Budgeting systems that provide flexibility and reward entrepreneurial behavior are likely to be the key to their success. In addition, units may need freedom from the traditional constraints of organizing in order to meet the requirements of the broader societal network of individuals and organizations who are their customers and provide the resources for their survival.

Traditional functional bureaucracies often dominate the administrative and staff support service areas of higher education. Areas such as budgeting, financial services, contact administration, maintenance, and student services tend to be functionally centralized and not focused on particular customers, but more of a focus on the customer and closer ties between these centralized services and the units they serve are possibilities. As will be discussed later, several ways of doing this exist, including treating many central services as businesses that have to earn their revenue and satisfy customers.

Meeting Customer Requirements

The logic of traditional bureaucracy calls for job descriptions and for the evaluation of individuals against the details of the job description. In the stable world of the bureaucratic organization, with good top-down coordination of effort, this model makes sense. Indeed, if the organization is well designed and all employees perform their jobs well, the organization most likely will be effective. Problems occur, however, when the environment becomes dynamic and the organization must focus on the changing needs of the customer. Undoubtedly, the strongest influence in moving organizations to a customer-focused approach has been the Total Quality Management movement (Deming 1986; Juran 1989). This movement points out that the key issue is not fulfilling job requirements but meeting customer requirements, because customers provide the revenue and must be satisfied by the services or products.

The Total Quality movement goes even further and emphasizes the existence of both internal customers and external customers. Not everyone has an external customer, but most people have internal customers. In response to this idea, corporations such as Xerox, Motorola, and Federal Express have performed extensive evaluations of internal and external customer satisfaction, holding employees accountable for the results of these measurement programs (Schmidt and Finigan 1992). An obvious advantage of these programs is that employees are focused on results directly related to their activities—a more meaningful measurement than simply meeting the objectives in the job description.

A number of colleges and universities have begun to apply Total Quality principles, often with the support and encouragement of the private sector (Chaffee 1990; Sherr and Teeter 1991; Sink 1993; Teeter and Lozier 1993) . Many institutions of higher education have made small steps toward identifying customer requirements and implementing customer satisfaction measures. Typically, students are asked to evaluate their satisfaction with particular courses and faculty members. In some schools, the results of these evaluations play a significant role in determining promotions and pay increases. Students should also be asked to evaluate the overall university experience—the advising services, the housing, the food services, the registrar's office, and the total experience they had. This is a much needed and logical extension of the whole idea of focusing on customers and customer satisfaction. In addition, universities could focus more on internal customer satisfaction by asking students, faculty, staff, and others how well they are served by specialty groups such as building services and the library. The critical issue with all of the services should be how well they meet customer requirements.

An important insight that comes from applying Total Quality ideas to higher education is seeing students as customers who receive not just classes but a whole variety of services from the university. Consequently, the university must be sure students are satisfied with the quality and nature of these services. Another possible insight would be to expand the concept of customer from simply students to the organizations that ultimately hire those students. These organizations rely on the knowledge produced in universities and are key customers that provide some of the resources necessary to university survival. Their satisfaction could be regularly and systematically measured, and their requirements ascertained as well.

Organizing into Teams

Inherent to the traditional approach to organizing is the idea of individual job descriptions and individual accountability. This idea is rapidly giving way to extensive use of teams who are collectively responsible for delivering services or creating and manufacturing products (Lawler, Mohrman, and Ledford 1992; Mohrman 1993). A wide variety of reasons fuel this change, including the recognition that in today's complex business world, individuals cannot do a great deal because of the complexity of products and services. Virtually anything for which accountability and identity can be established requires the coordinated efforts of a number of individuals. Traditionally, extensive and often expensive hierarchical coordination devices have managed interdependence among individuals. Teams, on the other hand, can handle some of these coordination issues themselves without the reliance on hierarchy and its associated costs and slowness. Companies such as Hewlett-Packard and Motorola routinely use cross-functional teams to develop their new products. Similarly, insurance companies such as Aid Association for Lutherans and IDS handle the servicing of their existing customers with teams that are focused on particular customer segments.

Institutions of higher education generally have not used teams. Two exceptions are the occasional use of team teaching and the use of team research. Greater use of teams in higher education has tremendous potential for faculty teaching and research as well as for staff support areas. Many staff areas are the equivalent of such service organizations as IDS and SAS Airlines, which already use teams extensively. With decentralized control and financial accountability, particular teams can be held responsible for their cost performance as well as their delivery of services. Potentially, the same thing could be done in institutions of higher education with the creation of service delivery teams that are focused on particular groups of students and particular internal customers. Of course, to make this work, those teams must have measures of their effectiveness and their costs. In addition, budgeting systems must be flexible enough to permit locally developed innovations that result in efficient and effective service delivery.

Doing Only What You Can Do Best

The traditional approach to organizing has created organizations that are vertically, and in many cases horizontally, integrated. The automobile industry provides a classic example. Historically, some auto manufacturers made their own steel and glass, transformed these raw materials into a finished product, and sold the product through their own dealer network. In other words, they were highly vertically integrated, doing all aspects of manufacturing a product. They were also horizontally integrated because within their organization, they had all the necessary staff functions and support services needed to create an effective organization. The logic supporting this approach is rather straightforward and led to the bureaucratic organizations that exist today: in essence, the assumption has been that a large, well-run organization like IBM, Ford, or General Motors can do virtually anything better than anyone else, so why trust others to do it? In addition, if producing a particular part or providing a particular service generates a profit, why shouldn't the large organization make that profit? Contracting with someone else means that the other organization will gain a profit that should have been retained.

The problems with trying to do everything are becoming increasingly apparent to most corporations. In a complex environment, the simple fact of the matter is that performance demands in all areas are constantly going up and that the expertise needed to do things well is constantly increasing. Thus, regardless of its resources, any corporation has difficulty being good at a variety of things. At the extreme, this situation has led to networked organizations in which each does just one aspect of developing a product or delivering a service (Miles and Snow 1986). Each organization is very good at its particular aspect. The network is generally held together by an organization that performs the key integration function that differentiates the product or service in its market environment.

Nike exemplifies this type of network organization. It does no shoe manufacturing because it judges that someone who specializes in manufacturing can do a better job. Nike simply designs, advertises, and markets products. This has allowed it to become an extremely successful corporation with an enormous amount of revenue despite a relatively small employee population. Nike's success depends on its being able to orchestrate a network of suppliers and distribution channels in a way that assures the success of all network members.

Similar thinking has prompted many other organizations to outsource some traditional support services, such as data processing and legal services. The decision to outsource requires an analysis to attribute costs to particular activities involved in producing the product or service and a customer orientation perspective to emphasize how well different pieces of the organization are serving other parts of the organization. This internal perestroika approach to accountability opens the possibility for external competitors to bid on things like information processing, maintenance, personnel, and other staff support services and for the organization to use costs and service as the criteria for the "make or buy" decision. A good cost accounting system provides critical information on how much a service costs in the open market versus what costs are associated with having an internal group deliver it.

Institutions of higher education would appear to be fertile ground for outsourcing support services. Universities may never be particularly good at running many of the staff and other support services that a large campus requires. Most large campuses in fact resemble small cities that require legal services, police protection, maintenance, trash disposal, and a host of other support activities. That universities can run and deliver these services as well as firms specialized in these activities seems unlikely. At the very least, universities should receive competitive bids for many support services and price them against their existing internal monopolies. This would force the surviving internal monopolies to focus on costs and customer satisfaction.

Whether universities should look toward a network approach with respect to certain kinds of educational activities raises some interesting speculations. Arguably, most colleges and universities cannot offer a full range of courses and programs at a world-class level. This point has become more meaningful as higher and higher levels of knowledge have developed in most disciplines, and as the cost of maintaining excellence in particular disciplines has escalated with the price of such resources as laboratories and support facilities. As an alternative, some universities have specialized in a few areas and targeted students interested only in those areas. Yet another alternative model could be an alliance that combines the strengths of one institution with those of another, so that students do not have to make premature choices about their education. By narrowing their offerings and specializing in particular industries, functions, or other areas in which they excel, schools can save money.

A *Wall Street Journal* article by Gilbert Fuchsberg quotes Dean Rosenblum of the University of Virginia's Business School as stressing the importance of alliances. According to Rosenblum, "collaborations and alliances are going to be a way of life. No school, however successful and well-financed, can do everything alone anymore." The article also describes new innovative MBA programs being developed in which students split time between different universities that have different expertises. In the business school world, this would seem particularly appropriate for students interested in international management, especially if alliances can be formed across national boundaries. Business schools can use alliances and new relationships to go global. They can combine their best areas of expertise to offer joint programs in international markets where alone they would have trouble finding the necessary expertise and resources.

Overall, many universities and colleges may have to make critical choices about what particular kinds of competencies they want to maintain and develop (Prahalad and Hamel 1990). As resources decrease and the cost of maintaining competencies increases, institutions will have to make hard choices. These choices do not necessarily imply that students will be limited in the type of education they can obtain at a particular institution. Indeed, if new organizational models are adopted, both educational choice and quality could potentially increase.

Control through Involvement

The traditional hierarchical approach to organizing assumes that control derives largely from hierarchical authority. This authority is manifested in supervisor-subordinate reporting relationships, job descriptions, and reward systems that are tied to the effectiveness of individuals as measured against their job descriptions. Clearly this approach has a number of advantages and remains the most appropriate approach in a variety of work environments, but it tends to encounter significant problems when performance must simultaneously emphasize low cost, high quality, and speed. The traditional approach also encounters difficulty when teamwork is required. Decision-making processes tend to be slow because of the need for hierarchical clearances; costs tend to be high because of the cost of control; and, quality is often lost because the individuals actually doing the work or delivering the service are disassociated from the customer or not involved in the production of the total product (Lawler 1992).

An alternative to the command and control approach is the high involvement approach (Lawler, Mohrman, and Ledford 1992). Considerable evidence shows that many corporations are moving to a high involvement approach. Basically, this approach emphasizes moving information, knowledge, power, and rewards to the lowest level of the organization. In the typical example, small groups, teams, or business units are given financial resources as well as the knowledge and power to make a particular product or to serve a particular customer group. The teams are then rewarded based on how well they produce their product or satisfy their customer group. Companies at the forefront of adopting this approach include Union Pacific, Xerox, ABB, and a host of other organizations that need to increase their performance in the face of difficult competitive environments. Describing in detail how a high involvement approach to management can be implemented and where it works particularly well is beyond the scope of this chapter. In many respects, however, high involvement is consistent with many of the new organizational approaches that have already been discussed. It requires, for example, creating small units, focusing on products or services through customer requirements, and adopting a dynamic or learning approach to organizing. High involvement management is also quite consistent with the idea of outsourcing many products and services while making internal providers compete with external providers of the same services.

Institutions of higher education are an interesting combination of traditional hierarchical management and a certain kind of involvement. Traditionally, faculty have had high autonomy and a strong influence on organizational policy. They have a tremendous amount of leverage in determining how they do their work, and they have had great access to learning opportunities with respect to their discipline and subjects of expertise. In a sense, faculty have operated as if they were part of a high involvement organization. What has been missing, however, are systems that hold faculty accountable for performance. As a result of tenure and other award system practices, they have had to neither focus on customer satisfaction nor compete against outside vendors in terms of the quality of their services. Overall, moving faculty to a high involvement organization would require influence on decisions with respect to budgeting and greater reward system accountability for the effectiveness of their programs and courses.

The situation for nonfaculty in most institutions of higher education is quite different from the one that exists for faculty. Increasingly, nonfaculty are unionized and managed in a clearly traditional hierarchical manner. They are usually highly specialized by job function and not focused on customers and products in a way that would allow them to be involved in broader aspects of delivering services and controlling the way work is done. As has been suggested throughout this chapter, nonfaculty could be organized and managed in a much different way, just as many profit-making organizations are being reorganized and redesigned. Nonfaculty could be organized in teams that have considerable control over how they deliver services. These teams could be held accountable for their financial performance and rewarded in terms of their cost effectiveness and the quality of their services. Actively using external competitors when available to compete with operating internal monopolies can help facilitate this change.

In short, relatively self-managing internal businesses could be created if universities were willing to realign how they handle information, knowledge, power, and rewards. This could result in employees being much more involved in their work area or units. If successful, this movement for employee involvement could lead to not only cheaper services, but also less hierarchy, and ultimately, fewer control problems in the organization.

Opportunities for Higher Education

Undoubtedly, the world of higher education will undergo demands for continuous change and continuous improvement. Customers are demanding better service in all areas, and universities are unlikely to be immune from this pressure. In addition, the funding basis of many universities has become increasingly demanding. The federal government is demanding better return on its research dollar; tuition-paying parents and students are asking for lower costs and higher quality; and of course, state legislatures are concerned about the costs of higher education. Just as the private sector has responded to similar pressures from its customers and supporters, universities will need to look at the way they organize as a possible response to new competitive environments.

Many of the same organizational changes that have been adopted in the corporate world are appropriate to higher education. Adopting a dynamic learning environment, being simultaneously large and small, focusing more on customers and customer requirements, outsourcing more services while concentrating on what the institution does best, and finally, getting all employees more involved in the business of the university are concepts that appear to be broadly applicable. How they are applied in a particular situation must reflect the realities of the local environment and the strategy of particular institutions. These changes may in fact provide some institutions of higher education with the same kind of competitive advantages that effective adopters in the corporate world have gained. Of course, laying out a precise template of what specific principles organizations should adopt is impossible. Each institution needs to decide how it wants to face its environment and which approaches fit its particular strategy. The challenge for institutions of higher education, therefore, is to develop an approach to organizing that positions them well in the increasingly competitive environment that lies ahead.

REFERENCES

Chaffee, Ellen Earle. 1990. "Strategies for the 1990s." *New Directions for Higher Education* 70:59–66.
Deming, W. E. 1986. *Out of the Crisis*. Cambridge, MA: Addison-Wesley.
Fuchsberg, Gilbert. "Education: Business Schools Team Up With Rivals to Enrich Offerings But Keep Costs Down." *Wall Street Journal*, Tuesday, August 18, 1992, sec. B, 1.
Galbraith, Lawler, and Associates. 1993. *Organizing for the Future*. San Francisco: Jossey-Bass.

Hammer, M., and S. Champy. 1993. *Reengineering the Corporation*. New York: Harper.

Juran, J. M. 1989. *Juran on Leadership and Quality*. New York: Free Press.

Lawler, E. E. 1992. *The Ultimate Advantage*. San Francisco: Jossey-Bass.

Lawler, E. E., S. A. Mohrman, G. E. Ledford, T. G. Cummings, and Associates. 1985. *Doing Research That Is Useful for Theory and Practice*. San Francisco: Jossey-Bass.

Lawler, E. E., S. A. Mohrman, and G. E. Ledford. 1992. *Employee Involvement and Total Quality Management*. San Francisco: Jossey-Bass.

Miles, R. E., and C. Snow. 1986. "Organizations: New Concepts for New Forms." *California Management Review* 28:62–73.

Mills, D. Q. 1991. *Rebirth of the Corporation*. New York: Wiley.

Mohrman, S. A. 1993. *The Lateral Organization*. In Galbraith, Lawler, and Associates *Organizing for the Future*. San Francisco: Jossey-Bass.

Mohrman, S. A., and T. G. Cummings. 1987. *Self-Designing Organizations*. Reading, MA: Addison-Wesley.

Ouchi, W. 1981. *Theory Z*. New York: Avon.

Peters, T. J. 1992. *Liberation Management*. New York: Knopf.

Peters, T. J., and R. H. Waterman. 1982. *In Search of Excellence*. New York: HarperCollins.

Pinchot, G. 1985. *Intrapreneuring*. New York: Harper and Row.

Porter, M. E. 1990. *The Competitive Advantage of Nations*. New York: Free Press.

Prahalad, C. K., and G. Hamel. 1990. "Core Competence of the Corporation." *Harvard Business Review* 68, no. 3: 79–91.

Schmidt, W. H., and W. Finigan. 1992. *A Race without a Finish Line: America's Quest for Total Quality*. San Francisco: Jossey-Bass.

Senge, Peter M. 1990. *The Fifth Discipline*. New York: Doubleday.

Sherr, Lawrence A., and Deborah J. Teeter, eds. 1991. *Total Quality Management in Higher Ed. New Directions for Institutional Research*. San Francisco: Jossey-Bass.

Sink, D. S., ed. 1993. "TQM in Higher Education." *Quality and Productivity Management* 10, no. 2.

Teeter, Deborah J., and G. Gregory Lozier, eds. 1993. *Pursuit of Quality in Higher Education: Case Studies in Total Quality Management*. San Francisco: Jossey-Bass.

Womack, James P., Daniel T. Jones, Daniel Roos. 1990. *The Machine That Changed the World: Based on the Massachusetts Institute of Technology 5-Million Dollar 5-Year Study on the Future of the Automobile*. New York: Rawson Associates.

CHAPTER 7

Revenue Responsibility Budgeting

Jon Strauss, John Curry, and Edward Whalen

Written by pioneers in the field, the three short pieces in this chapter provide firsthand insights on revenue responsibility budgeting. As we noted earlier, systems of revenue responsibility budgeting are sometimes called responsibility center budgeting or responsibility center management. Jon Strauss discusses some of the principles of responsibility center budgeting and gives examples of how decentralized data can be used even at institutions that' do not practice decentralized budgeting. John Curry narrates the actual process of adopting a university-wide responsibility center management system at the University of Southern California in the early 1980s. Finally, Edward Whalen considers the case for adopting responsibility center budgeting at public institutions.

The WPI Experience

Along with Edward Whalen and Robert Zemsky, Jon Strauss was one of the originators of revenue responsibility budgeting and has written extensively on the subject. Strauss helped implement responsibility center budgeting first at the University of Pennsylvania in the 1970s as a budget and finance officer, and then at the University of Southern California in the mid-1980s as senior vice president for administration. While he was president of Worcester Polytechnic Institute (WPI), Jon Strauss encountered resistance to implementing responsibility center budgeting but nevertheless believed that the principles of decentralized management are applicable to a small college environment. In the segment that follows, he presents a brief review of the underlying principles followed by an example of a prototype decentralized management model at WPI. Subsequent sections describe budgeting under decentralized management, potential benefits and pitfalls, and guidelines. He then describes the kind of decentralized management data being used at WPI, to show that even institutions that do not practice responsibility center budgeting management

163

*can learn from data constructed around decentralized principles. Jon Strauss is currently vice president and chief financial officer of the How-ard Hughes Medical Institute.—*ED.

Underlying Principles

Experience at the University of Pennsylvania demonstrated that three management principles guide the application and effectiveness of de-centralized management in higher education: openness, localness, and merit.

> *Openness.* One of the fundamental tenets of academic freedom that forms the foundation of the entire collegiate experience is free and open exchange of ideas and information. Traditionally, ten-ure and academic custom have allowed faculty to be largely self-determining: they generate their own support, set their own schedules, recruit their colleagues, and govern their institutions. As a rule, institutions that are dedicated to a management struc-ture that builds upon this foundation are best able to recruit and retain productive and satisfied faculty members—professors who contribute enthusiastically to the attainment of plans they have helped formulate and for which, as a result, they take ownership. Openness is thus a requirement for faculty involvement in the planning and management of the institution.
>
> *Localness.* If decentralized management can work in the for-profit environment where hierarchical control enjoys a much deeper tradition of respect, then local governance should be a natural in the academic community. In the most radical view, local colle-giate governance suggests giving departmental faculties responsi-bility for their entire academic operations—planning, developing opportunities, generating resources, and achieving excellence, all in addition to their prescribed obligations for instruction, re-search, and service. Contingent upon the acceptance of these responsibilities, of course, are the authority and the rewards that accompany such a system.
>
> An important benefit of local governance is its simplicity. Because decisions are made by individuals who are in a position to understand best the issues involved (who, incidentally, are often not on the top rungs of the hierarchical ladder), problems can be viewed without complicated models or explanations. The decision makers know at the outset of responding to a challenge that they will be involved in implementing solutions and will

be held accountable for outcomes. As a result, decisions tend to emerge more quickly and prudently, and the faculty can adapt their solutions to ever-changing conditions both on campus and off.

Merit. Decisions of the greatest merit are made and implemented openly and at the most local level of the organization. On merit alone are grades awarded, papers published, research support won, salaries earned, promotions made, and tenure granted; moreover, faculty are not only comfortable with, but generally insist upon, using merit to determine alternate courses of action. Merit also provides the principle to weigh several possible local alternatives. Even in the most effective decentralized organizations, overall resources must be allocated in accord with institutional priorities and the performance-risk assessments of "competing" local plans. In the final analysis, academia can no more ignore the principles of financial costs and benefits than the most aggressive Fortune 500 corporations. Moreover, for resource allocation to be effective in an environment of open information and local planning, relative merit must guide every decision.

These three basic management principles framed the set of organizational principles for the implementation of the University of Southern California's Revenue Center Management System.

The closer the decision maker is to the relevant information the better the decision is likely to be.

Stable environments facilitate good planning.

Responsibility should be commensurate with authority and vice versa.

A clear set of rewards and sanctions is required to make operational the distribution of responsibility and authority, as well as to effect their coupling.

While fiscal performance criteria are seductively easy to quantify, achievement of academic excellence requires that academic performance criteria be quantified as well.

The degree of decentralization of an organization should be proportional to its size and complexity.

Successful decentralization requires a centrally maintained management information system providing local and central managers with timely and accurate performance reports.

The central administration should retain sufficient academic and fiscal leverage to facilitate the achievement of institutional goals.

A Specific Example of Decentralized Management Data
at the Departmental Level

To give a sense of the major features of policies, procedures, and funds
flow in a typical decentralized management system, consider the actual
1991–92 financial results in table 1 for a WPI department under a prototype decentralized management model.

Under this system, the department sees its full revenue and expense
activity, restricted as well as unrestricted. Both revenue and expense are
further classified as direct and indirect, with direct being under the
direct control of the department and indirect being set from outside. The
basic logic is that revenue-producing centers will be budgeted and managed with expenses balanced to revenues, and that the financial activity
of the revenue centers will sum to the financial activity of the institution.

Individual categories of revenues and expenses are distributed according to the following rules: Tuition revenue is distributed 75 percent
to the teaching department and 25 percent to the enrolling department.
Restricted scholarship revenue, a distribution of the restricted revenue
from all sources of financial aid, is matched to the restricted expenses for
financial aid distributed proportionally to tuition. Reimbursed salaries
accounts for coverage of committed salaries budgeted as unrestricted
from restricted funds.

Financial aid is shown as an indirect expense but more correctly
should show as a discount on revenue. The financial aid costs, both
unrestricted and restricted, are distributed proportionally to tuition.
Some will argue that financial aid should be assigned with the individual
student, but this averaging approach reflects the notion that the student
is a member of the university and not just the department.

Departmental administration ICR represents that portion of the
indirect cost recoveries from restricted activities that are justified based
on unrestricted departmental costs, as discussed below. Research incentives, set at 25 percent of the total ICR, are monies the department is
allowed to spend based on a historical incentive at WPI. Indirect expenses incurred in the administrative service centers, listed as academic
support (library, academic computing) through public service and information, are charged back to the departments based on their use (e.g.,
metered utilities), or potential use (e.g., proportional share of the president's office), of the services. Restricted and unrestricted activity is
counted in the proportional distribution of these indirect expenses. Cost
sharing of research is the costs of the restricted research program of that
department borne by the unrestricted budget under agreement with the
sponsor. Indirect cost recovery is the indirect cost recoveries from all

TABLE 1. Total Resource Management, Revenue and Expense Summary, 1991–92 Fiscal Year

Description	Unrestricted	Restricted
Tuition and fees (undergraduate)	2,399,643	
Tuition and fees (graduate)	733,240	
Endowment revenue		
Scholarship revenue		340,134
Gifts and grants		5,496
Sponsored research		233,152
Other income		
Auxiliary income		
Participation	(783,221)	
Subvention	642,834	
Total revenue	2,992,496	578,782
Faculty salaries	712,629	25,540
Staff salaries	150,405	1,800
Benefits	212,306	6,726
Reimbursed salaries		
Graduate stipends	89,100	60,324
Student help	18,235	5,163
Total compensation	1,182,675	99,553
Graduate assistant tuition	90,620	48,320
Materials and supplies	59,895	21,300
Equipment, expensed	57,947	4,794
Travel	13,667	5,970
Telephone	6,088	
Departmental administration (ICR)	(2,179)	
Research Incentives	17,320	
Total other direct expenses	243,358	80,384
Total direct expenses	1,426,033	179,937
Academic support	219,928	
General administrative	169,296	
Debt service	40,812	
General institutional	36,497	
Depreciation	60,669	
Building repair and maintenance	32,550	
Plant operations and maintenance	145,517	
Departmental utilities	37,433	
General utilities	19,632	
Student services	210,889	
Public services and information	86,362	
Financial aid	563,410	340,134
Cost sharing of research	3,552	(3,552)
Indirect cost recovery	(60,084)	62,263
Total indirect expenses	1,566,463	398,845
Total direct and indirect expenses	2,992,496	578,782

sponsored research activity in the department less that justified and accounted for departmental administration. The ICR are shown as negative unrestricted indirect costs to emphasize that their purpose is to cover the indirect costs associated with supporting the sponsored research activity.

Participation is a charge of 25 percent of direct unrestricted revenue. This charge helps fund the reallocation (subvention) pool. Subvention is a discretionary allocation to account for the different unit costs of different program activities historical, intrinsic, or desired. (In this after-the-fact presentation, the subvention is set to balance revenue to expenses.) If a particular department suffers rapid loss of student interest and income, for example, the central authority (general) can help phase the impact by increasing that department's subvention. In responsibility center budgeting, subvention is the primary means of institutional-level budgeting and control.

Table 2 presents an overview of the funds flow for the total institution in this decentralized financial model for 1991–92. The six columns identify academic operations (departments), other educational (summer school, continuing education, etc.), auxiliary operations (residences, dining, bookstore, etc.), general, administrative services, and total. Notice that at the institutional level, participation transfers revenues (25% of unrestricted) from the revenue centers to general (subvention pool). General collects revenues from participation, unrestricted gifts, and unrestricted endowment and transfers them to the revenue centers as subvention.

Indirect costs are generated as the net costs of the administrative services and distributed to the revenue centers by indirect cost type (academic support, general administrative, etc.) using consistent algorithms based on use or potential use. The total column corresponds to the audited financial results, except indirect cost recoveries are shown as a reduction of indirect costs to emphasize that while the recoveries may be accounted as unrestricted revenues by FASB, they truly are not discretionary in purpose.

By normalizing the financial data, one can produce physical equivalents from which a number of interesting analyses can be made, both geographically (across schools or departments) and temporally. One could generate, for example, tuition equivalent student/salary equivalent faculty ratios by department or subvention ratios by department. The notion, of course, is not that these ratios should be identical across departments. Different teaching methodologies, lifestyles, laboratory needs, and histories all contribute to very different measures. The important point is that these measures should be consistent with quality percep-

TABLE 2. Total Resources Management, Revenue and Expense Area Summary, 1991–92 Fiscal Year

Description	Unrestricted						Restricted			
	Academic Oper.	Other Educ.	Auxiliary	General	Administrative	Institutional	Academic Oper.	Other Educ.	Administrative	Institutional
Direct revenue	41,993,658	2,737,229	6,349,005	5,983,153	342,218	57,405,263	14,688,841	611	330,664	15,020,116
Participation	(10,498,419)	(684,308)	(1,587,252)	12,769,979						
Subvention	14,871,969	986,208	2,930,849	(18,789,026)						
Total revenue	46,367,208	3,039,129	7,692,602	(35,894)	342,218	57,405,263	14,688,841	611	330,664	15,020,116
Direct expense	20,489,405	1,979,930	5,417,298	391	30,021,851	57,908,875	8,628,417	611	5,594,563	14,223,591
Dept. admin. ICR	(33,472)				(975)	(34,447)				
Indirect expense	18,112,601	1,059,199	2,275,304	(82,641)	(20,930,275)	434,188	(464,338)		(26,509)	(490,847)
Financial aid	8,721,517				(8,721,517)		5,265,231		(5,265,231)	
Indirect cost recovery	(922,843)			(1,299)	(26,866)	(951,008)	1,259,531		27,841	1,287,372
Total expenses	466,367,208	3,039,129	7,692,602	(83,549)	342,218	57,357,608	14,688,841	611	330,664	15,020,116
Variance				47,655		47,655				

tions or expectations and priorities. If they are not, explicit actions should be taken to align these measures over time. Organizing data in a responsibility center budgeting format thus provides a lot of useful, financially consistent information even if departments are not managed according to strict RCB principles.

Budgeting under Decentralized Management

To this point, most of the emphasis and all of the examples have been after-the-fact presentations of where revenues were earned and how they were spent. While this is an important educational tool, the real benefit of decentralized management is in prospective planning and budgeting. The general approach employed at both Pennsylvania and USC to budget the subsequent year is as follows:

1. Project the full institutional budget for next year(s) and make preliminary decisions for the trade-offs of tuition rates, enrollments, salaries, benefits, new programs, and reallocation.
2. Decide on the general parameters for the administrative service centers and set their outline budgets.
3. Distribute the indirect costs for the next year based on the algorithms using data from the previous year.
4. Project tuition revenues for the next year based on the new rates and the expected enrollments.
5. Set subventions to reflect history, priority, and ability to change to achieve the goals of the strategic plan.
6. Ask the revenue centers to balance their budgets with particular care for enrollment assumptions.

Once this logic is in place, various refinements can be added to do planning and subvention settings over longer time periods. The institution also needs a mechanism, perhaps an intercenter bank, to hold centers responsible for deficits and to allow other centers to profit in future years from prior year surpluses.

Potential Benefits

Over the years, the following sorts of benefits have been realized at the University of Pennsylvania, USC, and elsewhere by measuring budget performance on the basis of revenues and expenses, indirect as well as direct, at the school and department level.

Accountability for both the full revenues and expenditures of a budget center has had several effects. Perhaps most important, the centers themselves now have incentives both to enhance revenues and control costs. Cost-benefit analysis is encouraged. On the revenue side, responsibility center budgeting focuses more attention on the importance of tuition revenue and on the professors or courses likely to attract that revenue. In addition, members of a budget center are encouraged to seek out gifts and grants from both philanthropic and governmental sources.

On the cost side, the members of a center become more aware of the total costs of the enterprise including benefits, financial aid, and overheads, since these are no longer charged to other units in the accounting. In fact, explicit charges for space related costs may cause a reappraisal for the need or value of space. Explicit charges for space and depreciation also emphasize the need to provide resources for maintaining the physical plant, making the cost of deferring those repairs more apparent. Finally, explicit portrayal of indirect costs helps reinforce the notion that indirect cost recovery is not discretionary income but rather income to cover real, and often frustratingly high, administrative costs.

Portrayal of revenues and expenses at the school or department level involves the faculty substantively, not just as consultants, in academic and financial policy issues where they can make a difference. Public presentation of all the data (except individual salaries) for all centers encourages peer pressure for appropriate behavior. The explicit, public identification of the sources and uses of indirect costs creates pressures to provide services more efficiently. At both Pennsylvania and USC, general administration and general institutional indirect costs were reduced dramatically relative to total expenditures in the years following the introduction of decentralized management. Moreover, at USC departmental administrative costs were reduced as well. Finally, allowing centers to carry forward surpluses and requiring them to be responsible for deficits at year-end provide incentives for prudent long-term operations.

Potential Pitfalls

Implementing responsibility center budgeting also gives rise to dangers that must be avoided. These systems facilitate management but do not automate it. Consequently, the chief academic officer, in particular, must be vigilant in emphasizing the incentives for good academic performance and in discouraging possible unfortunate side effects in the schools and departments. Among these possible side effects are centers restricting students from taking courses in other schools in order to retain their tuition, trying to attract students from other schools with gut courses, restricting interdisciplinary activity in order to retain tuition revenue or indirect cost recoveries, and finally restricting use of necessary administrative or academic support services in an attempt to minimize indirect cost allocations that are based on measured use.

In addition, subvention raises some problems of its own. Subvention provides a net measure of the relative unit costs of different programs both intrinsic and as a result of institutional history. Further, subvention can be used to express priority and to provide discretionary funding for new ventures. Unfortunately, this system can also lead to invidious comparison between peers over who is most favored. The chief academic officer must be prepared to defend the subvention distribution in terms of the relative academic benefits provided. Many deans and department heads will try to win this budget game by arguing with the rules rather than concentrating on performance. The correct response must be that subvention is based on a certain set of rules and any changes will be problem invariant.

A few other potential weaknesses remain. Department chairs elected by their faculty for short terms may have difficulty in providing the strong financial management needed with decentralized management. While the costs of central services should be tested against the marketplace and changes made where appropriate, care must be exercised to assure that these changes are not too precipitous and that institutional considerations are brought to bear when services are outsourced.

Most important, as with all budgeting, the strategic plan must drive the tactical budget and not vice versa.

Guidelines

For those adventuresome enough to contemplate installing decentralized management at their institutions, here are some guidelines:

Keep it simple! Folks will argue both sides of any algorithm to distribute revenues or allocate costs.

Try to generate broadly based involvement and acceptance for the underlying concepts early on.

Maintain as much discretion as possible in the allocation of subvention.

Derive all reports directly from official information systems and make certain that reports reconcile. One simple mistake or inconsistency can destroy confidence for a long time.

Emphasize that while the numbers reconcile to the official information systems, the underlying decisions reflect academic priorities and judgment.

Display and budget restricted activity as well as unrestricted to emphasize the role of restricted funds in advancing the mission of that academic unit.

Avoid the temptation to deal solely with the direct revenues and expenses as this precludes the benefits of knowing the overheads, no matter how imprecisely they are allocated.

Never (ever!) compromise the principle that units must be responsible for their performance.

Embed the annual budgeting process in a multiyear strategic planning process.

Present all the data (except individual salaries) for all centers publicly to encourage comparison and preclude suspicion.

The president and chief academic officer must believe! (i.e., walk it as well as talk it!)

Another Approach

While the examples given to this point are derived from a decentralized presentation of WPI's financial performance on a departmental basis, WPI is not being managed on a decentralized basis. As at most colleges and universities, the WPI departments exercise significant authority over their expenditures and negotiate their annual expenditure budgets based on historical precedent and qualitative analyses of the academic benefits that will result. To date at least, the department heads have been skeptical of what benefits might accrue from taking responsibility for generating revenue and particularly for balancing expenses to revenues during an academic year. Moreover, they have been most reluctant to be held responsible for indirect expenses they don't control.

The attitudes encountered at WPI with respect to decentralized management are not peculiar; they were encountered at both Pennsylvania and USC. The enormous success of decentralized management at improving financial and service management, however, suggests potentially significant benefits for departmentally based decentralization in a small college environment similar to WPI if ways can be found to overcome these kinds of objections. Another approach based on responsibility center budgeting was undertaken at WPI with the full cooperation of the department heads.

Table 3 presents the reconfigured results for the department described in table 1. Data from the registration systems from which student revenue can be computed are displayed as revenue statistics. The unrestricted

TABLE 3. Decentralized Departmental Data for Budgeting Purposes

Revenue Statistics	Actual FY 1991	%	Actual FY 1992	%	Preliminary FY 1993	%
Undergraduate majors	209	7	186	7	211	8
Undergraduate advisees	200	7	185	7	206	7
Undergraduate courses	72	7	58	6	71	7
Undergraduate course credit	4,998	6	5,160	6	4,851	6
I Q P projects	35	4	61	8	48	7
I Q P credits	255	4	603	11	320	6
M Q P projects	87	7	100	9	65	6
M Q P credits	375	6	488	8	369	6
Other undergraduate projects	17	4	38	8	8	4
Other undergraduate project credit	44	1	131	4	23	1
Graduate majors	109	12	115	14	139	17
Graduate advisees	110	15	105	16	126	19
Graduate courses	24	11	26	13	16	14
Graduate course credits	1,104	14	1,449	18	832	21
Graduate projects (Thes/PhD/Dr/Isg)	44	10	36	9	20	11
Graduate project credits	250	10	188	9	84	9

Direct Expense Categories	Actual FY 1991	%	Actual FY 1992	%	Budget FY 1993	%
Tenure track faculty salaries	624,903	6	666,200	7	696,780	6
Non-tenure track faculty salaries	66,000	7	97,619	8	86,300	11
Staff salaries	94,818	6	99,215	6	103,040	6
Benefits	180,716	6	212,306	7	217,986	7
Reimbursed salaries					(10,000)	2
Teaching assistants	84,500	11	89,100	11	103,032	12
Student help	12,012	6	18,235	9	5,516	3
Total compensation	1,062,949	6	1,182,675	7	1,202,654	7
Graduate assistant tuition	85,536	11	90,620	11	107,232	12
Materials and supplies	77,962	8	59,895	6	51,550	6
Equipment, expensed	81,621	22	57,947	15	66,055	18
Travel	17,348	8	13,667	6	12,050	6
Telephone	6,566	5	6,088	5	5,400	5
Total other direct expenses	269,033	11	228,217	9	242,287	10
Total direct expenses	1,331,982	7	1,410,892	7	1,444,941	7

Employee Totals	Actual FY 1991	%	Actual FY 1992	%	Budget FY 1993	%
Tenure track faculty	12.50	6	12.00	6	12.00	6
Staff	4.00	7	4.00	7	4.00	7
Teaching assistants	11.00	11	11.00	11	12.00	12

direct expenses are the same for the individual categories as in table 1. Indirect expenses are not presented, but specific employee counts from the human resource system are included.

This approach has some of the advantages of full decentralized management in that departments are alerted to the characteristic features of their direct revenue and expenditure patterns and can compare their behavior to others. This approach, however, neither establishes a logical tautology for setting expenditure levels relative to revenue nor facilitates peer-based control of indirect costs. This method does provide, however, the beginnings of an approach that may prove effective for departmentally based decentralized management, and is presented here as a possible intermediate step. The difficult times facing higher education now and for at least the next decade have stimulated general interest in better, more participatory financial management in public as well as private institutions. Decentralized management has provided demonstrated benefits, but a major challenge remains in bringing this system to individual academic departments.

The USC Experience

Currently Vice President for Business and Finance at the California Institute of Technology, John R. Curry was instrumental in implementing responsibility center management at the University of Southern California (USC) in the early 1980s. As executive director of the university budget, he first helped establish the School of Dentistry as a pilot program for decentralized budgeting, and then enlisted the help of Jon Strauss in 1980 when USC decided to implement responsibility center management on a university-wide basis. In the lively account that follows, he recalls the process of changing from a centralized budgeting system to a decentralized one and identifies five stages of implementation. His managerial perspective serves as a useful blueprint for understanding how principle translates into practice. —Ed.

In the first section, Jon Strauss discusses principles that underlie both academic governance and the management of complex organizations. His three academic principles of *openness, localness* and *merit* indicate why decentralization should be a natural state in universities. The eight companion organizational principles are normative: they state what ought to be the characteristics of a functional decentralized university; that is, they characterize the decentralization—the end product—not the *decentralizing*—the act or process of change. It is the *process* of change that I discuss here, beginning with the conditions at the University of Southern California in 1980–81 when decentralization became a salient issue. A backward looking cultural assessment runs the risk of self-serving revisionism, yet I believe the effort will prove worthwhile.

At the beginning of 1980, dissidents and dissonance were on the rise. Lore about who was financially supporting whom, or who was exploiting whom, was lurid. Most deans were saying, "The more money I find (in the form of enrollment or sponsored research), the more they (the ubiquitous despised *they*) take away." The deans had specific and colorful examples. Central administrators, especially those in financial positions, held an equally flattering view of deans and faculty, saying, "If we didn't shut them down in the comptroller's office, they would spend the university into ruin." The administrators also had specific and colorful examples. Virtually every dean and faculty member believed that the athletic program was robbing the academic program blind.

Several deans, knowing that their revenues exceeded expenses (they could count enrollments and knew the research dollars their faculty had won), claimed bitterly and resentfully to be carrying everyone else around on their shoulders (thus suggesting that altruism is an unnatural act in the academy). Such claims were possible since neither fringe benefit costs nor indirect costs were included in their back-of-the-envelope calculations of net revenues, so no deans really knew the full costs associated with the revenues generated. Without that knowledge, everyone could proclaim the injustice of their forced role of benefactor. The word *disincentive* dripped from nearly everyone's lips.

On the other hand, numerous side deals licensed entrepreneurship and sometimes lunacy. The School of Medicine had a return-of-indirect cost recovery deal as an incentive to go after sponsored research. The School of Business had a tuition revenue deal as incentive to increase undergraduate enrollments. Some schools had Class II budgets that, if authorized, returned 80 percent of the marginal revenue to the finders for program support. Finally, having begun its transformation in 1977, the School of Dentistry had become a successful responsibility center pilot modeled after the system at the University of Pennsylvania. Lots of local entrepreneurship hovered around the edges.

The institution was learning a lot about entrepreneurship without accountability. Except for the School of Dentistry, there was not much local responsibility. For example, those entrepreneurs who had established Class II budgets, thus getting expenditure authority prior to realizing marginal revenues, were never sanctioned if they exceeded their expenditure authority, if they failed to deliver the revenue, or if the revenue they promised had already been promised elsewhere in the budget—a form of internal revenue piracy. Supposedly, budgets should have predicted financial outcomes with rewards for good fiscal behavior and sanctions for bad. Experience, however, too often proved otherwise. When entrepreneurial ventures failed financially, central administrators talked about deadbeat deans, but sanctions were not forthcoming. The sense of mismanagement was widespread and growing.

At the same time, senior management was putting the question of who was supporting whom to the test. In the smoke-filled rooms of central administration, the university had already begun to understand itself as a set of responsibility centers. For several years, at the fiscal close, the budget director had recreated the university in responsibility center guise, allocating all revenues and indirect expenses to the colleges, schools, and auxiliaries. Revenues minus all costs (direct plus indirect) had a name: net financial contribution (NFC). Some NFCs were positive, indicating exportation of a center's revenues; others were negative, denoting importation. The sum of all NFCs equaled the change in current fund balance in the university's year-end financial statements. Thus, revenue and cost allocation algorithms were in place, and some knowledge about the internal economy of USC was emerging.

A considerable barrier to campus-wide decentralized management, however, was the university's financial accounting system. Given that one could tell at a given time approximately where the university stood financially two months before, one wag suggested that a sophisticated model was needed just to forecast the past. And so the conversation went, "When you can't tell where you're going, how can you be held responsible for getting there?" Lewis Carroll would have written about this!

Many of these other conditions could have been ignored if it weren't for the university's financial condition. Dramatic enrollment growth in the late 1970s provided enough money to mollify the administration bashers. Grousing about disincentives, rip-offs, and what the infamous "they" were doing was background noise when the money was coming in faster than it could be spent. But when revenue growth attenuated and began shrinking in 1978, 1979, and 1980, and centrally imposed spring hiring freezes became as predictable as the swallows' return to Capistrano, the background noise came to the fore as a clear signal. An incredible number of things seemed in need of fixing.

Into the midst of this discontent came a new senior administration: a new president who had been charged by the board of trustees with rationalizing the organization; a new provost who immediately and intuitively grasped that neither he nor anyone else could micromanage the complexity of a university comprising twenty-one colleges and schools and a farm club for the NFL; and an administrative vice president from the University of Pennsylvania who was a carrier of the decentralization virus. All three readily grasped the principle that decentralization should be proportional to size and complexity. All three understood that accountability measured by outcomes is preferable to accountability measured by controlling inputs. And the dean of the School of Dentistry was there to proclaim their perspicacity: the successful pilot of a system founded on these principles, he was an articulate and animated fan. He had begun affecting other deans.

In the process of decentralization at USC, the School of Dentistry was an important model for the rest of the university. During the 1970s, Zohrab Kaprielian, the executive vice president of USC, began to suspect that the School of Dentistry was losing money. Dental school tuitions at other schools were rising faster than undergraduate and other professional school tuitions while the dean at USC resisted all efforts to raise his school's tuitions. The dean had also resisted improving revenues in the school's clinical operations. Aware of the responsibility center system at the University of Pennsylvania, Kaprielian commissioned a full allocation of revenues and expenses to the schools and auxiliaries. Sure enough, revenues attributable to the School of Dentistry failed to cover expenses by more than a million dollars.

I was dispatched to the University of Pennsylvania to learn in depth about managing and living in their system. What were the incentives, the rewards, the sanctions? What were the disincentives, the pathologies? Having accounted for the USC schools and auxiliaries as responsibility centers, should we operate them that way? I returned an advocate and an enthusiast. We established dentistry as our first pilot in 1977, giving the school the goal of eliminating the annual revenue imbalance in three years. The pilot was a resounding success, although hiring a new "entrepreneur" dean was required.

All these various conditions contributed to *preparedness:* the cultural readiness for effecting change. By 1980, USC had reached the great conjunction: a high level of discontent, of lurid and unflattering lore about "this place," of accumulated anomalies; emerging awareness, if only centrally, of resource transfers among schools; a growing anxiety about financial well-being of the university, perhaps a sense of fiscal crisis; a confluence of interests in and zeal for decentralization among key new senior administrators who were still in their honeymoon period; and a successful pilot program, with other entrepreneurs wanting access to a predictable reward structure. Several of us knew that the times and timing were right, and we are certainly ready today to proclaim it with twenty-twenty hindsight: the great conjunction gave rise to a full tide.

Anyone wanting to alter an organization's direction needs to know the desired future state: the goal, the new paradigm, the "fortune."

Knowing the goal and having an agenda, the change agent tries to determine when the right time has come in the affairs of the organization, when the organization is ready for change. Determining whither and when is never easy. The following guidelines can help establish a time of preparedness:

Be prepared for the end outcome—have a solution awaiting the definition of the problem.

Seed the culture with indications of what the organization would be like if the desired outcome were already in place.

Create from within or attract from without intellectual allies.

Take advantage of external influences when they create pressure internally for change (for example declines in college age populations or changes in government funding).

Stay attuned to the culture: seek the right tide and the right time.

In the foregoing discussion of preparedness, I reflected on seeding the culture as a prerequisite to, or necessary condition for, change. Among the techniques of seeding a culture are: conversion of colleagues into intellectual allies, recruiting allies into the organization, simulating a new system to show how current problems would be solved, forming ever-expanding workgroups or focus groups to diffuse the new concepts and to refine understanding of their application. For example, the dean of the College of Letters, Arts, and Sciences became an ardent supporter of RCM when he discovered that his school had been bringing in increasing tuition revenues without receiving any additional expenditure benefits. This second phase of adopting change, closely linked to preparedness, is *permeation:* the systematic but informal introduction of new management concepts into an organization.

When the senior leadership at USC decided in 1981 that they wanted to implement RCM, and that the university's culture was ready for change, implementation had to move from the informal to the formal stage. In a university, that means: a committee! They were ready to begin the next stage—*prototyping.* President Zumberge appointed the Budget Incentives Task Force in the fall of 1981, comprising the "power deans" of the campus, proponents of RCM, representatives of the faculty senate, faculty members with expertise in management, and administrators whose service-unit budgets would be exposed under RCM as indirect costs. The task force was charged with defining a decentralized budget and financial management system with incentives for revenue generation and expenditure management and with sanctions for failure to comply with budget plans. One of the primary purposes of the task force was the facilitation of broad ownership of whatever system was defined.

President Zumberge appointed Robert Biller, then dean of public administration and a known master of process management, to chair the task force, and appointed me as staff to the chair. When Bob and I met to discuss the first meeting, he shocked me by saying, "Write the report; write it for the first meeting." This didn't sound quite like due process to me but Bob persisted: "You know a lot about RCM-like systems; you've helped create one here. So write a concept paper, but write it as if it were our report. That will really facilitate debate. Give task force members something hard to push against."

So I did. But being a mathematician, I liked to derive systems from "first principles." I set about to write down those organizational or management principles from which our incarnation of RCM should flow.[1] They are:

P1. Responsibility should be commensurate with authority, and vice versa.

P2. Decentralization should be proportional to organizational size and complexity.

P3. Locally optimal decisions are not always globally optimal: central leverage is required to implement corporate (global) priorities.

P4. Outcome measures are preferable to process controls.

P5. Accountability is only as good as the tools that measure it.

P6. Quantitative measures of performance tend to drive out qualitative measures (a variant of Gresham's law).

P7. Outcomes should matter: plans that work should lead to rewards, plans that fail should lead to sanctions.

P8. Resource-expanding incentives are preferable to resource-dividing ones.

P9. People play better games when they own the rules.

Borrowing heavily from Penn's approach, I then specified a typical revenue and expense statement for a "center," proposed model revenue and indirect costs allocation rules, and described an internal banking system to account for year-end surpluses and deficits. I further specified

---

1. I listed a refined version of the original 1981 principles in my chapter, "Revenue Center Management at USC," in Edward Whalen's *Responsibility Center Budgeting: An Approach to Decentralized Management for Institutions of Higher Education* (Bloomington: Indiana University Press: 1991).

how revenues would be shared between the centers and central administration. Finally, I showed how each aspect of the proposed system was consistent with the above set of principles.

At our first task force meeting, Bob Biller handed out my concept paper (which had been reviewed by the two senior vice presidents for whom I worked) saying something like, "Curry here has written a paper that—if you like it—will be our report. If you find any problems, however, we'll have to meet a few more times." We met a lot more times. The report that emerged from the task force some four months later bore remarkable resemblance to the original concept paper, yet it represented a significant advance. For example, P6 above was not in my original paper. Reminding members of the task force that you get what you measure, management professor Steve Kerr urged us to introduce academic measures of performance along with the financial. Hence we connected the review of the performance of academic plans with the performance of annual budgets developed to implement them. Thus we added P6, a variant of Gresham's law, to the original principles in the final report.

By the time the task force fulfilled its charge, I was convinced of Bob Biller's wisdom: the power of a *prototype*, or straw report was undeniable. The more the prototype is based on principle, and the more internally consistent it is, the more likely its adoption in some consistently refined form. When individuals objected to some aspect of the prototype, typically over whose ox might be gored by changing to the new system, we could ask, "How would you change this aspect and still retain consistency with our principles?" or, "Are there some principles we should change?" As one colleague observed, the axiom-theorem-proof approach of the concept paper "elevated the debate from the plane of petty politics to the plateau of principle."

I distinguish this type of *conceptual prototyping* from *behavioral prototyping*. Both were indispensable to successful change implementation. The latter, creating the School of Dentistry as a pilot using a borrowed approach, created internal precedent, and allowed us—and most important, the dean and faculty of the school—to say, "it works!" In organizations characterized by multiple and conflicting goals, "organized anarchies" as Cohen and March characterize universities,[2] precedent from elsewhere and especially from within is powerful.

The conceptual prototype guided the broad deliberation required to move from one example to systemic implementation. Indeed, conceptual

---

2. Michael D. Cohen and James G. March, *Leadership and Ambiguity: The American College President* (New York: McGraw-Hill, 1974).

prototyping was contemporaneous with *participation*, yet another phase of implementation. Participation came in the judicious selection of task force members, and in their many debates leading ultimately to their ownership of the final report in December of 1981. The report defined USC's version of RCM: We called it Revenue Center Management to distinguish it from its forebears. The report was accepted by the president and adopted by the council of deans.

The length and quality of the decision process (really from 1975 to 1982) rendered implementation relatively swift. RCM went live at USC with the 1982–83 budget. There was much to learn thereafter. From the time of the task force report, business managers from over sixty departments across the campus had to be trained; at the same time, they participated in specifying a new budgeting and financial accounting system required to enable them to take on their new authority and responsibility. As we lived with the system, we learned that some rules had unforeseen consequences and needed changing; that central administration cannot abrogate the system without consequence; that the rewards have to be honored, the sanctions enforced. We learned that some heads of revenue centers really didn't want responsibility. They preferred authority all by itself! And, above all, we learned that implementation never ends: rational systems, too, harbor disincentives, but when a system is explicit, anomalous behavior can be associated with specific rules, and the rules can be altered to improve outcomes. We kept the original task force in place for almost two years as an adaptation team. We should have kept it longer. Almost four years of living with the system passed before most of us agreed it had taken hold, that it was the way USC did business.

Persistence during that time paid off: preparation and implementation are more process than moment. The *persistence* phase of implementation is just as important as the permeation phase. The organizational propensity to recidivism, the regression to an old mean, is powerful indeed, and should not be underestimated.

The phases of implementation chart (fig. 1) summarizes most of the ideas discussed thus far, and allows us to extract additional insights into the management of change. First, although assessing the culture may be the earliest phase, it is continuous throughout the implementation process. The same is true of each successive phase. Indeed, they all should continue beyond the right-hand boundary of the chart! Second, the informal phases of implementation—assessing the culture, preparing the culture, and behavioral prototyping—occupy 86 percent ($^6/_7$) of the time to cut over, while the formal phases—conceptual prototyping, participation, and decision—occupy only 14 percent. Building the momen-

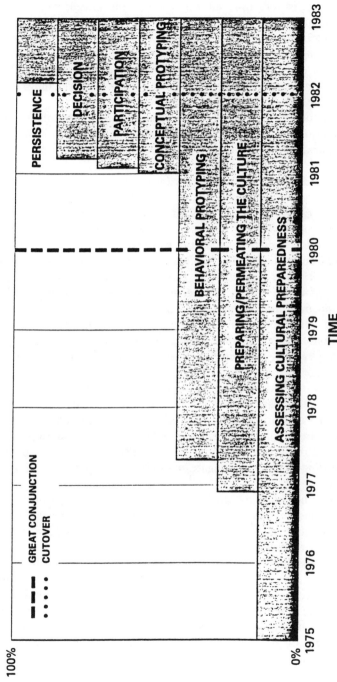

Fig. 1. Phases of implementation

tum for change is very time intensive, but if the time is well chosen, formal implementation occurs relatively rapidly. The chart also suggests an important behavioral consequence to this time asymmetry. As the talk (and gossip) about change increases, and as more people become carriers of the change virus, frustration builds in the organization. People begin feeling as if something tangible should be happening, when nothing tangible is. If the informal phases are left adrift—that is, if leaders wait too long to introduce formal implementation measures— then momentum declines and the peak moment may be lost. More than one administration has drowned in a tidal wave of expectations.

The Case for Adoption by Public Institutions

Currently vice chancellor for administration and finance at the University of Houston, Edward L. Whalen has written extensively on implementing revenue responsibility budgeting systems at public institutions. His book, Responsibility Center Budgeting, *provides a detailed account of Indiana University's adoption of responsibility center budgeting in the late 1980s. Whalen served as assistant vice president and university director of budgeting during the transition on the eight-campus public system, and the book is filled with firsthand insights on the challenges of translating theory into practice. In the following piece, Whalen continues to address concerns specific to implementing revenue responsibility systems at public institutions.*—ED.

In *Responsibility Center Budgeting*, we made the observation that, in the United States, there are about 2,000 four-year public and private institutions of higher education. Fewer than 600 of them are public; the rest— over 1,400—are private. That more private institutions than public ones have adopted responsibility center budgeting should not be surprising, since according to these aggregate numbers, more private institutions exist.

On the other hand, public institutions tend to be larger operations than private institutions, in terms of both enrollments and dollar volume. The number of public institutions with enrollments of more than 10,000 is four to five times larger than similarly sized private institutions. Responsibility center budgeting has greater applicability for larger and more complex institutions, since for a small college or university, managers of operating units (and for that matter, individual faculty and staff members) sense how their efforts contribute to the well-being of the whole enterprise. Their incentives tend to be consistent with those of the university. That sense of community tends to be lost in a big university with tens of thousands of students, hundreds of academic and support units, hundreds of millions of dollars of revenues and expenditures, and a wide variety of funding sources. In such an environment, implementing a decentralized budgeting and management system that motivates deans and heads of support units with incentives promoting the institution's objectives can offer real advantages. Nevertheless, in most cases, the budgeting and management structure of most large universities tends to resemble that of small liberal arts colleges more closely than that of the select institutions that have moved to responsibility center budgeting.

Why haven't public institutions taken the lead in moving toward responsibility center budgeting techniques in managing their affairs? Five possible areas of explanation occur to me:

Governing boards
Executive management
State funding arrangements
State administrative requirements
Coordinating boards or state legislature, executive branch

Other areas may exist as well. Although I shall explain the possible impediments to responsibility center budgeting linked with each area named above, I do not believe that any of these impediments to be insurmountable.

Governing Boards

Leadership is key. When moving to a new form of revenue and resource management and budgeting, a commitment at the top, the very top, is vital. And the very top of the university or college hierarchy is the board of trustees or board of regents. Although the university's president executes the move to responsibility center budgeting, the governing board must fully understand and enthusiastically endorse it. A president or provost or vice president who attempts to make such a change without the complete involvement of the board will find him or herself undone. Unless the board, a group of individuals, acts as one entity, the multitudes who resist change will corrode the vision, undermine the foundation, and compromise the structure.

The composition of governing boards of independent universities may be more receptive to the promise of alternative management techniques than that of public institutions. A business orientation may be more common in the former, while the latter must address a wide variety of societal and cultural concerns. Financial viability is seldom an item on the agenda of a public institution. In the case of the independent, however, survivability is not assured, so good business practice is more of a consideration.

Because responsibility center budgeting is a major change in the way institutions do business, governance must not only be strong but also continuous. Turnover in membership of public institutions' governing boards may sometimes be rather rapid. Because of changes in the political orientations of the governor's office and of the legislature, attitudes, philosophies, and backgrounds of new board members may differ markedly from their predecessors and incumbents. Thus windows of opportunity for the installation of responsibility center management or its counterparts may not last long.

The scope of responsibility that many governing boards of public institutions face may prevent the boards from focusing on the issue of expeditious internal management. In the public arena, a governing board often oversees a system or collection of universities. In certain cases, the governing board presides over a statewide system. Rarely are such systems composed of homogeneous units with common problems. With such broad and diffuse responsibilities, directing the attention necessary to reforming the internal management of a few of the largest and most complex units requires extraordinary resolve.

Despite the problems that governing boards of public institutions may pose, none, either alone or in combination, precludes a move to responsibility center budgeting. Especially during times like these, when states are confronted with serious financial exigencies and when taxpayers are resistant to revenue enhancing tax levies, publicly appointed board members may be more disposed to entertain promising structural and management changes. Turnover of board membership may actually serve to capture the moment. An active governing board of a public institution with a vision for innovative management need not be entirely passive in identifying prospective new appointees, even in situations where a change in political fortunes has occurred.

Executive Management

Leadership is key. The principal role of a governing board is not to implement responsibility center budgeting but to select and support a chief executive officer (president or chancellor) who will. That individual, in turn, must surround him or herself with those who will carry out its installation and inspire, convince, and cajole others about its merits. Both the governing board and the chief executive officer must share a common belief in responsibility center budgeting, but the chief executive officer and his colleagues must develop the vision for its installation.

No inherent character or personality differences appear to exist between the presidents of public institutions and those of private institutions. Indeed, some individuals manage in the course of their careers to serve as the chief executive officer of both types of institutions. So the scales should be fairly evenly balanced insofar as the predilection of public and private university presidents toward responsibility center budgeting is concerned.

While the predilection may be balanced between the two types of institutions, it's also liable to be uniformly low. Generally, chief executive officers are selected from among the academic ranks, and relatively few academic disciplines are concerned with management effectiveness and operating efficiencies. Rarely are management effectiveness and operating efficiency top priority selection criteria for faculty-dominated search and screening committees, so an institution's governing board may have to take the lead in identifying such a candidate. This difficulty, however, is common to both private and public universities.

Funding Arrangements

While the characteristics of chief executive officers do not differ significantly between public and private institutions, these institutions differ obviously and measurably in terms of their funding sources. Public institutions are public because of their access to public funds, which depend on political considerations rather than market forces. Does the nature of state support carry with it any conditions that impede the adoption of responsibility center budgeting?

At a time when fiscal difficulties have caused state appropriations to decrease in a number of examples, some argue that the inherent instability of public support precludes the adoption of responsibility center budgeting. I am not one of them, for the following two reasons.

First, fluctuating revenue creates a need for a responsibility center budgeting arrangement. At the University of Southern California, that incentive-based budgeting system is called revenue center management. Fluctuations in major revenue require an incentive-based approach that enlists the ingenuity and participation of deans and division heads in enhancing their own revenue opportunities and in adjusting their expenditures to what they perceive to be the resources available to them. Under traditional centralized approaches, dips in revenue are deemed to be central administration's problem until edicts are issued attempting to curtail expenditures of operating units. Responsibility center budgeting provides a mechanism for weathering a financial storm with minimum damage to the academic enterprise.

Second, fluctuations of state appropriation do not distinguish it from other revenue sources. Anyone who over an extended period of time has managed an investment portfolio or who has attempted to forecast student enrollments knows that endowment income, tuition, and student fees are also subject to substantial fluctuations, often in response to determinants that are very difficult to anticipate. Public institutions have no corner on the market of fickle sources of revenue.

Although the nature of state appropriation per se does not obstruct the implementation of responsibility center budgeting, the conditions under which that appropriation is made available to public institutions may. Under responsibility center budgeting, major operating units— such as schools, colleges, support units—retain the income they earn, and at the end of a fiscal year any unspent balances (and deficits) are retained by them. Those two features, the ability to earn income and to retain year-end balances, are essential. An institution can hardly extend those features to its operating units if it does not possess them as well.

Conditions for implementing responsibility center budgeting in a public institution of higher education are propitious if it is recognized as a separate and independent financial entity able to supplement its state support with earned income and to retain unspent balances at the end of a fiscal year. On the other hand, if a public university's tuition, fees, and other revenues are swept into the state's general funds or if at the end of a fiscal year unspent balances revert, that institution's ability to implement responsibility center budgeting is seriously compromised. These ground rules, however, can be changed.

Once again, leadership is key. The university's president and the members of its governing board are not without influence and have access to the governor and members of the legislature. At a time when the public is concerned about efficiency in the public sector and is unwilling to accept additional tax burdens, public officials tend to be receptive to well-reasoned ideas for improving management. Decentralized budgeting techniques offer opportunities for developing pie-expanding incentives rather than pie-dividing incentives. Today's financial conditions make such techniques attractive to state legislators and other decision makers.

State Administrative Requirements

State appropriation sometimes arrives with various limitations on the ways in which it can be used. Sometimes expenses are classified by type of expenditure: so much for personnel, so much for supplies, so much for equipment, and so on. In other cases, functional categories are specified: so much for administration, so much for instruction, so much for academic support, and so on. Those conditions are awkward and tend to impede management discretion, but they are not as important for responsibility center budgeting as an institution's ability to earn income and retain its unspent balances. Certainly, such limitations on income are not unique to state appropriations. Administration of grants and contracts often labor under similar restrictions; private donors rarely dispense their philanthropy in the form of unrestricted gifts. Such impediments are common to both the private and public sectors of higher education.

Unlike private institutions of higher education that handle all their administrative functions, some of the administrative functions of certain public institutions are carried out by other state agencies. Examples of such functions include purchasing, personnel management, financial reporting, payroll, construction, and long-term debt financing. The existence of such service units operating outside the institution's management would require adaptation of responsibility center budgeting but does not prohibit it.

Coordinating Boards

A private university can adopt responsibility center budgeting, and since it is independent, the choice is unlikely to make anyone outside of the university uncomfortable. Not so with a public institution. Public institutions are like bananas: they are found in bunches. When one public institution distinguishes itself from the rest, other members of the bunch tend to become uncomfortable. Those who tend the bunch—higher education coordinating boards, other state reviewing agencies, legislative staff and committee—may be uncomfortable if these institutions are out of step with their counterparts in other states.

As a result, for the chief executive officer of a public institution and his colleagues, driven by a governing board keen on responsibility center budgeting, the process of communicating the nature of the new approach has to be extended to external constituencies. Public officials, the governor, key legislators, members of the coordinating board and other reviewing agencies, and legions of career state bureaucrats have to be informed of the approach.

If the Indiana University experience is any indication, receptivity to the idea will be high. One of the by-products of responsibility center budgeting is management information that addresses many of the key questions of interest to reviewing agencies and legislative committees, such as how much programs cost and how state funds are being used. The data are available automatically.

Full disclosure is a requirement of responsibility center budgeting. Such openness should not be restricted to those within the institution. A public university is accountable to the public who supports the institution: that public deserves to be informed as well.

Selling responsibility center budgeting, that is, generating a feeling of participation in state government, may not be such a problem. Constraining enthusiasm may be the greater hazard. Some will maintain that responsibility center budgeting should be adopted universally and immediately. Some will want to help by appropriating state support according to the internal allocation patterns among academic units—for example, directly on the basis of student enrollments without consideration of broader institutional needs. In any event, involvement and oversight of state government in a public institution's activities do not appear to present obstacles for responsibility center budgeting.

Conclusion

Can responsibility center budgeting work at a public institution of higher education? Of course, it can. What is required is leadership and the ability of an institution to earn income and retain unspent balances. And of the two, leadership is by far the most important.

Part 4
Other Contexts

CHAPTER 8

Lessons from Health Care

William F. Massy and David S. P. Hopkins

Higher education is not the only sector where rising costs, concerns about quality, and inadequate access for low-income groups have triggered public concern. Indeed no institutions receive more public scrutiny and greater cost-containment attention than those in the health care field. The health care experience offers important lessons for higher education.[1] Teaching hospitals and medical school clinical practices have been particularly hard hit, because they represent the confluence of health care cost-rise factors and higher education's lattice and ratchet.

The critics' concerns in higher education and health care are remarkably similar. According to Thomas Langfitt, president of the Pew Charitable Trusts and former vice president for medical affairs at the University of Pennsylvania:

> Critics argue that the excessive increases in hospital rates and physicians' fees—and in the fees charged by colleges and universities—are used to make larger and larger reinvestments in the firm and to pay bonuses in the form of facilities and higher salaries to retain and attract the most highly visible and productive physicians and faculty. According to this line of thinking, the financial structures of health care and higher education institutions are becoming more and more like for-profit service companies that compete in the marketplace for both talent and revenues.[2]

---

1. Morgan discusses some lessons from health care for higher education. A. W. Morgan, "Cost as a Policy Issue: Lessons from the Health Care Sector," *Journal of Higher Education* 54 (1983): 279–93.

2. Thomas W. Langfitt, "The Cost of Higher Education: Lessons to Learn from the Health Care Industry," *Change* 22, no. 6 (November/December 1990): 8.

Langfitt goes on to describe the root cause of the public's concern, which is based on a decline in trust due to a growing gap between expectations and perceptions of reality.

> The public expects physicians and faculty to behave differently than people who make their living in the marketplace. They provide vital services that are not measurable in the same terms as tangible goods or the kinds of services provided by a plumber or a financial adviser.

> The relationships between the physician and the patient and the teacher and the student are different from other relationships. In the eyes of the public, both the physician and the teacher possess indefinable powers that contribute to their success in making the patient well or inspiring the student to extraordinary accomplishments. The figures who often loom largest in the minds of many people are the doctors who saved their or their loved ones' lives and the teachers who forever changed their attitudes and aspirations.[3]

Alas, the public sees too many doctors as income maximizers and too many faculty not as great teachers but as just another professional pursuing his or her own goals. Although not necessarily pecuniary, these goals divert resources from broad and inspiring social aims to narrow goals that often are difficult to understand and appreciate.

The Health Care Ratchet

The tremendous advances in biotechnology since World War II, coupled with America's economic dominance during most of the period, produced great progress and unbridled optimism. The medical profession's venerable moral imperative, "do no harm," became "do all you can." The general economic affluence and the structure of the health care payment system produced the tag line, "regardless of cost." Soon this, too, achieved the status of a moral imperative, an entitlement, as health care professionals arose in righteous anger against efforts to apply economic constraints.

Every system is limited by some kind of constraint. For a long time, the cost of health care was limited by what could be done—that is to say, by scientific knowledge and technology, and by the inability of some socioeconomic groups to obtain access to the system. Scientific and technological breakthroughs combined with progress in solving the ac-

---

3. Ibid., 9.

cess problem changed all that. In the 1980s, it became apparent that the cost of health care as a percent of GNP was rising at a rate that could not be sustained. (Health care was 6 percent of GNP in 1965, 9 percent in 1976, and a projected 14.4 percent in 1993.)[4] Clearly, to offer everything to everyone would nullify other important public and private priorities.

The true nature of the medical care ratchet and its driving forces eventually became apparent, starting with the "do all you can" imperative. Health care professionals are motivated not just by money, but also by the intrinsic value of reaching clear-cut diagnoses and, wherever possible, curing the sick. Medical interventions that promised benefits with few side effects were applied without debate—the costs were determined and settled up later. Whole generations of doctors were trained to think this way, and these values became deeply embedded in the health care culture.

Accelerating scientific breakthroughs and technological growth reinforced the trend. The best doctors kept up on the latest developments and deployed the latest equipment and medications. Certification agencies pressed for the adoption of new interventions, and medical schools enthusiastically mounted profitable continuing education programs. Equipment salesmen and drug "detailers" vigorously pursued their vested interests in technological advancement. These developments produced much desired medical progress, which raised the public's expectations to ever higher levels.

Rising expectations for health care efficacy and the increasing litigiousness of American society locked in successive rounds of medical advancement and their resulting cost increases. The public demanded better hospitals, high-tech equipment, and access to highly trained specialists. Government programs stimulated further research and development and sought to remedy the shortage of doctors (e.g., in rural areas). People—and their lawyers—came to expect perfection in care and, increasingly, in outcomes. The best defense against malpractice suits became to do everything possible regardless of cost. Doctors and hospitals were expected to continue life as long as they could, by all means available, regardless of the psychic and economic hardship.

The financial objectives of health care providers also fueled cost rise. The Medicare legislation authorized payment of "usual and customary charges," but soon this standard became a rapidly rising target. Doctors' incomes soared as prices rose and the number of medical

---

4. Evelyn Christian, et al., *Factbook: Health Personnel, U.S.*, March 1993, Department of Health and Human Services, Publication Number HRSA-P-AM-93-1 (Washington DC: U.S. Government Printing Office, 1993), 74.

procedures multiplied. Shortages of trained health professionals at all levels further fueled the escalation. Hospitals, including the nonprofit ones, increased their volume and then raised prices to provide funds for new capacity and technology.

Such cost-plus pricing was the creature of two structural arrangements peculiar to the health care industry. The rapid growth of medical insurance meant that the patient did not participate directly in paying for services received. Co-payments generally were small or nonexistent during the 1950s and 1960s. Insurance premiums were not a large factor in peoples' budgets, partly because employers paid such a big portion of the cost. Beginning in the 1960s, the federal Medicare and Medicaid programs provided "zero-premium insurance" for the elderly and many low-income citizens. While amply justified in access terms, the programs created expensive entitlements and further decoupled the receipt of services from the economic trade-offs required to pay for them.

Few people worried about the cost of health care, and those that did found their hands tied by entitlements and union demands for better medical benefits. Providers found it easier to pass their costs along than to optimize the trade-off between service and cost—if, indeed, they were motivated to optimize in the first place. Insurance carriers found themselves in a competitive marketplace that placed a premium on generosity of terms, which were visible to subscribers, relative to cost, which was heavily subsidized by employers. The medical economy became badly overheated, enabled by cost-plus pricing and driven by the force of progress and the private objectives of those operating the system. Perceived property rights in the resulting benefits made the process difficult to reverse—the classic ratchet.

Policy Solutions

The federal government, private employers, and insurance carriers responded to cost escalation with a variety of policy initiatives. First were state governments' attempts to constrain the proliferation of expensive facilities and equipment through the passage of "certificate-of-need" laws. These attempts failed largely due to the inability of the political system to say "no" to any hospital with a constituency of its own. (And what hospital is without a constituency?) Other proposed solutions were designed to contain costs by regulating medical decision making, building price resistance, or changing cost reimbursement procedures. They fell into the following categories: (1) utilization reviews, (2) co-payments and preferred provider programs, and (3) prospective payment systems. The results of applying these health care policy remedies are not completely evident, but they certainly have slowed the rate of medical cost increase. Debate about cost containment continues in the wake of the demise of President Clinton's health care proposals.

Higher education has much to learn from health care. First, some of the policy solutions have analogies in higher education. By analyzing their performance in health care, we can gain insight into their applicability to colleges and universities. Second, hospitals have had to change their management processes and relations with physicians in order to cope with cost containment measures imposed by payers. The analog here is that colleges and universities also rely on highly independent and mobile professionals—the faculty—for their mainline production work.

Utilization Reviews

Utilization reviews represent the direct approach to cost containment—regulation of service decisions. Insurance companies or employer groups engage experts to decide whether a given medical intervention is necessary, given the patient's symptoms and the other circumstances surrounding the case. The results determine whether payment is authorized. Utilization review represents an application of economic agency theory's specific responsibility option.

Utilization review may take place either before or after service is provided. In before-the-fact review, the doctor or hospital seeks prior approval to perform the procedure. This generates the kinds of problems normally associated with micromanagement—in this case the direct cost of the review, delay of service, and potential degradation of decision quality as judgments are made far from the scene of the action. Experience shows, however, that before-the-fact review is effective in reducing overutilized procedures. After-the-fact review, where payers decide whether to reimburse the provider for costs already incurred, provides many of the benefits of prior review without the attendant delays and disempowerments. Retrospective denial of payment triggers organizational learning, which means the provider will be less likely to perform the procedure again under similar circumstances. The incidence of after-the-fact reviews has led many hospitals to institute *managed care programs,* in which the hospital routinely interposes itself into the doctor-patient relationship—in effect, providing its own prior review.

Utilization review's applicability to higher education seems quite limited. In the most direct analog, the funding authority would review each student's program for cost-effectiveness according to preset criteria, and then pay the school or not depending on what it found. Such utilization review, however, would disempower students and faculty, and would be resisted strongly. While other analogs come to mind, they seem equally far-fetched or else completely commonplace. For example, funding agency budget review on project proposals might be viewed as prior utilization review, but we gain no insight from this analogy.

Co-payments and Preferred Provider Systems

Making people pay a higher fraction of the charges for services received generates price resistance and thus pricing discipline. In health care, insurance pays most or all of the cost, the residual being born by the patient as a *co-payment*. The larger the co-payment, the greater the price discipline, but unfortunately, the greater the financial hardship on those with limited means. Therefore, co-payment policies must balance the need to bring costs and benefits together in decision making with the need to insure access.

Co-payments vary, but patients usually are responsible for about 20 percent of the first dollar of charges. The payments are capped to limit financial exposure in case of catastrophic illness. Insurance with lower co-payments and higher caps generally costs more, which encourages people to be cost conscious when choosing among medical plans. Many employers now screen insurance plans for service quality and then pay only the cost of the lowest-priced acceptable plan; employees are free to choose a plan that offers more service at a higher price, but they must pay the difference. Such policies work well and are equitable despite the fact that most people are uncertain about the balance between the costs and benefits of actual medical treatment.

In *preferred provider programs*, insurance companies contract with hospitals and doctors to become preferred providers for their clients, which means giving service at a discount price. Co-payments are reduced or waived if the client chooses a preferred provider. (Special exceptions are made for out-of-area emergency service.) The insurance company induces providers to offer discounts by promising substantial patient volume and requires good quality as a condition for maintaining preferred provider status.

Co-payment policies must balance access with price discipline, and higher education has a mixed record in this regard. Financial aid based on need, offered by some private colleges and universities, represents the best approach. In principle, these plans equalize financial sacrifice in relation to income and assets, so everyone's co-payment is the same, relative to means. Merit-based aid reduces co-payments for a few students, but it does not attack the broad problem of access. Public institutions receive state subsidies that ease the middle class's financial burdens but do little to internalize the relation between true cost and individual benefits received. Federal financial aid is capped at such a low level that for many students, going to even a moderately priced school requires supplementary financial aid or great personal sacrifice.

Higher education policymakers can learn little from health care's experience with co-payments. Concerns about the relation between federal student aid and cost escalation notwithstanding, the tuition "co-payment" demanded of most families whose children attend colleges and universities dramatically exceeds the 20 percent found to be sufficient in health care. The average higher education co-payment could be increased by converting the state institutional subsidies to student aid based on need, but this would encounter formidable political obstacles, and in any case the state governments are not oblivious to the cost of education. Contrary to the assertions of former Education Secretary Bennett, federal financial aid programs are probably not a significant cause of escalating tuitions. These programs are analogous to benefits plans where the employer pays for the lowest-cost insurance coverage, while individuals are responsible for the incremental cost of higher-priced plans. As noted above, these plans are judged to have a positive, not negative, influence on cost containment. The caps on federal aid packages would have to be increased significantly before they would be likely to stimulate cost-plus pricing.

Prospective Payment Systems

American medicine has traditionally operated in terms of piecework. Doctors bill on a fee-for-service basis, and usually the fees are broken down into small increments—so much for an office visit, so much for a lab test, and so on. Hospitals also itemize most of their charges, so patients and their insurance carriers are confronted with massive statements that often add up to staggering sums. Fee-for-service provides ample opportunity for cost-plus pricing, since the large number of posted rates makes market comparisons difficult. Doctors and hospitals also may provide unnecessary services. They have no incentive to economize; in fact, the prospect of additional profits and the fear of malpractice suits gives them an incentive to do everything that is at least arguably useful. Utilization review and co-payment requirements may inhibit the use of unnecessary procedures as defined in macroterms—for example, open heart surgery as opposed to angioplasty—but the number and size of microlevel line-item charges for necessary procedures remains essentially unmonitored. Error rates are high; in the mid-1980s, for example, studies showed that hospital bills had errors 99 percent of the time. "Reasonable and necessary fees" also exhibit large geographical differences. The fees for a gall bladder removal varied from $500 in the West to $1,250 in New York City[5]—a range far beyond what can be explained by salary and other input-cost differentials.

Prospective payment systems were invented to deal with un-monitored line-item charges. The essential concept is that the client's payment should be determined *before* the service is rendered, before the myriad of decisions about service specifics and often independently of the provider's standard piecework rates. There are three basic types of pro-spective payment systems: (1) capitation, (2) per diem payment, and (3) the so-called diagnosis-related group (DRG) system. Capitation, used mainly by health maintenance organizations, covers both doctor and hos-pital charges. State Medicaid authorities and some private insurance carri-ers use per diem hospital payment systems. The federal Medicare pro-gram uses DRGs—so far only for hospital payments, but extension to physicians' services is now under consideration.

Health maintenance organizations (HMOs) are designed to internal-ize responsibility for outcomes and the financial costs of medical decisions within the provider organization itself, with the health plan members and/ or their employers making a single prospective monthly payment. In the simplest capitation model, doctors pool their resources and form a clinic to provide care on a fixed-price basis. Clients pay a fixed amount per month, regardless of whether they are sick or well. The clinic provides or arranges for all care, including hospital care, and takes all the financial risk. Since few clinics own hospitals, most HMOs contract for service with local hospitals, using their ability to direct large patient volumes to extract price discounts. The patient sheds all financial risk and, in return, relin-quishes decisions about choice of specialist and hospital. The HMO tries to keep its clients healthy, since preventive care is less expensive than curing illness once it occurs—especially if a hospital stay is involved. The doctors share the clinic's profits and also retain some of the savings from reduced hospitalization, so they have a stake in cost containment. Cost-plus pricing is inhibited, because the HMO's rates are determined in the competitive marketplace. Competitive conditions permitting, the HMO can require co-payments to limit capricious utilization.

The most serious deficiency of the capitation system is that it places the risk associated with the incidence of illness squarely on the individ-ual physician group. This represents questionable public policy since single physician groups are usually in a poor position to diversify away

5. J. H. V. Brown and Jacqueline Comola, *Improving Productivity in Health Care* (Boca Raton, FL: CRC Press, 1988), 115.

the risks of illness: for example, an epidemic of an expensive disease in a particular area could cause severe hardship for the capitated local providers. Both increasing the size of the HMO's covered population base and purchasing "stop-loss" insurance from a large insurance carrier can reduce this risk.

Per diem systems reimburse at a flat rate for each day a covered patient spends in the hospital. The illness doesn't matter, nor does the amount of resources the hospital employs on behalf of the patient, unless the resources shorten the length of stay. California uses a per diem system. Hospitals decide whether or not to contract with the state for Medicaid patients, but once contracted, reimbursement is at a prospectively negotiated per diem rate for all. Many hospitals believe their negotiated rates have been unfairly limited to the marginal cost of service, leaving fixed-cost coverage and capital replacement to others. Their only choice at present is to try to recoup these losses by increasing charges to other, charge-paying patients. In effect, this transfers the financial burden of caring for sick poor people to other sick people who are insured or otherwise able to pay. (The addition of co-payments to medical insurance policies exacerbates this problem.) The state, on the other hand, can spread the cost to all taxpayers, most of whom are well at any given time. Clearly, this payment mechanism raises legitimate concerns about equity from a public policy standpoint.

Per diem reimbursement systems are also deficient from a risk-sharing standpoint. They, too, expose individual providers—in this case, hospitals rather than physicians—to the risk of "case mix" variation that is beyond their control. Since some diseases are far costlier to treat than others, a prospective reimbursement system that is not adjusted for case mix unfairly penalizes those hospitals that experience an unfavorable change in case mix.

Medicare consultants designed the *diagnosis-related groups* (DRG) system to relieve hospitals of the risk associated with case mix while maintaining the cost-control incentives of the per diem system. Invented by academic researchers, the system categorizes illnesses requiring hospitalization into about five hundred DRGs in twenty-three major illness categories. The group definitions are quite specific, and in many cases they represent different treatments as well as different kinds of illness. The weighting scheme used to establish DRG prices is derived from observed data on relative costs. Medicare then uses these weights to set its reimbursement rate for each DRG. Hospitals classify their patients according to DRGs (there now are "expert system" computer programs to help with this task), and the federal government reimburses for Medicare patients at these prospective rates. For example, a primary diagnosis of atrial fibrillation and a secondary diagnosis of rheumatic heart disease in a sixty-eight-year-old female falls in DRG 139, which in 1987 carried an expected length of hospital stay of fourteen days and a reimbursement of $2,207 regardless of the actual charges or length of stay.[6] The reimbursement rates are revised periodically to reflect inflationary forces and whatever changes in technology and treatment modality the government wants to recognize. Hospitals are free to use more costly technologies and methods, but they must do so at their own expense.

Prospective payment systems require a documentable output quality measure for performance accountability. While the quality of medical care is subject to much debate, the results are observable in the end: the patient gets better or not, and if not, one usually can find assignable causes. Cadres of professional evaluators and accreditors—not to mention malpractice lawyers and whistle-blowers—are ready to find fault if fault is to be found. The HMO or PPO that prices below market and makes up the difference by shortchanging quality of care runs a significant risk. Detection means loss of contracts, regulatory intervention, malpractice suits, and in extreme cases, loss of license or criminal prosecution.

Performance accountability is critical because without it, the potential competitive pressure on prices and the drive for surpluses is effectively unlimited even in a nonprofit organization. Absent accountability, ethical values might not be enough to maintain the quality of care. For example, a few providers might cut prices to attract more business and then reduce quality to make this financially feasible. The increased competition would force other entities to follow suit, withdraw from the market, or go bankrupt. (Some people say the fierce price competition resulting from airline deregulation has eroded safety. In the most competitive industries, where the fighting is tooth and nail and social values cannot be imposed through regulations, companies are often terrible polluters.) In health care, however, a combination of moral imperative ("do no harm"), accreditation, and the risks of malpractice seems sufficient to balance the pressures for cost reduction.

Today's higher education environment does not include malpractice risk, and accreditation standards generally are not as stringent as those imposed on hospitals. The external quality assessment measures now being used in the United States are rather blunt instruments, as the experience of the few states with formal systems demonstrates.[7] Likewise, students and their parents find making fine quality distinctions

---

6. Ibid., 120.
7. Pat Hutchings and Ted Marchese, "Watching Assessment: Questions, Stories, Prospects," *Change* 22, no. 5 (September/October 1990): 12–38.

difficult. Institutional prestige remains a key determinant of demand: student demand depends more on the achievements of those who graduated generations earlier, the self-fulfilling prophecy of application-enrollment ratios and test scores, and research output than on current instructional quality. The moral imperative does exist in the mind of many faculty, but, especially in regard to undergraduate education, that imperative does not penetrate as broadly or deeply as does the moral imperative in medicine.

How likely are faculty to maintain educational quality in the face of resource constraints and cross pressures on objectives? Unfortunately, the problematic nature of performance accountability suggests that the answer is "not very likely." Temptations to cut corners to maintain life styles and research output in the face of revenue constraints can be overwhelming. While the quality erosion might eventually undermine an institution's prestige, and hence student demand and goodwill, neither the institution nor its constituents might realize the danger until it is too late. Alternatively, if all the institutions in a given sector are forced to reduce cost, the result may be a general quality reduction that keeps individual schools in the same relative position while leaving the public worse off. Such concerns are not far-fetched, since resource constraints will be endemic in higher education for the foreseeable future.

What can be done? One answer is to improve the situation incrementally, by such examples as adding assessment programs at the margin, balancing faculty incentives for teaching and research, and reforming resource allocation systems. Resource allocation reform is, of course, the theme of this book, and we address the matter of incremental change in other chapters. Now, however, we shall suspend disbelief and commitment to the "art of the possible," letting our imagination run free and asking radical what-if questions. In particular, we ask how higher education could be reengineered to take advantage of the experience from Medicare's DRG system and how such a reengineered structure might work.

Medicare's DRG System

Before developing our what-if model, we must analyze the DRG system's operating characteristics and the kind of research used to bring it into being. We begin our analysis of Medicare's DRG system by dissecting it into its basic elements, starting with the DRGs themselves. Then we shall analyze the system in terms of the nonprofit decision model described in chapter 3. Finally, we shall describe how the DRG system was developed.

How the System Works

What is a DRG? The definitions were developed so that the range of diagnoses and treatment options for each DRG is limited, but not so limited as to deprive doctors and hospitals of the ability to exercise on-the-spot professional judgment. For example, several different DRGs are defined for patients being treated for heart disease. One set of DRGs is for those patients who undergo surgery for their heart disease, while another set is for those who are treated without surgery. Within the first set, individual DRGs are assigned according to the type of surgery being performed (coronary artery bypass graft, valve replacement, etc.), while the DRGs in the nonsurgical set are distinguished by the particular diagnosis (acute myocardial infarction, congestive heart failure, etc.). No treatment factors are included in the definition of DRGs beyond the type of surgery that is performed.

The DRG model works as follows:

1. a patient presents with a set of symptoms;
2. the doctor develops a diagnosis, which produces a tentative assignment to a DRG;
3. services are provided;
4. the episode ends with (a) a successful outcome, as when the patient is cured, or (b) an unsuccessful outcome, as when the patient dies, or (c) the patient shifts to another DRG, and the process is repeated; and
5. the DRG assignment is finalized and costs are reimbursed according to a prospectively determined rate schedule based on the DRG, regardless of the services provided or the outcome.

As an example, let us follow the course of a patient who is admitted to the hospital with chest pain. If the patient is suspected of having suffered a heart attack, at the time of admission he would most likely be assigned to DRG 121 (acute myocardial infarction). Initial treatment would most likely involve medication combined with observation in a coronary care unit. If the patient fails to respond to the treatment, further tests and even surgery may be considered. Perhaps a cardiac catheterization is ordered and the blocked blood vessels feeding the heart are opened up by balloon angioplasty. At this point, the appropriate assignment would be to the DRG that includes angioplasty, DRG 112. Now suppose the patient suffers a second heart attack during the procedure and is rushed to the operating room for an emergency coronary artery bypass graft (CABG). This procedure in combination with the angioplasty has a different DRG code, namely DRG 106. Assuming all goes well for the patient from this point on, he will recover from the surgery and will be discharged from the hospital. The hospital's reimbursement will be based only on the prospective rate for DRG 106. The same would be true if the patient had died during the CABG surgery, even though the hospital would not have incurred the cost of the postsurgical recovery period.

Step 3 in the above model represents the key issue for analysis: how do the caregivers decide what services to provide? The more services provided, the better the treatment quality but the higher the costs. Treatment quality and patient outcomes can be assessed with reasonable accuracy, because the episode ends a relatively short time after the services are provided and the nature of the ending is readily observable. Certain cases exist where the ultimate consequences of treatment are not clear, but these are the exceptions rather than the rule. As noted earlier, quality is assured by individual medical ethics, supplemented by peer review, whistle-blowers, and malpractice lawyers. Furthermore, to a first approximation, the individual provider's definition of quality does not differ significantly from that of the patient, the government, and the general public. The cost-containment problem arises because providers want to provide more quality than the public wants to pay for, not through any disagreement about what constitutes quality.

Economic Analysis

The theory of nonprofit enterprises offers important insights about the workings of the DRG system. To simplify matters, we make the strong assumption that the health care provider is a monolithic entity. This admittedly represents an oversimplification. In particular, we assume that physicians, who are largely responsible for determining the utilization of hospital services by their patients, decide on the basis of what is best for the hospital. In reality, the relation between physician incentives and hospital costs under DRGs is indirect at best, although it is becoming stronger due to the physicians' own interest in seeing their hospital survive. The isomorphic assumption implies that the marginal utility of output quality is the same for both the doctor and the hospital.

We also assume that health care providers and Medicare value outcomes in essentially the same way. That is, they put roughly the same utilities on different degrees of recovery success and failure. Their marginal utilities of money may differ, however, because payers and providers have different obligations and opportunities outside the health care sphere. The marginal utilities affect the payer's and provider's decisions.

According to the nonprofit enterprise theory, the decision maker achieves maximum utility when:

$$\frac{\text{marginal utility of outcome}}{\text{marginal utility of money}} + \text{marginal revenue} = \text{marginal cost}.$$

We can write this more simply as:

$$EMU + MR = MC,$$

where *EMU* stands for "effective marginal utility of outcome," the ratio of the marginal utility of outcome to the marginal utility of money. The marginal cost (*MC*) is determined by technology and the prices of inputs, and the marginal revenue (*MR*) is determined by the DRG system itself.

We can see the advantages of the DRG system by comparing it with the older, cost-plus, fee-for-service system.

> *Cost-plus system.* The provider can increase revenues until its *EMU* goes to zero—that is, where all that can be done has been done. *MR* equals *MC* at this point, which is the provider's optimum.
>
> The above result is not optimal from Medicare's point of view, however. We assume for the sake of exposition that Medicare's *EMU* equals zero, the same as the provider's (this assumption is not necessary, however). Medicare's *MC* equals the provider's *MR*, since the former's payment is the latter's revenue. However, the government's revenue is not increased by the extra service, so its *MR* equals zero. Therefore, Medicare's decision equation is unbalanced: the left side is zero and the right side is positive.
>
> *DRG system.* The provider receives a fixed sum once the patient is assigned to a DRG, regardless of the level of service. Hence his *MR* equals zero, but his *MC* remains positive, as before. The provider will stop adding service when his *EMU* equals *MC*, which is well short of the point where *EMU* equals zero.
>
> While the DRG reimbursement rate is fixed as far as the provider is concerned, for Medicare it is the decision variable. Therefore, Medicare's *EMU* and *MC* relate to changes in the reimbursement rate. Medicare's *MR* equals zero, so it will increase the rate until its *EMU equals MC*. By using DRGs, the Medicare authorities can bring the system to a global optimum

despite the fact that the provider's utility function is unbounded. DRGs present a perfect example of overall pricing responsibility as described in chapter 3 in connection with economic agency theory.

The DRG system applies revenue constraints to limit the level of service to that which Medicare wishes to fund. The scenarios demonstrate only income effects, not substitution effects. Substitution effects are generally not important because tight controls on quality make it difficult for hospitals to subsidize services within one DRG at the expense of those in another. Furthermore, the close alignment between Medicare's and the providers' utility functions acts to limit the incentive for such cross-subsidies. Some private payers remain under fee-for-service, and thus pay higher prices that cross-subsidize DRG patients, but fewer cross-subsidies across medical treatment categories exist.

Although the DRG system focuses mainly on income effects, substitution effects are not beyond its reach. Suppose, for example, that Medicare wants to discourage a certain surgical procedure. By setting the procedure's DRG reimbursement rate below the rock-bottom marginal cost, hospitals are encouraged to place patients in an alternative DRG where the payment is better in relation to cost. Whether this mechanism will work depends on the following considerations:

Providers must have some degree of latitude over DRG assignments, as when the DRG definition depends not only on the patient's symptoms, but also on the choice of treatment. For instance, a person with heart disease might be diagnosed as needing a bypass operation (one DRG) or nonsurgical balloon angioplasty (another DRG).

The alternative DRG must be of proven worth, lest Medicare be accused of forcing poor medical treatment and the provider be sued for malpractice.

The second method for inducing substitution effects involves changing the DRG definitions themselves. For example, an innovative procedure with high cost-effectiveness can be encouraged by creating a new DRG whose reimbursement rate exceeds marginal cost. An existing procedure can be discouraged by merging its DRG with the DRG of one offering the same benefit at lower cost; the hospital will choose the lower-cost procedure, once the revenues are equal.

How the System Was Developed

The original research leading to the development of the DRG system was carried out at Yale University by Robert Fetter and John Thompson in the 1970s. They were attempting to define groupings of patients who placed similar demands on hospital resources, so that variations in resource utilization patterns among hospitals might be studied for these relatively homogeneous groups. Ultimately, their classification scheme became the basis for the Prospective Payment System (PPS) implemented by Medicare in 1983.

They began by compiling a large data base of hospitalized patients. These data were drawn primarily from computerized records submitted by hospitals in New Jersey, although some records were obtained from other geographical areas as well. In all, the database contained approximately 700,000 patient admissions. The information relating to each patient admission included demographic variables, such as the age and sex of the patient, and specific diagnostic and procedure codes.

They then started to develop a classification scheme that would explain variations in utilization as measured by the patient's length of stay in the hospital. Length of stay was chosen as the dependent variable because it was well defined, readily available, consistently measured, and known to be highly correlated with the utilization of hospital resources. Using this indirect measure of resources was necessary since data on costs were not generally available.

The first step in their modeling process was to assign all possible diagnoses to one of eighty-three mutually exclusive and exhaustive Major Diagnostic Categories, or MDCs. A team of clinical experts set the specifications of the MDCs, thereby ensuring that the initial classification of patients would be medically meaningful. The researchers then subjected the patient records in each MDC to a statistical analysis in which different variables were used to group or partition patients into those categories that were most homogeneous with respect to the length of stay. The variables used to partition the patients included primary and secondary diagnoses, primary and secondary surgical procedures, age, and clinical service area. Only some of these variables were used to partition patients within any particular MDC. Also, the clinical experts were involved at each stage of the partitioning process to ensure the credibility of the results. This process resulted in the definition of a total of 383 DRGs. Subsequent refinements, based on a revision to the diagnostic coding standards and the analysis of a nationwide sample of computerized patient records, reduced the number of MDCs to twenty-three and reformulated the DRGs, among other things, to first partition the patients within every MDC according to whether or not surgery was performed.

The Health Care Financing Administration used the resulting set of 470 DRGs to determine its prospective prices. The average cost for Medicare patients within each DRG was calculated on a national basis and then wage indexes were developed to adjust for regional differences in the cost of hospital labor inputs. Due to the expense of the research involved, the determination of average cost by DRG was made only once to determine the prices to be paid in the initial year of PPS. Subsequently, the price schedule has been updated annually using an across-the-board price increase rate determined by the U.S. Congress. By setting the rate of increase well below the rate of inflation for health care, the government has stimulated hospitals to operate more efficiently.

To give hospitals a reasonable period in which to adjust to the new payment system, PPS was phased in over four years by blending together an increasing proportion of the appropriate regional DRG rates with a decreasing proportion of the hospital's own historical costs. Also, certain costs, such as those for capital-related items and direct medical education, were excluded from the initial DRG rates and continued to be reimbursed directly. Capital costs are now being added to the DRG rates on a separate phase-in schedule. Interestingly, PPS has also provided a separate "indirect medical education adjustment" for teaching hospitals. This formula-derived add-on payment is intended to recognize the higher costs teaching hospitals incur due to both a more intense case mix and the additional costs of interns and residents. Finally, PPS provides some measure of relief against cost "outliers" (i.e., individual patients whose length of stay or total cost greatly exceeds the norm) and for so-called disproportionate-share hospitals that have a significantly higher proportion of low income or Medicare patients than the national average and are therefore less able to cost-shift to other payers.

DRGs Applied to Higher Education

The DRG system has worked to reduce costs and increase accountability in health care, so we are justified in asking whether it might also work in higher education. At the outset, though, we should note that the cost-containment problems are different. Schools do not receive "usual and customary charges" for whatever services they decide to provide for students or for sponsored research projects. In the broad sense of the term, prospective payment already exists in state appropriations and tuition rates. Structural changes, such as committing to tuition increases before determining budgets needs[8] or adopting responsibility center or value-based budgeting, would help make the payments truly prospective. One need not adopt a DRG-type system, however, to achieve these benefits.

To answer the question of whether the DRG concept can be applied to higher education, we must first adapt the design to colleges and universities and then work through a thought experiment to test its efficacy. Finding the higher education analog to the medical diagnosis-related group is the natural starting point for this analysis.

Program-Related Groups

DRGs were developed to define a more uniform product and to set fixed payment rates based on efficient production of services. In education, the analog to patient is student and the analog to symptoms is preparation, interests, and circumstances. Diagnosis-related group means the set of treatments whose common characteristic is efficacy for the stated diagnosis. The analogous concept in colleges and universities is rooted in academic program structure. Therefore, we will postulate a set of *program-related groups* (PRGs). We shall argue presently that academic programs such as pursuit of the bachelors degree or even majoring in a particular subject are too broad to serve effectively as the basis for PRGs. Therefore, we shall define PRGs in terms of academic program *modules,* collections of courses in a particular subject area that lead to a prespecified accomplishment level.

A PRG, then, will represent the conjunction of a program module with student type and also, perhaps, institutional mission as it defines the kind of services provided. *Student type* refers to such attributes as field of study (e.g., major), level of study (e.g., undergraduate, terminal masters, other masters and doctoral), mode of study (e.g., full-time versus part-time, traditional versus nontraditional age cohort), and preparation for study (e.g., well prepared or needing remediation). *Mission* might refer to the sector of higher education (e.g., community college, state college, or state university). Thus, we propose the use of mission as a proxy for the breadth, depth, and purpose of the institution in which the program module is offered.

The educational module should define an identifiable subject-matter collection associated with reasonably well-articulated learning outcomes. Examples might be Western culture, mathematics through intermediate calculus for scientists and engineers, micro-and macroeconomics with

---

8. "Double Trouble," *Policy Perspectives* 2, no. 1 (September 1989): 7.

policy applications, writing skills, introduction to computer science and computing, and accounting for business majors. While the learning outcomes of a module might be satisfied by a single course, much would be gained by defining modules in terms of groups of courses—so that faculty would work together to define objectives, develop assessment measures, and continuously improve the courses themselves.[9] The module concept's defining feature, though, lies in the identification of key learning outcomes in operationally meaningful terms, which in turn opens the way for judging success in achieving them. This is inherently easier at the module level than at the degree or major level, where learning outcomes are more diffuse, agreement on assessment methods harder to obtain, and quality is more difficult to associate with identifiable faculty teams.

Carrying the module idea one step further leads to the introduction of mastery learning, wherein a student works at his or her own pace until he or she is able to demonstrate a predefined level of learning performance. Students not achieving mastery in a reasonable period of time might be failed or charged a financial penalty to compensate for the extra resources consumed. Better yet, incentives based on degree-of-achievement assessments (not just whether a threshold is achieved) could lead to case-by-case optimization of the trade-off between learning and the time (and resources) committed. We are intrigued with the applicability of mastery learning to the PRG concept but feel that course-based modules are sufficient for the present discussion.

A particular module may fall into more than one PRG. For example, the mathematics sequence mentioned above might be required for all physical science and engineering majors, just as the hospital's intensive care facility is needed for many kinds of surgery. Moreover, mathematics instruction may have to start at an earlier point for students who enter with less high school preparation, and it may need to be structured differently for nontraditional students who spread their college program over six to eight years instead of the traditional four years.[10] Each combination of need and treatment falls into a different PRG. The PRG definitions remind us that academic program is not the only descriptor of educational production—the combination of raw material (student type) and instructional process (program module) is the important thing. Going back to health care, we see that a combination of disease (e.g.,

---

9. Certain higher education systems abroad already use the module idea. For example, the two polytechnics in Hong Kong rely extensively on modules to organize their academic programs.

10. "Breaking the Mold," *Policy Perspectives* 2, no. 2 (January 1990): 3.

angina) and treatment (e.g., angioplasty or bypass surgery) is sometimes used to define a DRG.

The PRG definitions are loosely related to the programs of "Planning, Programming, Budgeting" (PPB), a budgeting system popular twenty years ago in government and, to some extent, in higher education.[11] PPB organizes expenditures by program; planning and resource allocation take place at the program level. For example, business schools recognized MBA education, doctoral education, executive education, and faculty research as separate programs. One problem with PPB was that the program definitions could not be disaggregated by student type, yet as we have seen with PRGs, student type is an important consideration for resource allocation. Second, PPB required that a given element of cost be associated with one and only one program. For example, the business faculty salaries attributed to the three educational categories plus research had to sum exactly to the school's faculty salary budget. This meant that operating units had to develop and manage a complex system of cost allocations—so much faculty time attributed to each activity, for instance. Faculty members complained that these allocations did not reflect the true nature of academic work, in which they devote a great deal of time to *joint* activities benefiting multiple programs simultaneously. PPB never caught on in colleges and universities because its underlying assumptions were not realistic. Though also based on the concept of a program, the PRG system does not require expenditure categories to be mutually exclusive. A professor's efforts can benefit more than one program simultaneously. The PRG system focuses on income, leaving entities to control their expenditures any way they like.

The so-called unit costing models popular in higher education in the early 1970s also are distant cousins of the PRG concept. (We discuss the modern approach to constructing such models in chapter 10.) For example, college officials and state authorities used the Resource Requirements Prediction Model (RRPM) to compute average costs per unit of instruction, broken down by field, type of course, and level of student.[12] The approach suffered from two shortcomings. First, the model was too complex to be implemented or interpreted easily. Second, for all its complexity, it ignored the unsponsored research component of depart-

11. U.S. Senate, Subcommittee on Economy in Government, *The Analysis and Evaluation of Public Expenditures: The PPB system*, 91st Cong., 1st sess., 1969, serial 12834, 2.

12. Warren W. Gulko, "The Resource Requirements Prediction Model I (RRPMI): An Overview," Technical report no. 17 (Boulder, CO: National Center for Higher Education Management Systems, 1971).

mental output. When the computed "unit costs of instruction" were compared across institutions, the research universities fared quite badly because their costs included unsponsored research. They protested vigorously that the cost differences simply reflected instructional quality differences, an argument that eventually won the day in many cases. However, the arguments presented in chapter 3 cast doubt on whether the extra cost improves educational quality, as opposed to fueling an output shift toward research.

The possibility of output shift requires us to add research to the list of PRGs. Let us define a set of "cost centers" in which research is performed. These will include academic departments and also important interdisciplinary laboratories and institutes. (Other interdepartmental units might be partitioned into their constituent cost centers, or simply assigned to one of them.) As discussed in chapter 10, funding for unsponsored research will be separated from that for instruction and allocated to each cost center on the basis of the center's track record.

Ideally, one should define a quantum of research in terms of incremental knowledge created, but this is not feasible. A number of surrogates suggest themselves—for example, numbers of publications, perhaps adjusted for the amount of work involved and the frequency of citation. While publication counts are dangerous when used to review individual faculty performance, they do provide a reasonable measure of aggregate research output. Only within-field comparisons are valid, however, because the standard of what constitutes a publication of given quality varies markedly from field to field. Another surrogate can be built on the faculty's record in the competition for sponsored research projects. One can also look to the number of professors who are active in research, where *active* is defined as achieving a certain output threshold. While such assessments are far from perfect, recent experience in the United Kingdom and Hong Kong suggests that the approach is feasible and that it can make a positive difference in research quality. (See chaps. 9 and 10.)

The PRG Pricing Scheme

Since the purpose of this exercise is to examine a DRG-type prepayment scheme for higher education, we propose to associate a fixed price with each distinct student type/academic program module/mission combination: that is, the PRG price should equal the observed cost for the most efficient resource combination that can achieve the desired results. Then, by paying just this amount, one could hope to arrest or reverse output shifts and induce the less efficient institutions to become more efficient, just as was done in health care. Each PRG would carry an expectation of a certain amount of funding from which tuition would be deducted to calculate the government contribution. Intended mainly for state public funding of HEIs, the PRG system would keep financial aid separate to help students with fewer financial resources. One could imagine a system where federal grants to colleges and universities might also take account of PRG; however, federal funding is currently capped at such a low rate that the issue is moot.

Having defined our PRGs in the most complete way, we now introduce an important simplification. Suppose one assumes that price should be primarily associated with educational value added. Conventional wisdom holds that students with better backgrounds cost more to educate, and therefore one might think that those PRGs should cost more. No evidence supports this assertion; indeed, one could argue convincingly that remedial education should cost more. Students with better backgrounds often attend more prestigious universities, where the subsidy from teaching to research is higher, thus distorting the cost of education. In the PRG model, research would be funded separately, thereby eliminating those costly cross-subsidies. More research is needed to determine whether different levels of student preparation would incur different levels of cost. Until that time, a more equitable system might be to fund PRGs initially at the same level without regard to institutional mission and its correlate, student characteristics. Thus, we are led to speculate that our prospective payment system for higher education would function well without making the distinction between the different missions. The three variable model can be reduced to a two-dimensional array in which prices need only be given for student type/academic program category combinations, irrespective of the type of institution. The simplification works, however, only when research is separated out and funded specifically. Otherwise, research funding will be confounded with mission, so that dropping mission from the unit-cost definitions would risk gutting research quality.

Expected Operating Characteristics

Our hypothetical system takes the PRG as the unit of public funding. Funds would flow in proportion to the number of students enrolled in each PRG, rather than enrollment in degree programs or in the institution as a whole. This provides a helpful degree of fine structure in the funding unit and adds a more refined student type dimension. PRGs are rooted in academic program modules, but the mapping is unique only in one direction. Each PRG is associated with one and only one module, but a module may serve students from more than one PRG.

How would the PRG system affect institutional performance? How would it affect the behavior of faculty responsible for the academic program modules? We would expect the following.

1. A student presents herself for matriculation with a certain profile of preparation, interests, and circumstances.
2. The school assesses the student's needs and assigns her to a particular PRG and, by implication, an academic program module.
3. The module's faculty provides instructional services.
4. The service episode ends with (*a*) a successful outcome, (*b*) an unsuccessful outcome, or (*c*) transfer to another PRG.

We define a successful outcome as achieving the educational module's desired outcomes, that is, "attainment." Unsuccessful outcomes involve dropping out or repeating the work. Transfer to another PRG occurs when the student changes programs or schools while in good standing. These steps are identical to the first four steps of the health care DRG scenario.

In health care, payment is based only on the final DRG; the outcome is not considered. But that might not provide the right incentives for colleges and universities. Resource allocators could encourage schools to provide access for students with particular characteristics by defining an appropriate PRG and paying whenever the school matriculates someone in that PRG. Let us assume, however, that the authorities want to improve attainment as well as access. The student who begins a module only to drop out partway through the first year may not be viewed as representing educational accomplishment. Attainment can be taken into account by making payment, the fifth step in the scenario, dependent on the observed outcome.

5. Costs are reimbursed according to a prospectively determined rate schedule based on the PRG, scaled to reflect attainment.

For example, schools might be paid at three times the base PRG rate for students who move to the next attainment level, at twice the base rate for those who have to repeat courses, and at the base rate for those who drop out.

Our putative PRG system could be an attractive vehicle for spurring particular kinds of actions by colleges and universities. With PRGs, the central authorities can provide outcome-based incentives (such as for minority student attainment), and they can control income effects by adjusting the average level of PRG payments. Hence PRGs may prove useful for stimulating specific programs. The use of a PRG system on a broad scale, however, will be optimally successful only if the quality of education can in fact be assessed.

Imagine what would happen if attainment were judged only on a pass-fail basis, with no quality assessment above the "pass" threshold.

1. A student presents herself for matriculation with a certain profile of preparation, interests, and circumstances;
2. The school assesses the student's needs, and assigns her to a particular PRG.
3. Educational services are provided. However, the faculty may maximize their research effort subject to the constraint that student attainment just meets its threshold. This contrasts with health care, where a combination of moral imperative and diligent discipline leads to service maximization within the budget limit for the DRG.

Steps 4 and 5 are as described earlier.

The scenario demonstrates clearly that—absent good educational quality measures—the PRG system does not preclude cross-subsidies from education to research. While the revenue supplied for each PRG would be strictly limited, nothing requires expenditures to track the distribution of revenues. Figure 1 depicts the situation graphically. In the left-hand panel, the cost-containing DRG system presses down against the medical staff's desires to improve service—and thus increase cost. Each up-arrow represents the pressure for quality in a different DRG. The arrows point straight up, partly because of the "do all you can" imperative and partly because quality is externally policed. In higher education, the service-quality arrows will be slanted as shown in the right-hand panel to the extent that faculty value research over teaching. The upward (total expenditure) force is constrained by the PRG system, but the horizontal (cross-subsidy) force is not. Over time, the whole system slides toward the right side of the diagram, which metaphorically represents research. The extent of cost-rise is limited by the PRG system, but schools are free to substitute research effort for teaching effort. Such strategies need not be Machiavellian; indeed, they may be so gradual that people aren't even aware of them. The very invisibility of the sideways force makes the academic ratchet so difficult to control.

This is one of the reasons that the Higher Education Funding Council of England has remained adamant about the need to assess teaching

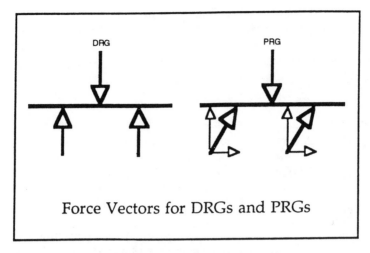

Force Vectors for DRGs and PRGs

Fig. 1. Forced vectors for DRGs and PRGs

quality even in the face of operational difficulties and widespread opposition. Without such assessments, the fact of research assessment—with substantial sums riding on the outcome—would shift attention from education to research. Hong Kong's University Grants Committee deliberately limited its research assessment to determining threshold activity levels, in part because the companion teaching effectiveness measures were still under development.

The analysis of teaching assessment is beyond our scope, but we conclude with these observations. First, the exercise is undoubtedly difficult. Teaching is not only subjective but also tends to be conducted behind closed doors.[13] Some progress has been achieved, however, and teaching assessment does not appear to be out of the question for serious-minded institutions.[14] Second, certain process indicators can provide indirect evidence about teaching quality. For example, departments that spend a significant amount of time and energy working together on teaching and curriculum are likely to do a better job than ones that rarely consider these questions explicitly.[15] Finally, the further one goes in defining educational modules in terms of learning outcomes, the easier it will be to assess quality. Redefining the unit of instruction from the

13. Lee S. Shulman, "Teaching as Community Property: Putting an End to Pedagogical Solitude," *Change* 25, no. 6 (November/December 1993): 6–7.

14. Hutchings and Marchese, "Watching Assessment," 14.

15. William F. Massy, Andrea K. Wilger, and Carol Colbeck, "Overcoming 'Hollowed' Collegiality," *Change* 26, no. 4 (July/August 1994): 10–20.

input-oriented course or credit-hour to the outcome-oriented educational module, and perhaps even shifting from time-based to a mastery milestones, may well hold the key to educational quality assessment and the associated changes in academic productivity.

Conclusion

Escalating health care prices and alarm about the percentage of GNP going to health care have spawned major reforms in how the industry goes about its business. Aimed at cost containment, the changes are profoundly affecting not only costs but also the way medical services are provided, their relative prices, and access for different groups. What may at first have seemed to be narrow cost-motivated reforms are producing a fundamental restructuring.

Many observers believe that "now it's higher education's turn." Cost-rise pressures are worrying government funding agencies as well as students and their families, and in some states, enrollment-increase pressures amplify the concerns. This chapter examines the health care experience to show how a prospective payment system for HEIs might be designed and implemented.

Defining the appropriate unit against which to apply prospective payment represents the key first step in system design. We envision the program related group, or PRG, as playing this role. Analogous to Medicare's diagnosis-related group (DRG), the PRG conjoins student characteristics and academic program characteristics. Academic programs would be defined in terms of modules, each comprising a body of subject matter and specified attainment thresholds, and each taught by designated faculty teams. State funding agencies could assign base prices to PRGs. HEIs would be paid according to PRG enrollments or better, enrollments adjusted for attainment.

The PRG system would control costs in the same way the enrollment-driven formulas do now. It would use a more refined funding unit (the PRG), however, thus relieving the institution of financial risks associated with variation in students' programs and preparation. Moreover, attainment-based prices would more closely align institutional and funding-agency objectives.

A PRG system could not, however, assure educational quality by itself. Prospective payment does not assure health care quality, either, but works because quality already is policed by accreditation, malpractice, and other factors. In the higher education prospective payment context, faculty might well be tempted to maintain or increase cross-subsidies favoring research. Indeed, these stronger and more intrusive cost constraints might trigger stronger efforts to defend research in the face of dwindling resources but at the expense of educational quality.

To be truly effective, one should accompany a PRG system with a program of educational quality assurance. The use of academic program modules would help: we have argued that they represent a better level of aggregation for assessment than either individual courses or the more nebulously defined degree or major. Institution-wide quality processes, in which faculty quality audit teams examine quality processes at the module level, will play a role as well.

We conclude that while no panacea, the PRG concept holds enough promise to warrant continued study. We hope this essay will help stimulate such work.

ANNOTATED BIBLIOGRAPHY

Bentley, James D., and Peter W. Butler. "Measurement of Case Mix." *Topics in Health Care Financing* 8 (Summer 1982): 1–17. A good summary description of DRGs and other proposed case mix classification systems. Also describes how Medicare's case mix index, using DRGs, is derived.

"Breaking the Mold." *Policy Perspectives* 2, no. 2 (January 1990):3.

Brinkman, Paul T. "Formula Budgeting: The Fourth Decade." *New Directions for Institutional Research* 43 (September 1984): 21–44. Describes the evolution of state formula-based budgeting strategies for public colleges and universities. Discussion of addressing the quality issue with formulas.

Brown, J. H. V., and Jacqueline Comola. *Improving Productivity in Health Care.* Boca Raton, FL: CRC Press, 1988.

Christian, Evelyn, et al. *Factbook: Health Personnel,* U.S. Department of Health and Human Services HRSA-P-AM-93-1, Washington, DC: U.S. Government Printing Office, 1993.

"Double Trouble." *Policy Perspectives* 2, no. 1 (September 1989): 7.

Fetter, R. B., Y. Shin, J. L. Freeman, R. F. Averill, and J. D. Thompson. "Case Mix Definition by Diagnosis-Related Groups." *Medical Care* 18 (February Supplement 1980): 1–53. Gives a complete description of how the preliminary DRGs were constructed.

Gulko, Warren W. "The Resource Requirements Prediction Model I (RRPMI): An Overview." Technical report no. 17. Boulder, CO: National Center for Higher Education Management Systems, 1971.

Hutchings, Pat, and Ted Marchese. "Watching Assessment: Questions, Stories, Prospects." *Change* 22, no. 5 (September/October 1990): 12–38.

Langfitt, Thomas W. "The Cost of Higher Education: Lessons to Learn from the Health Care Industry." *Change* 22, no. 6 (November/December 1990): 8.

Massy, William F., Andrea K. Wilger, and Carol Colbeck. "Overcoming 'Hollowed' Collegiality." *Change* 26, no. 4 (July/August 1994): 10–20.

McGovern, James J. "Perspectives for Management Control and Program Budgeting," prepared for the deans of the Medical College of Virginia, Virginia Commonwealth University (1988). Discusses the processes and terms that are used in making budgeting decisions. Includes centralized vs. decentralized budgeting, block vs. responsibility budgeting, all sources planning-programming-budgeting.

Millett, John D. *Resource Reallocation in Research Universities.* Washington, DC: Academy for Educational Development, 1973. Studies five research universities' (not identified) actual practices of resources allocation. Findings: there was a general consensus that extensive efforts had to be made to bring income and expenditures into balance, that increases in expenditures should be reduced to the level of the slowdown in increased income, and that curtailments in expenditures should be made on a programmatic basis.

Millett, John D. *Allocation Decisions in Higher Education.* Washington, DC: Academy for Educational Development, 1976. Discusses political and economic frameworks and how they are used to analyze allocation decisions within institutions and in the context of the general economy. Benefits and problems of market price mechanisms outlined.

Milter, Richard G. "Resource Allocation Models and the Budgeting Process." *New Directions for Institutional Research* 49 (March 1986): 75–91. Describes a computer-based approach to university resource allocation. Integrates technique with group process methods to assist top-level administrators make difficult choices. Examples from a case study included.

Morgan, A. W. "Cost as a Policy Issue: Lessons from the Health Care Sector." *Journal of Higher Education* 54 (1983): 279–93.

Mortimer, Kenneth P., and Barbara E. Taylor. "Budgeting Strategies Under Conditions of Decline." *New Directions for Institutional Research* 43 (September 1984): 67–86. Describes resource reduction and reallocation strategies. Analysis of the content and impact of budget cuts and the effectiveness of different strategies.

Peterson, Marvin W., with J. Michael Erwin and Richard Wilson. "State-Level Performance Budgeting." *New Directions for Institutional Research* 16 (winter 1977): 1–34. Case study of state performance budgeting in Hawaii and Washington. Includes current practices, performance measures, and issues. Findings: the two states presented striking contrasts in the development of a performance-oriented approach to budgeting. Hawaii was highly centralized; Washington was loosely coordinated.

Putney, Frederick B., and Stephen Wotman. "Organizational Constraints and Goal Setting." *New Directions for Institutional Research* 17 (spring 1978): 13–32. Discusses cost analysis techniques used to set operational and capital goals at Columbia University's School of Dental and Oral Surgery. Findings: decentralized decision making and planned change were stressed. Presents academic unit program cost and revenue grids.

Shulman, Lee S. "Teaching as Community Property: Putting an End to Pedagogical Solitude." *Change* 25, no. 6 (November/December 1993): 6–7.

Thompson, John D., Robert B. Fetter, and Charles D. Moss. "Case Mix and Resource Use." *Inquiry* 12 (December 1975): 300–312. Describes pilot study to develop a crude set of diagnosis-related groups for explaining variations in hospital length of stay. Study was based on data collected from eighteen Connecticut hospitals. Case mix differences among the hospitals are examined, and a crude form of reimbursement model is proposed.

U.S. Senate, Subcommittee on Economy in Government. *The Analysis and Evaluation of Public Expenditures: The PPB system.* 91st Congress, Ist session, 1969. Serial 12834, 2.

CHAPTER 9

Britain's "Performance-Based" System

Elaine El-Khawas and William F. Massy

Through a series of actions, the British government has clearly demonstrated the beginning of a new day for universities in the United Kingdom. In a major restructuring, polytechnic institutions have been accorded university status. New funding patterns have been implemented, based on new funding councils and a panoply of new categories and qualifying criteria. New procedures for quality assessment and quality assurance also have been established, most of which have direct links to funding. These are substantial changes in a short period. Indeed, the government has acknowledged the degree of change by offering transition adjustments (or "safety nets") for institutions facing an extraordinary cumulative impact of recent policy changes.

Underlying these changes is a new view of the role of higher education in the United Kingdom and, especially, a new view of the role of government funding of universities. The 1991 White paper, *Higher Education: A New Framework*,[1] is a pivotal document, outlining the government's new philosophy and approach to higher education. Fundamental is its commitment to widened access, a recognition that the economic and social well-being of the United Kingdom requires that higher education accommodate more than one-third of each year's high school graduates, a substantial increase from the 15 percent or so who have been accommodated in the recent past. Also fundamental is the recognition that funding for higher education cannot increase commensurate with increased participation; costs per student must decrease as participation widens.

The government's emerging principles for public funding build on these harsh realities. The clear message is that universities should expect limited funding from government and that some portion of those funds

---

1. *Higher Education: A New Framework* was issued in a 41 page brochure along with another White paper, *Education and Training for the 21st Century*, by the British government in 1991.

will be awarded differentially among institutions based on the quality of their performance. During 1992 and 1993, numerous new directives were announced, followed by consultations with higher education representatives.[2] Much still remains to be worked out. The broad framework has been established, but continuing debate and revision have become the order of the day.

Understanding the new funding initiatives and following the course of their implementation should be instructive for American audiences. The British government has put some fundamental issues about funding and accountability squarely on the table. In one form or another, most other industrialized countries and universities are facing similar problems, although responses have usually been more incremental than the British approach. In Australia, for example, the government has begun a new program for funding higher education and has implemented a plan for supplemental funding linked to quality assessment; however, the quality-linked supplement involves a relatively small amount of funds, and quality is not linked to an institution's basic government grant. Australia also has introduced a program in which extraordinary quality will be rewarded with additional funds.[3] Hong Kong has developed a new funding model and assessment approach broadly modeled on the British experiment, in order to place higher education funding on a performance basis prior to the transition of 1997.[4] In the Netherlands, the government launched a new approach during the 1980s, based on conditional financing of research, that shares similar purposes with the British plan. More recently, the Dutch have implemented a new, output-drawn system for higher education funding.[5] Because the British have undertaken the more radical experiment, monitoring the experiment's effects should offer valuable lessons for other countries where such issues have not yet been fully addressed.

---

2. Cf., The Higher Education Funding Council of England, "The Funding of Research by the Higher Education Funding Council of England," Consultation Paper (July, 1992); The Scottish Higher Education Funding Council, "Assessment of Quality of Provision of Education in Higher Education Institutions," Consultation Paper (August, 1992); The Higher Education Funding Council of England, "Quality Assessment," Consultation Paper (October, 1992); Scottish Higher Education Funding Council, "Consultation on Aspects of Current Research Funding," Consultation Paper (October, 1993)

3. Cf., Committee for Quality Assurance in Higher Education, *Report on 1993 Quality Reviews* (Canberra: Australian Government Publishing Service, 1994).

4. See chapter 10.

5. Cornelius A. Hazeu and Peter A. Lourens, "Changing Patterns in the Funding of University Education and Research: The Case of the Netherlands," in Philip G. Altbach and D. Bruce Johnstone, eds., *The Funding of Higher Education: International Perspectives* (New York: Garland Publishing, 1993), 189–206.

This chapter reviews several core elements of the funding approach for higher education institutions in England as it has evolved between 1993 and 1995 (which differs in some respects from the systems being followed in Wales and Scotland). Our comments focus especially on the government's decisions about methods of resource allocation and its new methods for assessing quality. We offer observations more than judgments, and we seek constructive insights and policy analysis more than specific critiques of this still-evolving approach. We view the recent British policy decisions as choices made, as informed judgments that policymakers must make about how best to solve real problems.

The New Funding Approach for British Universities: A Brief Profile

In the past, British universities received annual funding for the general support of their operations through intermediary agencies, initially the University Grants Committee and, more recently, the Universities Funding Council (hereafter, UFC) for the university sector and the Polytechnics and Colleges Funding Council for the nonuniversity sector.

Since 1992, separate funding councils have been established for England, Scotland, and Wales. The "new" universities, that is, the former polytechnics, receive their funding through the same council and on the same terms as the older universities. This chapter focuses on the Higher Education Funding Council for England (hereafter, HEFCE), which officially took over the responsibilities of the UFC in April 1993. Its offices, its chief executive, much of its staff, and many of its administrative operations continue from the arrangements of the Universities Funding Council and the Polytechnics and Colleges Funding Council.[6] According to Graeme Davies, HEFCE's Chief Executive, "The mission

---

6. Preparation of this chapter was informed by discussions with Graeme Davies, Chief Executive of HEFCE, discussions with a number of vice-chancellors, and a visit to HEFCE headquarters in Bristol, England. Bibliographic sources include the consultation papers cited in footnote 2 plus the following materials: Committee of Vice-Chancellors and Principals (U.K.), "The Costing of Research and Projects in Universities: Report and Guidance for Universities" (July, 1988); The Higher Education Funding Council of England, "The Funding of Teaching by the HEFCE in 1993–4," Circular 1/92 (August, 1992); The Higher Education Funding Council of England, "Assessment of the Quality of Education," Circular 3/93 (February, 1993); Graeme Davies, "The HEFCE: Where Do We Go From Here?" presentation to the Committee of Vice-Chancellors and Principals (September 23, 1992); Graeme Davies, "Some Current Observations for the Sector," HEFCE Annual Conference (April 6, 1993); and Graeme Davies, "Restructuring in the UK," presented to the Stanford Forum for Higher Education Futures, Pacific Grove, CA (November 7–8, 1993).

of HEFCE is to promote the quality and quantity of learning and re-search in higher education institutions, cost-effectively and with regard to national needs."[7]

From an American perspective, one of the most significant features of HEFCE's new allocation model is the separation of funding for teaching and funding for research. Teaching is funded through a "core and margin" model, based on student enrollments, while research is funded through a formula based on research assessments. Although funding is calculated incrementally on a field-by-field basis within each institution, HEFCE distributes these funds to the institutions in the form of unrestricted block grants. Separate from both teaching and research funds are "nonformula" funds, designated for unusual circumstances or activities outside the spheres of teaching and research. HEFCE thus allocates funding in three categories: teaching, research, and nonformula funding.

The funding model for teaching has a built-in drive toward efficiency. Each year, HEFCE calculates the AUCF, or Average Unit of Council Funding, for each of forty-four cells (each cell represents a subject area, an undergraduate or graduate level, and a full-time or part-time mode). Each year, the AUCFs are adjusted upward, based on the government's inflation forecast, and then downward for productivity improvement. The productivity improvement factor, set by the government at between 1 percent and 3 percent, represents an expected increase in efficiency. Core funding is enrollment driven: the number of students multiplied by their respective AUCF factor yields institutional funding levels. The core funding is also adjusted for special circumstances, such as the higher cost of living for schools in London.

Marginal funding redistributes the funds saved from the productivity improvement factor to institutions who prove themselves most efficient. Each year, HEFCE also calculates the actual costs for each institution in each of the forty-four cells (by subject, level, mode) and compares these to the AUCFs (a national average). Those programs with the lowest ratios receive marginal funding for extra student spaces; high-cost programs do not receive any additional spaces. In this way, efficient programs are encouraged to expand while inefficient or expensive programs are penalized. This measure anticipates the increased participation rates in higher education and attempts to channel new students to more efficient programs.

Both core and margin funding apply only to teaching and together account for 62 percent, the largest portion, of HEFCE funds. The gov-

7. Graeme Davies, "Restructuring British Higher Education," *Executive Strategies* (NACUBO and the Stanford Forum for Higher Education Futures), 2 (1995): 3.

ernment also encourages long-term proposals for core funding projects in certain desired areas, such as two-year vocational degree programs and targeted enrollment in certain geographic areas. The core funding is intended to provide stability, and the teaching assessments only influence marginal or growth funding—and that, only if the assessment is negative.

Research funding from HEFCE, on the other hand, is directly linked to the results of a process of research assessments. This new approach determines the level of HEFCE funding to support the ongoing research activities of academic departments—what is often termed "departmental research." As such, this represents a major departure from conventional academic practice in the United States. These funds are no longer simply built into the enrollment-driven core funding; in fact, whether a department receives any funds for research activity and how much funding it receives now depend on the department's rating by external assessors and on the number of staff active in research. This model removes a sizable amount of funds from a predictable formula basis and gives it a new performance-determined basis, with external assessors acting as gatekeepers for these funds.

Almost one-quarter of HEFCE's funds go to research. In the United States, these funds would be earmarked for departmental research: they pay for research faculty salaries, basic laboratory costs, and the like. In England, research is funded through a dual-funding principle. In addition to the HEFCE's research funds, which pay for departmental research, the government also sponsors several research councils, much like the National Science Foundation or National Institutes of Health in the United States, that fund research on a project-by-project basis. The research councils allocate funding through peer review panels, which evaluate proposals for particular projects. Unlike HEFCE's unrestricted block grants, these funds are strictly for the development of those projects.

Outside of teaching and research, HEFCE also allocates approximately 13 percent of its funding to nonformula funding for such activities as special museum collections and research reactors. In 1993, a portion of this funding also offset transition costs as the new changes were implemented, to help cushion institutions from any harsh changes.

Observations on the New Allocation Model

As an approach to funding university operations, England's new funding plan incorporates many elements of what might be considered cutting edge thinking on good practice in resource allocation. The plan stresses efficiency: it examines unit costs closely and signals policy aims through fiscal levers. It makes substantial use of financial incentives and sanctions, all designed to influence the behavior of universities toward the government's policy goals. The plan also parallels much recent policy thinking in its dramatic moves toward differential funding based on performance and in its redirection of responsibility to the basic operating units of institutions.

This funding approach also is relevant to some long-term funding realities being faced in the United States and other countries. The same pressures, for example, have framed the current debate in the United States on national policies for health care. (For a more thorough discussion of health care, see chap. 8.) The general issue—how to allocate limited funds to serve wide needs—extends to a whole range of areas of social spending, from elementary schools to social welfare. The "new" view in such policy debates assumes an acceptance of budgetary limits and the necessity of linking funding decisions to measures of program efficiency and effectiveness. The underlying belief is that while funds from governmental sources will not increase, productivity must nevertheless increase because social demands have increased. The motto has become: Accomplish more with less.

The British system represents an effort to achieve institutional accountability for performance quality through the funding allocations, without detailed regulation or micromanagement. Institutions continue to receive a block grant—covering departmental research activity and other special allocations as well as their core activities—which they can divide among programs and activities according to their best judgment. The fruits of these expenditures will be evaluated in the next assessment cycle, and the results will influence funding in future periods. This is a classic case of ex post accountability: that is, accountability without the disempowerment associated with traditional before-the-fact approval processes. The system's efficacy will depend on whether the assessment mechanisms do in fact reward achievement and penalize failure with respect to mutually agreed upon criteria.

Two additional factors unique to the British scene influenced the funding plan's design. First, merging the councils for universities and polytechnics and converting the latter to university status threatened the viability of the extant universities funding system. Conventional funding models either are incremental in nature or driven by student-place allocations and policy decisions about student-staff ratios. The historical patterns, however, would have been severely challenged in the merged system, as the polytechnics pressed to develop their research programs. Separating the core educational funding from research and allocating the latter on the basis of arms-length peer assessments will, one hopes, avoid the political tendency to level student-staff ratios based on political and "equity" considerations, and at the same time give the polytechnics an opportunity to compete for scarce research funding on a reasonably level playing field.

The second factor derives from the relatively large scale of the English higher education system. (The Scottish, Irish, and Welsh systems are much smaller, which accounts for some of the differences in approach.) The Higher Education Funding Council for England must apportion funding among some 131 institutions, which span the spectrum from the ancient classic universities to the newest polytechnics and special-purpose schools. HEFCE officials stress the impossibility of digesting and making judgments about planning documents from such a large and diverse group of institutions. The chosen solution amounts to: (1) focusing upon assessable outcomes rather than plans, promises, and assertions; and (2) dividing the assessment work into separate educational and research components, each of which is evaluated on a field-by-field basis. The resulting division of labor produces summary ratings that drive the allocation model and influence the council's decisions about special allocations. Once again, time will tell whether these efforts to deal with scale, heterogeneity, and change in an era of limited resources will improve cost-effectiveness in higher education.

Using Assessment as an Allocation Tool

By late 1993, the HEFCE had several assessment activities well under-way. The first component, research assessment, already had considerable experience, and a file of data on the research quality of academic units existed at all universities in England. The second component, quality assessment of teaching and learning effectiveness, began in 1993, with assessments first completed for four subject areas—chemistry, history, law, and mechanical engineering.

Before commenting on each assessment component, we note that the British quality assessment procedures involve two significant decisions:

first, the decision to link funding levels directly and immediately to the judgments made about quality; and
second, the decision to separate research from teaching in making quality judgments and funding allocations.

Both are major policy decisions. Each represents a sharp departure from previous practice, not only in Britain but in other industrialized countries as well.

The direct link between quality judgments and funding levels has already gained wide attention and strong criticism, amidst predictions that such institutions will modify their responses to fit the announced rules. On the other hand, it responds to the criticism—widespread in the United States as well as the United Kingdom—that the traditional system lacks accountability.

Clearly, the apparent sharpness of the decision served a major symbolic role. Whether for good or ill, these decisions gave a strong signal about the government's serious commitment to quality assurance and its determination to change allocation methods to reflect accomplishment. These decisions also signaled a change in how the government would operate vis-à-vis the universities: a stronger fiscal hand, less negotiation and compromise.

Beyond philosophical and strategic issues, the direct link between quality judgments and funding may actually have limited financial consequences for universities in any single year. In the assessment of teaching and learning, for example, institutional funds are in jeopardy only if an academic subject area is found to be performing unsatisfactorily; funding would be affected only for that specific area and would initially affect only the unit's funding allocation for growth. Core funding would be withdrawn only after a probationary interim period brings about no improvement. This is not a harsh result.

In the assessment of research, the effects are more immediate and potentially more severe; a unit with a low score loses a portion of its general funding. There is no probationary period in which to rectify problems, and so far, no process for appeal. (There is a safety net to limit the reduction in any one assessment cycle.) The HEFCE could amend these procedures, of course, and court challenges may lead to some modification. Nevertheless, apart from the dislocation of an abrupt cutback, results have generally not been severe. Units with a rating of 1 received no research-based funding for 1993–94, but most of these were former polytechnics and, in the past, did not have funds for research activity. Most units with higher research ratings were funded at levels similar to or better than what they had before for research. Even if a unit received a cut in research funds, this did not affect core funding based on enrollment numbers.

The second major decision—to separate the funding of research from the funding of teaching—is a significant departure from conventional policy approaches to academic institutions. Particularly from an American perspective, this approach is unorthodox, as it overturns the presumption in the United States that a professor's general teaching and research responsibilities are inseparable components in the funding allocations made to schools or departments. Yet, apart from some initial awkwardness in implementing this distinction, it seems that the separation does in fact offer a potentially cleaner way to fund teaching and what is often called "departmental" research. In contrast, American practice generally depends on distinctions in teaching load to accord some faculty more time than others for research activities. As a result, however, faculty research time has very weak forms of accountability attached to it. Moreover, departmental research tends to be viewed as a faculty right, and few mechanisms are available for determining whether departments utilize the funds effectively or for changing funding levels on the basis of performance.

Assessing Research

The research assessment exercise in England has been developed in greater detail and has acquired more actual experience than the procedures for assessing teaching quality. In addition, the procedures have been changing with experience: HEFCE solicits detailed criticism from both assessors and institutions after each exercise. Previous changes have included simplified forms and audits; a future consideration is a finer rating scale than the current 1–5 scoring system. Thus, although we shall discuss several aspects of the research assessment exercise, the approach is certainly still subject to modification.

Aside from the radical departure of separately assessing teaching and research, the details of the research assessment are rather traditional and conservative. The general procedure follows conventional academic practice: in each of the seventy-two assessment units, a panel of five to eight experts reviews written materials and convenes to arrive at a rating. Although the panels are informed by a range of objective information, such as data on publications, numbers of staff, and external research funding, the concept of the "active researcher" lies at the core of the research assessment methodology. Each unit decides which members of its academic staff to name as active researchers. In the 1992 exercise, each active researcher then cited two best publications and two best "other public outputs" between January 1, 1989, and June 30, 1992. (This period was extended by one year for the humanities to reflect the longer gestation time for research in these disciplines.) Based on this collected data, or return, the panels assign a quality rating from 5 (high) to 1 (low).

The choice of which faculty member to nominate as active researcher turns out to be crucial for institutions because the research funding depends on the product of quality and quantity, not on either alone. More precisely, the level of research funding in a given field equals: the quality rating minus one, times the number of active researchers. (Note that a unit receiving a score of one receives no funding.) The more people nominated as active researchers, the lower is likely to be their average quality, since the best researchers will be nominated first. The system is calibrated such that a department with a core cadre of outstanding researchers will receive more money than one with a larger number of "average" researchers, which is consistent with HEFCE's desire to concentrate the resources in the best departments.

The criteria for judging researchers and rating research programs are straightforward and unidimensional, stressing a generalized standard of achieving national and international renown (see fig. 1 for HEFCE's research quality scale). Absent from the criteria, however, are factors that weigh the relevance of research to areas of national interest or factors promoting innovation. No guidance on interpretation was given to the assessment panels: it was assumed that the academic panelists responsible for the detailed work would know the objectives and associated standard for work in their field. The panels did not take resource differences into account, despite evidence for positive correlations between inputs and outputs.[8] Hence the research assessments must be viewed as providing absolute measures of research capacity—to be used in directing future investments—rather than measures of past cost-effectiveness. As might be expected, the quality assessment results are skewed toward institutions with mature research programs: based on the 1992 assessment, the top twenty institutions received some 75 percent of the funding.

In the 1992 assessment, the panels reviewed a total of 2,700 submissions from 172 institutions covering the research of more than 43,000 active researchers. About two returns per institution, or 10 percent of the total number, were audited through random selection and panel nomination. The total cost to HEFCE for the 1992 assessment was 1 million pounds, but since its findings are used to distribute 650 million pounds per year for the next four years, the cost only comes to 0.5 percent of the funds being distributed.

In some respects, the design for the research assessment parallels the design followed in the United States to produce reputational ratings of doctorate programs.[9] Both methods focus on academic units and

8. Geraint Johnes, "Determinants of Research Output in Economics Departments in British Universities," *Research Policy* 17 (1988): 171–78.

9. Lyle V. Jones, Gardner Lindzey, and Porter E. Coggeshall, eds., *An Assessment of Research-Doctorate Programs in the United States* (Washington, DC: National Academy of Sciences, 1982), four volumes.

Quality is judged on a scale from 5 (high) to 1 (low):

Rating 5:
Research quality that equates to attainable levels of international excellence in sub-areas of activity and to attainable levels of national excellence in virtually all others.

Rating 4:
Research quality that equates to attainable levels of national excellence in virtually all sub-areas of activity, showing some evidence of international excellence.

Rating 3:
Research quality that equates to attainable levels of national excellence in a majority of the sub-areas of activity, or to international in some.

Rating 2:
Research quality that equates to attainable levels of national excellence in up to half of the sub-areas of activity.

Rating 1:
Research quality that equates to attainable levels of national excellence in none or almost none of the sub-areas of activity.

Fig. 1. Research quality scale. (From Graeme Davies, "Restructuring British Higher Education," *Executive Strategies* **[NACUBO and the Stanford Forum for Higher Education Futures], 2 [1995], 12. Reprinted by permission of the Stanford Forum.)**

require that summary judgments be made on work that is, in fact, the separate work of individual scholars. Both approaches rely primarily on the expert judgment of other scholars in the same subject area, and the criteria for judging quality are broadly similar as well. For British universities, judgments are highly generalized, focused on whether the unit is performing research at an international level or at a national level in most areas or in some areas. In the United States, scholars assess each academic department according to a similar overall judgment: whether an entire department's scholarly quality is distinguished, strong, good, adequate, or marginal. Both the British research assessment and the American department ratings rely mainly on a single factor, scaled (coincidentally) from 1 to 5, which allows for easy comparison across units within a single university as well as for comparisons across universities for units in the same academic area. This encourages competition among units for high scores on research performance. In this context, it may be instructive for British audiences to observe that, despite the criticisms of a single measure that have been voiced for decades in the United States, an index of a single reputational score has been maintained in each update of the ratings. In the 1982 report, however, the ratings were embedded among a variety of other, more descriptive information.

The expert evaluations in the British system are developed by panels, in face-to-face meetings, rather than by survey. The panels met several times to develop criteria and judge specific areas of departmental accomplishment as well as to rate the department as a whole. The British process is much more labor intensive than the American one. For example, the panels are supplied with detailed documentation on each department and each research-active member of academic staff. (Some have discussed reducing the paperwork burden: some assessors considered it a heavy burden, and departmental units also judged it burdensome—like "filling out a tax return.") In a sense, then, the British research assessment panels can be viewed as receiving the kinds of multiple indicators touted in the 1982 U.S. report and then translating them into the single scores required to distribute funding. The scores are also published in "league tables," however, which may result in the myopia about which the U.S. committee was concerned.

Potential issues of credibility and acceptance—voiced as concerns about elitism or bias on the part of assessors—have been handled differently in the U.S. and British systems. The British have relied on the scholarly reputation of their assessors and on claims to the objectivity of the process, which includes documentation provided by each unit. The small number of assessors used in any subject area and the judgmental connection between documentation and final rating, however, make the process vulnerable to attack. This process has already been challenged legally in the instance of dental research, with questions raised about how the assessor panel reached a final decision when their initial votes on a unit were not unanimous; although HEFCE won the lawsuit, the judge expressed some concern about the dangers of making judgments without giving reasons. The U.S. approach, by relying on the "objective" results of a survey process, avoids the necessity of explaining why each judgment was made. (Of course, the problem of subjectivity is just pushed down to the level of the survey respondent.) In addition, as a practical matter, the U.S. ratings are expressed in fractional scores (e.g., 4.7 or 3.2), thereby resulting in many moderate changes. This may blunt some of the credibility problems inherent in a rating scheme.

Assessing Teaching and Program Quality

Comments about the specific decisions that are part of the assessment of teaching and learning quality are necessarily quite tentative. The assessment process, first implemented in 1993, was substantially revised during the first part of 1995 based on experience in the eight subject categories examined during the first two years.[10] We shall begin by evaluating the initial process and then describe the recent changes.

The basic approach (for both implementations) follows the general design of the research assessment: academic units are the focus, and assessors review materials and make summary judgments based on simple nominal scales. The assessment procedure has three steps. First, the department develops a statement of aims and objectives. Second, it performs a self-assessment, using its stated aims and objectives as a standard. The third step brings a site visit by an external assessment team: the team makes an independent evaluation, again based on the department's stated aims and objectives. The major difference between the original and revised process involves step three. Originally, concerns about the cost of assessment led HEFCE to limit site visits to departments where the self-assessment provided a prima-facie case for either excellent or unsatisfactory performance. Some 80 percent of institutions were judged "satisfactory" on the basis of desk reviews of their self-assessments. Since April of 1995, however, all departments in all institutions will be visited at least once every six years.

Institutional self-assessment's key role in teaching evaluation continues. According to Graeme Davies:

> HEFCE believes that the prime responsibility for maintaining and enhancing the quality of education rests with the institution. It [HEFCE] wishes to give full weight to an institution's own views of its strengths and weaknesses in the particular subject. Thus the second step, self-assessment, is key.[11]

The circular that HEFCE issued to describe the original plan devoted more than half its pages to advice for preparing a self-assessment. In an attempt to limit the paperwork burden, the self-assessment document was limited to no more than ten pages (with two additional pages for

---

10. "The Quality Assessment Method from April 1995," HEFCE circular 29/94 (December 1994), 25 pages.

11. Davies, "Restructuring British Higher Education," 10.

documenting claims to excellence). In the original system, institutions had to provide extensive additional documentation if they self-nominated themselves for an "excellent" rating or were suspected of providing unsatisfactory teaching.

Among the early concerns about the teaching assessments were that the qualifications for determining excellence had not been nationally standardized. In some cases, administrators complained that the standard of excellence was measured too rigidly against the goals described in the self-assessment, so that if an institution set forth more modest objectives, it was more likely to earn an excellent rating. Further, some have argued that the rating scheme should be two-dimensional, incorporating the relevant aims of the institution, rather than one dimensional. At present no distinction is made between a school that demonstrates excellent teaching of advanced students with a school that rates the same for at-risk students, yet it would be highly inappropriate for an advanced student to choose the latter school simply because it has an excellent teaching rating. The original system offered no way to counteract such misinformation. Finally, HEFCE assessors announced their judgment at the end of their visit, allowing them no time to compare departments on a national level before making a final decision. These combined factors led some to suggest a simple satisfactory-unsatisfactory system rather than the original three-tiered system with schools vying for the excellent rating. That recommendation was incorporated in HEFCE's recent changes in teaching assessment.

On a more general level, the perennial drawbacks that would result from using standardized categories as a focus of evaluation are especially pertinent for assessing academic programs. With research, which is based in disciplinary communities and requires in-depth attention to specialized topics, changes that would render categories unworkable do not often occur. With academic study programs, however, change and revision are frequent. They are mainly incremental, only occasionally substantial, but their cumulative effects can be significant. Academic programs are typically changed for good reason, sometimes to respond to external parties (professional communities, employers), sometimes to keep up with changes in technology and knowledge in the subject area, and sometimes to reflect faculty awareness of shortcomings in their current programs. In the United States, for example, many subject specializations have been revamped during the last decade to add an "applied" approach, to incorporate computer applications, to stress general competencies, or to reflect changing scientific understanding of phenomena.

An unintended effect to be watched for, then, is the danger of "deified" categories" that take on a life of their own. If judgments are made within set categories, administrators have a strong incentive to keep their programs in line with the established categories. Innovative academic programs are at a disadvantage because program guidelines, choice of assessors, judging criteria, and other assessment procedures are shaped (usually unconsciously) according to general images of each subject category. These problems are inherent in any classification scheme—especially when the scheme is unidimensional. Minor exceptions can be given special attention, and indeed, the HEFCE has indicated that an amendment for unusual programs might be made; however, this may not be sufficient to allow for academic program change, which should be valued and encouraged. Category-based assessment requires a serious trade-off: set categories, even with a special category, will influence and constrain program change, while innovative programs will be forced into categories that do not fit their circumstances.

This is a more serious issue for teaching assessment than for the research assessment. Supporting and encouraging program change should be a policy goal of government; such changes represent quality improvement. If anything, the pace of program change may need to increase in the United Kingdom to accommodate trends toward wider postsecondary participation and closer cooperation with business and industry. A more flexible program design might be considered, in which it would be made explicit that, after a certain period (e.g., as a new cycle begins; after five years) new categories would be developed. Responsibility for such decisions could rest with professional and disciplinary groups, possibly with special committees.

Responding to feedback from constituents, HEFCE has moved to simplify the output rating scheme while adding structure and texture to the assessment process itself. The current scheme simply classifies a department as "satisfactory" or "unsatisfactory," depending on the outcome of the assessment visit (recall that all units receive site visits under the new scheme). The assessment teams now rate each department, on a scale of 1 to 4, for the following six dimensions of teaching quality:

1. curriculum design, content, and organization;
2. teaching, learning, and internal assessment methods;
3. student progression and achievement (including attainment rates);
4. student support and guidance;
5. learning resources, including libraries and computational facilities; and
6. quality assurance and enhancement processes.

The assessors then make a summative judgment about whether overall quality is satisfactory. While the judgment is necessarily subjective, it is understood that receiving a "1" on any dimension represents grounds for an "unsatisfactory." Time will tell if this multicriteria approach can surmount the problem of deified categories—whether it will encourage the continuous improvement of teaching quality.

Graeme Davies describes how HEFCE will use these assessments:

> There needs to be particular caution about the impact of the link between funding and assessment. Where education is confirmed to be unsatisfactory, the institution will be ineligible in the first year after the assessment for any funding allocated by HEFCE for growth. It will also be informed that if quality does not improve, core funding and student places will be successively or immediately withdrawn.[12]

The institution will be encouraged to improve, but if improvement is not forthcoming HEFCE will respond by investing its scarce resources in places that offer better value for money. While the final rating is binary, with only a few departments expected to be judged unsatisfactory, incentives and accountability are enhanced by publishing the full assessment reports, including the scores on the six quality dimensions. The press and public will doubtless take great interest in these reports.

Viewed from an American perspective, the HEFCE teaching assessment may be evolving to resemble state-mandated program reviews in the United States. These state procedures require a detailed review of all academic departments on a multiyear, rotating cycle, based on a self-assessment report and a report by outside visiting teams. Typically, these assessments have consequences only at the extremes, when a department is shown to be very strong or unusually weak. Most academic departments in the United States consider program review to be a time-consuming chore without much meaning. Yet, for the state agencies, the procedures protect them by publicly demonstrating that quality assurance exists. This discrepancy—limited intrinsic utility but a payoff for external accountability—may evolve in the new British system as well. However, HEFCE believes its procedures really do add value in terms of accountability and by providing incentives and feedback to the institutions.

Questions about the purpose and cost-effectiveness of the quality assessments can also be raised. As with other public agencies, the gov-

---

12. Davies, "Restructuring British Higher Education," 11.

ernment agency responsible for higher education should choose a method of quality assurance that is appropriate for its target population. Because university offerings in the United Kingdom have low probabilities of serious flaws, a method of external scrutiny less labor intensive than the one now being used might warrant further consideration. Approaches relying on information reporting, possibly with occasional inspections, are sufficient for many such situations.

This also raises the issue of duplication of effort between the quality assessment carried out by the HEFCE and the quality assurance that is separately being carried out by the Higher Education Quality Council (HEQC), an autonomous body created at the same time and operated under the jurisdiction of the Committee of Vice-Chancellors and Principals. Although a distinction can be made between the actual focus of activity of the two councils (one on the assessment of specific academic areas, the other on quality assurance processes common to the entire university), critics assert that distinctions between them are too insignificant to justify the long-term continuation of both. Supporters argue that both kinds of evaluation are needed and that different methods are appropriate for assessing observed outcome quality and for auditing the processes that determine quality over the long run. In fact, whether the focus is on program-specific processes and results, as with the HEFCE approach, or on institutional procedures, as intended with the HEQC approach, the general result is that most programs will pass muster and only weak programs will be identified.

The compatibility between HEFCE's quality assessment and the HEQC's quality assurance remains to be determined. Because a sense of redundancy and undue burden is already part of public commentary, some have suggested a combined approach. This could offer a single system of academic program review, utilizing regular information reporting (both on quality assurance programs and on academic program outcomes) as well as a cycle of visits to academic units. Both university-wide and department-specific scrutiny could be combined. The emphasis could be on program improvement (i.e., identifying strengths and weaknesses; offering recommendations for improvement) with a provision for special treatment of programs identified as weak. The question of merger is a hot topic in England at this writing, and the issue is still in doubt.

Summary Observations

The changes in the British system amount to more than just a new system of resource allocation and assessment: they signify a sea change in the relationship between government and the university system. Whereas the government had previously held itself responsible for education as a public good, overseeing both planning and improvement as well as providing support, the government has now moved into the position of a procurer of educational services. Without hands-on governmental control, many worry that considerations about equity and improvement—desirable for the public good but not necessarily desirable from the institution's point of view—may fall by the wayside. Indeed, critics have claimed that the new system emphasizes funding over program and accountability over improvement.

Yet the path the British government has taken represents a sort of middle ground in a dilemma faced by many countries with increasing student populations and ever-limited funding. The more collegial, negotiating style of interaction between government and higher education formerly used in the United Kingdom remains the dominant cultural style in most countries, but this approach makes it difficult for government to hold institutions accountable for performance and leads to confusion and conflict when per-student costs rise faster than available increases in public funding. In the opposite extreme, some states have dramatically cut public funding of higher education while actively encouraging institutions to look for funding from the private sector. This privatization allows market forces to shape the university. The market provides accountability, as programs with no market value are severely curtailed. The British government, in contrast, has taken neither a laissez-faire nor a hands-on approach to funding.

In effect, the new policies have created a simulated market for higher education in which funding is linked to quality assessments. By granting polytechnics the same status as the universities, the government had made the old system of negotiating for funds untenable—there were simply too many schools. Markets, on the other hand, are inherently backward looking, focusing on performance-to-date; they do not respond strongly to plans and promises but operate rather as an arms-length system of control.

Further, the decision to fund teaching and research separately has created two separate simulated markets and encouraged institutions to differentiate themselves based on their strengths. Only the larger universities have strongly emphasized research while smaller institutions have focused on improving their teaching without the worries of losing funding. Due to the rigor of the research assessments and the strong links between those assessments and funding, research funding has been concentrated in twelve traditional English universities. This contrasts with the situation of higher education in the United States, where many institutions feel pressured to develop high-powered research programs, even though those programs may not be appropriate for their students.

In these simulated markets of British higher education, assessments of both teaching and research are crucial, for they provide the primary information by which the buyer—the government—makes its decisions. If the assessment systems work well, the simulated markets could perform better than a real market of higher education. In the United States, for example, many buyers of higher education, such as parents and students, make their choices on the basis of reputation, yet reputation depends on research rather than instructional quality and in any case often lags far behind actual changes in institutions. In principle, a panel of experts on teaching and research could provide more accurate measurements of quality, thus leading to better funding allocations.

Not surprisingly, some of the harshest criticism has been leveled at these assessment systems. The credibility of the new procedures is not assured. The research assessment may be especially vulnerable, based on its direct link between harsh changes in funding and the inherently "soft" mechanism of expert judgment by a few persons. Research ratings affect funding immediately, without any incremental decreases of funds or probationary period for improvement. The research assessment procedures, along with the swiftness with which these changes were announced, provoked many to proclaim that the government was overly concerned with fiscal accountability and not improvement.

Because of the nature of the simulated market system, however, those two goals need not necessarily be at odds. The government could choose to make concerns about improvement and equity—in other words, concerns relevant to the public good—more explicit in its evaluation criteria. At present, however, the assessment system offers relatively few mechanisms to spur improvement. Subject areas receive a rating on teaching quality and units receive a research rating, but otherwise they receive little feedback on what their strengths and weaknesses are. The units gain little insight from the assessments as to what specific behaviors will lead to good ratings in the next round of assessments. The research assessment, in particular, looks backward to a unit's recent performance with little attention to works in progress or to plans for worthwhile projects.

Although the British government may choose to incorporate more criteria specifically aimed at an improvement agenda, in a larger sense, it should be recognized that the new system has devolved the government responsibility for improvement to the institutional level. Because institutions still receive their funding in a block grant, they can choose independently to fund more innovative or far-reaching programs. The government as buyer may send signals as to what it might like to see, but the responsibility for an improvement agenda now rests with individual institutions and units. In time, one hopes that most institutions will learn how to take advantage of their newly empowered position. The new funding model relies on the idea that individual units in institutions, closer to research and teaching, may know best which projects to fund.

One further consequence of the simulated market approach is the absence of effective government policy guidance on how to maintain quality as participation rates rise. New inspection systems may not be a sufficient strategy for addressing the different challenges that arise when universities are called on to accommodate larger numbers of students from a wider band of socioeconomic backgrounds. Experience in the United States and other countries offers strong evidence that rising participation rates call for different institutional and instructional strategies if standards are to be maintained. Unless new strategies are developed, higher participation rates mean larger classes, less individual attention, less time for discussion and analytic feedback, and more emphasis on rote learning. University students may still pass exams, but employers will undoubtedly observe a difference in what graduates can do. Higher participation rates also mean greater diversity in student readiness for university study, if not in academic preparation then in motivation, self-discipline and study habits, and in the degree to which they must contend with distractions from their studies—the need to work, obligations to help family members, and so on. As British universities move toward higher participation rates, a focused campaign is needed to strengthen good teaching, introduce new teaching and learning strategies, and build up advising and other academic support services (including the library and computer support). Government could play a stronger role in promoting such innovations without abandoning or undermining its new funding methodology.

Part 5
Models

CHAPTER 10

Quantitative Funding Models

Harry Atkinson and William F. Massy

Many universities and higher education systems use quantitative funding models at some point in the resource allocation process. This chapter examines the alternative ways such models may be used, explains the design principles involved in developing them, and describes the process by which a funding model was actually developed and implemented by the Hong Kong University and Polytechnic Grants Committee, now the University Grants Committee.

We define a funding model as a set of computational procedures that give expression to a funding methodology and convert information about the expected outputs of a higher education institution or system into estimates of the resource levels necessary to produce them at historical quality levels. For example, if an institution is expected to service x-thousand enrollments, its annual funding might be estimated at y-thousand dollars. The resource "requirements" calculated by the funding model may represent the final stage of the resource allocation process—as in so-called formula funding systems—or, more appropriately, a starting point for the exercise of judgment. Likewise, the model's parameters may be based strictly on objective data or the objective inputs may be modified by subjective judgment.

The state of Ohio provides an example of a formula funding system: public funds flow to institutions according to a model based on the year's actual enrollments by student level and field. By way of contrast, New York's funding model uses objective data about enrollments and campus characteristics to establish funding baselines, which provide the starting point for judgments by the State University of New York Chancellor and his staff. In England, subjectively determined factors for research quality are provided as inputs, with the model's outputs used directly as the basis for funding.[1] In Hong Kong, the model incorporates subjective

---

1. See chapter 9 and also Graeme Davies, "Restructuring British Higher Education," *Executive Strategies* (NACUBO and the Stanford Forum for Higher Education Futures), 2 (1995).

research quality factors and judgment also is applied at other key points in the model. So far, neither system directly incorporates teaching quality judgments, though the results of teaching assessments are used in England to help determine student enrollment targets.

Applying judgment to a model's output is a good idea when the number of institutions being funded is small enough to make this practical. (The Higher Education Funding Council of England argues that their 131 institutions precludes such application.) Where systematic quality assessment procedures can be developed, these can be written into the model's structure and provided as judgmental inputs.

Funding models began to appear in the 1960s, with the development of RRPM (Resource Requirements Prediction Model) and CAMPUS (Comprehensive Analytical Methods for Planning in University Systems).[2] Thanks to the work of NCHEMS (National Center for Higher Education Management Systems), these models became quite popular with state higher education systems—which used their results as benchmarks to compare public institutions within and among the states. Some models were very detailed: requiring, for example, disaggregated enrollments to the level of the individual course. They required voluminous data, which made them expensive to develop and maintain, and virtually precluded use of judgmental elements within the model's structure. This also made the interpretation of results quite difficult, a problem that was compounded by the research universities' persistent complaints that the models did not adequately reflect resource requirements associated with research. The combination of expense, interpretative complexity, and problems related to research eventually led to the substitution of today's simpler model genre.

Funding models estimate an institution's overall cost of instruction and unsponsored research (that is, research paid for by general funds), including administration and support services, based on actual, predicted, or target enrollments. They do not tell policymakers how the overall cost should be divided among government, tuition payers, and other sources. The answer to this question must be determined outside the model. For example, government may choose to pay a certain proportion of overall cost, or fixed sums from tuition, endowments, and other sources may be subtracted from overall cost with government paying the residual.

---

2. See Warren W. Gulko, "The Resource Requirements Prediction Model (RRPM-1): An Overview," technical report no. 17, National Center for Higher Education Management Systems, Western Interstate Commission on Higher Education (Boulder, CO: the center, 1971). See also David S. P. Hopkins and William F. Massy, *Planning Models for Colleges and Universities* (Stanford, CA: Stanford University Press, 1981).

An important caveat should be kept in mind throughout our discussion. Though the model calculates discreet sums for departments, and possibly for education and research within each department, funding should flow to an institution as a block grant with no restrictions on how it is allocated internally. The detailed calculations comprise the model's internal workings as it builds an overall funding figure for the institution. The detail will always have more statistical error than the total, which averages the microlevel discrepancies. The funding body need not see the intermediate results, and it certainly should not rely on them for policy purposes.

Design and Usage Principles

Higher education's decades of experience with funding models permits substantial generalization about design and usage principles. We have identified five major issues: (1) the choice of analysis units for modeling; (2) whether research represents a separate output; (3) how unit cost is determined; (4) whether to base the model on actual, predicted, or target enrollments (enrollment policy); and (5) use of judgmentally determined performance assessment factors. The decisions taken with respect to these issues largely determine the model's structure and how it will be used.

Analysis Units

Models must be constructed from elemental building blocks, which we call "analysis units." Two types of analysis units can be identified: *cost centers* and *program categories.*

Generically, *cost center* means an accounting unit in which costs are accumulated. Examples include academic and administrative departments, though any identifiable unit can be set up as a cost center. For present purposes, we take cost center to mean a specific list of cost groupings for which data are accumulated and tracked separately within the model. *Program categories* refer to activity groupings defined in terms of outputs: for example, enrollments classified by student major. In contrast to cost centers, program categories need not represent well-defined account groupings. That is the difference between the two concepts: cost centers are defined in accounting terms and program categories are defined in terms of natural output groupings.

The choice of definition for cost center and program category definitions represents a key design decision for any funding model. Too great a level of aggregation produces a crude model lacking in face validity. Too much disaggregation balloons data requirements and makes the model difficult to understand and control. Academic departments or groupings of similar departments often represent good cost center definitions, though for large institutions the school or college (e.g., the College of Letters and Sciences) may be more practical.

Program category definitions exhibit more variation. The aforementioned CAMPUS and RRPM models disaggregated enrollments to the level of the individual course, which made them massive and unwieldy. Other models aggregate enrollments to the level of the whole institution, making no distinction between, say, science and humanities majors. But whatever the level of aggregation, program categories must be defined in terms of output units. Most instructional categories use enrollments as the output unit, for example, though the number of majors or the number of degrees remain possibilities.

The design trade-off, then, is to seek academic program categories and cost centers that are detailed enough to capture the institution's diversity but not so detailed as to make the model unwieldy. We advocate a middle approach which classifies enrollments by subject category. For example, Massy's and Zemsky's work on academic production functions disaggregates undergraduate arts and sciences enrollments according to five disciplinary domains (humanities, languages, mathematics, science, and social sciences).[3] The Hong Kong model, described later in this chapter, classifies students according to sixteen academic program groupings, four degree levels, and four modes of study.

Research

U.S. funding models typically bundle unsponsored research with teaching into the same program category. However, the recent work in Britain and Hong Kong recognizes that research and teaching represent different output categories—thus separating the two for modeling purposes. By placing instruction and research in separate program categories, these models open the possibility of different performance evaluations. At the very least, this strategy focuses policymakers on educational and research outputs as distinct quantities.

American universities distinguish departmental research, performed by faculty as part of their everyday duties, from organized research,

---

3. William F. Massy and Robert Zemsky, "Faculty Discretionary Time: Departments and the Academic Ratchet," *Journal of Higher Education* 65, no. 1 (January–February 1994): 1–22.

which always is separately budgeted. Organized research usually is externally sponsored, but institutional funding can be substantial—as in cost sharing on sponsored agreements and research development programs, for instance. Departmental research represents faculty time, paid out of the educational and general budget, above and beyond that needed for instruction, advising, course development, and other activities directly associated with teaching. Resources applied to departmental research are recorded under "instruction" on the university's books of account (if separately accounted for, such expenditures would be classified as organized research). But despite the lack of data about departmental research expenditures, it is clear that they vary inversely with the faculty teaching loads.

Conventional wisdom holds that departmental research represents a necessary precondition for quality instruction: in other words, that instruction and departmental research are joint products. To the extent this is true, it is sometimes argued that there is no reason to separate departmental research from instruction for modeling or any other purpose. However, recent thinking challenges the conventional wisdom. Indeed, the perceived positive linkage between research and teaching quality may be counter-factual in many institutions.[4] It has become apparent that, in many institutions, the effort devoted to departmental research exceeds that required to sustain quality teaching. The theory of the academic ratchet holds that faculty time utilization for departmental research grows steadily, driven by the quest for institutional prestige and individual career advancement, and the resultant pressures for faculty publication. Resources permitting, the ratchet produces ever lower teaching loads, which the faculty labor market propagates across institutional boundaries.[5] The ratchet increases departmental research, which escalates the cost of instruction but also allows faculty to publish more and to seek and manage more externally funded projects.

To the extent departmental research resources produce outputs (publications and prestige) that can be considered separately from educational outputs, there is a case for separating the two for modeling, and funding, purposes—even though instruction and departmental research cannot be distinguished in the university's accounting system. Britain

---

4. Robert Zemsky and William F. Massy, "Expanding Perimeters, Melting Cores, and Sticky Functions: Toward an Understanding of Current Predicaments," paper for the Cost of Undergraduate Education Project CUE 1995-1 (May 1995).

5. Massy and Zemsky, "Faculty Discretionary Time." See also William F. Massy and Andrea K. Wilger, "Productivity in Postsecondary Education: A New Approach," Educational *Evaluation and Policy Analysis* 14, no. 4 (1992): 361–76.

and Hong Kong believe that such a separation, and the separate evalua-tion of research and of teaching performance, is a good way to arrest the academic ratchet.

Unit Cost

Determination of the unit cost of output for each program category represents the computational core of any funding model. For example, enrollment-driven models require the unit cost of enrollment for each program category. Where departmental research is defined as a separate output, unit cost might be defined as the funding allowed per research-active faculty member. The total funding applicable to a program cate-gory will be determined by multiplying unit cost by the number of output units (enrollments or research-active faculty FTEs), perhaps with the addition of a fixed cost component.

The determination of unit cost begins with the analysis of cost cen-ters, not program categories. What costs to include represents the first design question. The analysis usually begins with the cost center's gen-eral funds budget—that is, funds provided by the institution's general resources. Separately budgeted research costs should be excluded, even if they were originally allocated from general funds (as under cost-sharing agreements, for example). Costs paid by restricted funds should be added if one determines that the activities represent a regular ele-ment of teaching and departmental research. Likewise, generally funded costs may be excluded if they do not contribute to these mainline activi-ties. One should ask about the activities that each cost element supports, looking to the activities' funds source only to provide clues about the purpose of the expenditure.

Whether the model should separately identify fixed cost presents a second major design question. Some costs, like the salary of the depart-ment chair and the department secretary, do not vary with the size of the cost center or its level of activity. Whether such fixed costs should be distinguished from variable costs like professors' salaries, secretarial support, and travel becomes a matter of modeling strategy, not of princi-ple. For example, fixed costs are insignificant in large cost centers, so they can safely be lumped together with variable costs. If an institution contains many small departments, however, fixed costs probably should be identified and tracked separately, even though that complicates the model.

Fixed cost can be identified statistically as the constant term in a regression analysis, or by analyzing departmental expenditures line by line and asking, for each line, whether the cost is invariant to output changes. The compensation of department chair and department secretary may well fall into the fixed category, for instance, whereas teachers' salaries would be variable with enrollments over the long run.

Stanford University has recently analyzed the incremental cost associated with additions to the faculty. The cost categories are as follows:

Pre hire/recruitment: the upfront costs of search, candidate interviews, and relocation.

Faculty salary and fringe benefits: committed compensation from institutional sources, plus housing allowance and similar items.

Start-up cost: initial equipment purchases, laboratory renovation, research program initiation, and initial summer salary.

Operating cost: recurring expense expected to continue during the faculty member's tenure at Stanford; includes secretarial and ongoing research support, library and information resources, supplies and travel, and (importantly) the square-foot cost of office and laboratory space.

The costs are based on assistant professor hires, with appropriate escalations for promotions and salary increases. The analysis, which produces total cost and present value figures for an assumed thirty-year faculty tenure in different academic fields, is being used to aid the provost in her determination of optimal faculty size.

The next step in funding model unit cost determination allocates the applicable cost center expenditures across the program categories the center supports. This can be done in many ways, some of which will be illustrated later in this chapter. However, the fundamental idea can be described in terms of a simple example. Suppose that half the English faculty's effort supports "writing across the curriculum," a part of the general education program, and half is devoted to teaching English majors. The general education half would be distributed across all the college's undergraduate program categories in proportion to their enrollments, while the English major half would be allocated to the humanities program category. The total cost for the program category, then, is the sum of the allocations from all the cost centers whose resources (e.g., faculty time) are used to produce the program's outputs. The calculations are done separately for fixed and variable costs if fixed costs are separately tracked; otherwise they are based on the total expenditure of the cost center. Dividing the total variable cost (or the total combined cost) by the number of output units for the category (e.g., enrollments) produces the desired unit cost.

Setting research out as a separate program category requires, as a first step in the analysis, that the cost center's expenditure be allocated between instruction and research. For example, if it is determined that publication-oriented research and scholarship represents 25 percent of the English faculty's activity, then 25 percent of the applicable cost will be allocated to research and the remaining 75 percent allocated to education. The research percentage cannot be ascertained from accounting records, but it can be set judgmentally—with the judgments being informed by discussions with faculty and, perhaps, by diary exercises that determine how professors allocate their time. Such diary exercises are not popular with faculty, but they have been performed successfully by a number of British institutions, including one of the most prestigious.

Enrollment Policy

Funding models generally use enrollment as the unit of educational output, but practice varies as to what enrollment figure should drive the model. Should the drivers be actual enrollments in the current year or some recent historical period? Should predicted enrollments be used? Or, should the funding authority decide in advance what enrollment levels it will support and then model institutional cost based on these targets?

Some states base public funding on actual enrollment levels—typically for the fall semester. The model multiplies actual enrollments by unit cost, and funds flow automatically based on these calculations. Such systems are justified by cost reimbursement principles: institutions receive a "standard" cost based on actual teaching effort. (A pure cost reimbursement system would pay according to auditable expense actually incurred; a model simplifies the system by determining a standard unit cost per enrollment, which serves as a surrogate for auditable cost.) Where enrollment predictions are based on recent institutional experience as adjusted for demographic trends, predicted enrollment can be used instead of actual enrollment without violating the cost reimbursement principle.

Systems based on actual enrollments have much to recommend them, but they possess two major flaws. First, government's commitment is open-ended, which makes it difficult to forecast and control expenditures. Second, institutions are provided an incentive to maximize enrollments in categories (e.g., fields and levels) where the model's unit costs most exceed perceived marginal cost. As funding models tend to provide greater reimbursement for doctoral than for bachelors degree enrollments, this can result in the production of too many doctorates—a situation that reminds one of the health care reimbursement problem discussed in chapter 8.

Substituting target enrollment for actual enrollment circumvents these problems. In England and Hong Kong, for example, the government decides in advance how many students in each category it wishes to fund, and then uses these figures to drive the model. Student numbers in excess of targets bring no additional funding. (Sometimes the excess numbers are limited by policy to avoid diluting educational quality.) By placing caps on total reimbursement, such systems mitigate the bias in enrollment mix and provide incentives for efficiency—just as in the cost containment strategies being adopted for Medicare and Medicaid. Institutions that fail to enroll the target numbers may be penalized through funding "clawbacks."

So-called core and margin systems may embrace the desirable features of cost reimbursement while mitigating the incentives problem. Core enrollments are determined from institutional history, policy targets, or a combination of the two, and these enrollments are funded on the basis of full average cost. Excess enrollments may be funded on the basis of marginal cost, perhaps subject to a predetermined upper limit.

A variation on the core-and-margin theme fixes total funding according to target enrollment numbers as long as enrollments fall within a preset band around the target. Variations outside the bands trigger funding adjustments, which may be based on either marginal or average cost. Such systems can be used to fine-tune incentives. For example, suppose government wants to expand certain student categories but is not in a position to increase unilaterally the institutional targets. Decreasing band size and funding at a generous rate would provide institutions with an incentive—but not a requirement—to expand output for these categories. Conversely, overcapacity might lead government to withdraw funds sparingly when enrollments drop below the target. Such options are rarely used in the United States, but they offer great power.

Performance Assessment Factors

Funding models can incorporate performance assessment factors at the program category or cost center level. For example, if departmental teaching assessment ratings are available, the model would multiply a department's calculated cost by its assessment rating and sum the results to obtain an adjusted figure for the whole institution. We consider the policy principles underlying such actions in chapter 12; our purpose here is to discuss how the principles can be incorporated into funding models.

The Higher Education Funding Council of England (HEFCE) assesses teaching quality for all subjects in all the institutions within its jurisdiction, according to the methodology described in chapter 9. The assessment produces a binary result: "acceptable" or "not acceptable." A "not acceptable" rating does not automatically result in a funding reduction. However, unless the problem is corrected, the institution is unlikely to be granted any additional target enrollment numbers in the subject area, and it may well see target numbers withdrawn. Since the English funding model uses average (not marginal) cost, this penalizes the institution financially as well as hurting its public image.

England's approach adopts the principle of symmetric incentives as discussed in chapter 12 but implements it in a way calculated to avoid the quality trap. The financial penalty is limited to the difference between average and marginal cost, multiplied by the number of student places withdrawn, which will be smaller than a unit cost reduction equal in percentage terms to the withdrawals. In other words, the public perception of "an x percent reduction" in student numbers will carry a smaller financial penalty than the same "x percent reduction" in unit costs. The approach also offers the advantage of simulating market action more directly than would unit cost changes—especially when the institution enjoys a certain amount of selectivity, and thus autonomy in tuition pricing.

Quality assessments at the institutional level also may be applied to the cost estimates obtained by modeling. For example, institutional quality audits, as performed by the Council of Vice-Chancellors and Principals of U.K. institutions (see chap. 9), could be used to shape funding. We mention this possibility for completeness, though the impact of institutional level assessments can be handled outside the model rather than being programmed into it. We should add that HEFCE operates a comprehensive research assessment scheme, also discussed in chapter 9, whose results are brought into their funding model as department-level multipliers.

A Case History of Funding Model Development

The two of us recently participated in the development of a comprehensive performance-based funding model for the Hong Kong University Grants Committee.[6] This section describes the process by which the

---

6. Massy is a member of the UGC and its Funding Model Working Group. Atkinson was the committee's consultant on the project and did most of the actual development. The Funding Model Working Group was chaired by Sir Ronald Oxburgh, Rector of

model was developed—in hopes that this will provide guidance for others wishing to develop similar models—and provides such knowledge about the model as resides in the public domain.

Background

The model was prepared as the basis for government funding of the seven of Hong Kong's higher educational institutions: the City University of Hong Kong (previously City Polytechnic), the Hong Kong Baptist University (previously Baptist College), Lignan College, the Chinese University of Hong Kong, the Hong Kong Polytechnic University (previously Hong Kong Polytechnic), the Hong Kong University of Science and Technology, and Hong Kong University. The institutions have widely differing histories and missions within an educational system based on that of the United Kingdom. The institutions receive most of their resources from the Hong Kong government through the University Grants Committee (UGC), established in 1965.

The objective of the new model was to provide figures for the funding requirements for both teaching and research through the years 1995–98, to enable the UGC to agree upon the recurrent grant for each institution; its goal was to be more output and performance oriented than previous models used in Hong Kong.

The development of the model entailed several tasks. First, developing the means to calculate the funding for teaching, based on the numbers of students and on unit costs for teaching; and, for research, on the number of academic staff judged to be research active according to certain criteria, on the unit costs for research, and on an element for other professional activities. Determination of the unit costs for both teaching and research was a major task in itself: the final figures used were based on historical data and on policy considerations.

An essential prerequisite to the funding calculations was the establishment of a new, comprehensive database of relevant statistics for each institution. This required the creation of program categories for student enrollment, cost centers for departmental expenditures and research, and headings for central expenditure. Finally, a research assessment exercise was conducted in which research was widely defined as all creative outputs that were not teaching or general scholarship related to teaching.

The funding model followed a number of the principles for university

Imperial College, London. Nigel French, Secretary General of UGC, also provided helpful guidance during the writing of this chapter.

funding developed in Britain in the mid-1980s by the United Kingdom's University Grants Committee, under Sir Peter Swinnerton-Dyer's chairmanship:

> the system is zero-based, rather than working with marginal changes from the previous year—although a safety net was provided when necessary;
> all activities are divided between two outputs: teaching and research;
> each of these carries a share of the indirect costs;
> the funding for research is determined, in part at least, by an exercise to assess research quality;
> research is funded through a dual system so that specific research projects compete for research grants from a body (a research council) that is separate from the body providing the general funding;
> in this system, research grants provide the marginal funds needed for the project (equipment and temporary staff), but not the costs of the time of the academics involved, or of the "well-found" laboratory—which are provided by the general funds of the institution itself.

Many of these principles were followed subsequently by the United Kingdom's University Funding Council (UFC) and, more recently, by the higher education funding councils for England, Wales, and Scotland.

One important difference between the British and Hong Kong funding models involves the split in funding between teaching and research. In the United Kingdom, the funds were split from the beginning into "pots of gold" for each of the units or areas in which research was assessed. These pots were originally established for the traditional universities; however, they were difficult to adjust when the polytechnics (funded through the Polytechnics and the Colleges Funding Council [PCFC]) were eventually brought together with the "old" universities within merged funding councils. In Hong Kong, instead of making an a priori division as in the United Kingdom, we have built up the teaching and research funds on the basis of historical financial returns, the research assessment exercise already mentioned, and policy judgments about how much money should be spent on research.

Otherwise, for the Hong Kong model:

> teaching funds are based on student numbers and on unit costs *that do not differentiate between institutions*. The funding is therefore

not directly related to the numbers or salaries of academic staff, or to fixed student-to-staff ratios;

research funds are based, inter alia, on the number of research-active academics; and on a wide definition of *research* (to include creative activities of academic staff other than traditional research);

quality and output can be rewarded in both teaching and research;

although the teaching and research elements of funding are calculated separately, a single block grant is given to each institution without specifying the amount which must be spent in either area.

Although the Hong Kong UGC's decisions on funding for each institution will be primarily based on results from the model, they would also take into account various overall policy factors, including the missions of the institutions and the impracticability of changing funds to individual institutions too rapidly. To allow for these judgments, the model enables the following adjustments to be made:

to the split of general funding between teaching and research;

within research, to the balance between the part based on the research assessment, and the part allowed for other professional activities;

to the unit costs (e.g., to favor some subjects, modes or levels);

to "top slice" overall funds, for example to reward teaching quality.

Data Collection and Calculation

As the basis for the model, we set up a new data collection system called the Common Data Collection Format (CDCF) for the Hong Kong institutions. This database groups information into:

Cost Centers, corresponding to the academic departments in which most staff are organized, through which most research is done, and in which most expenditure is controlled. Fifty-eight cost centers are used (table 1).

Academic Program Categories (APCs, sixteen in number), which stand for the academic teaching programs, which usually draw resources from a number of cost centers.

All student data are collected through a series of "student load matrices," whose columns are the Academic Program categories and whose rows are the cost centers. A different matrix is provided for each combination of mode and level.

The algorithm of the model itself is very simple. Funds are provided according to the sum of a number of elements, each being proportional to the product of three factors:

$$\text{volume} \times \text{unit cost} \times \text{quality}$$

Teaching

For teaching, it was decided not to introduce a quality factor at this level but rather to reward teaching and learning performance by other means. Thus, the algorithm for teaching becomes

$$\text{funding element} = \text{volume} \times \text{cost}$$

where volume is the number of full-time equivalent (FTE) students of a given academic program category, level and mode, and cost is the appropriate unit cost for that sort of student.

TABLE 1. Cost Centers

1.	clinical medicine	30.	surveying, land
2.	clinical dentistry	31.	surveying, other
3.	clinical vet studies	32.	mathematics and statistics
4.	nursing	33.	computer studies/science
5.	other para-medical	34.	law
6.	biological sciences	35.	accountancy
7.	pre-clinical studies	36.	public administration
8.	experimental psychology	37.	business studies (inc. management)
9.	other bio-sciences	38.	catering
10.	agriculture	39.	hotel management
11.	physics and astronomy	40.	economics
12.	chemistry	41.	geography
13.	materials science	42.	social work
14.	earth sciences	43.	other social sciences
15.	other physical sciences	44.	Chinese language and literature
16.	mechanical engineering	45.	English language and literature
17.	electrical engineering	46.	Japanese language and literature
18.	electronic engineering	47.	other languages
19.	chemical engineering	48.	translation
20.	production engineering	49.	communications and media studies
21.	marine engineering	50.	history
22.	biotechnology	51.	other arts/humanities
23.	materials technology	52.	art
24.	textile technology	53.	performing arts
25.	civil engineering	54.	music
26.	other technologies	55.	other creative arts
27.	architecture	56.	design
28.	building technology	57.	education
29.	planning	58.	physical education

Determining the number of FTE students can sometimes cause confusion because quoted FTE numbers can include weightings for costing purposes without that being explicitly stated. A full description of the student population requires specifying for each student the relative time he or she spends by mode, level, subject, and indeed, whether the student is in the first or last year of the program. In practice, however, some simplification is necessary. The easiest solution is to count the number of individual students registered at the institution—the head count. This approach produces misleading results, however, if many of the students are part-time (PT), since they do not need the same institutional resources as a full-time (FT) student. A somewhat more refined approach, used by the funding councils in the United Kingdom, models the number of enrolled students separately for each mode (FT, PT, etc.). This approach may also lead to error, however, if different part-time students spend different times completing a program, or if institutions have a modular system.

A more satisfactory approach involves counting the full-time equivalent (FTE) number of students. In general, this means the number of full-time students plus the number of part-time students, weighted by the fraction of time spent by each compared to the time for an equivalent full-time student. Thus, a PT student working half time in his or her program would count as FTE number of 0.5, while a third time student could count as 0.333 and so on. Different funding weights can be given to different types of student according to the costs of teaching each. Thus, it is not necessary to assume that two half-time students cost the same as one full-time one; nor that a full-time student pursuing a diploma at subdegree level costs the same as a full-time undergraduate.

In our data, we further assigned FTEs separately to each mode and level, for an even finer count. Although in practice many different modes exist in different institutions within the same funding group, for weighting purposes we lumped students together in a limited number of categories. Four modes and levels were used, as illustrated in table 2.

The total funding for teaching, then, is determined by the sum of

TABLE 2. Modes and Levels

Modes	Levels
Full-time, FT	Subdegree, SD
Sandwich course, SAND	Undergraduate, Ug
Part-time, PT (ex. PTE)	Taught postgrad, TPg
Part-time evening, PTE	Research postgrad, RPg

the funding elements for every combination of subject, mode, and level. Each of these combinations will, in principle, have a different unit cost. The method by which historical unit costs were determined is outlined later in the chapter. The unit costs are expressed relative to the cost of a full-time undergraduate in a fixed, low-cost, reference APC, to which the relative cost of 1 is given. The absolute cost of this reference APC is one of the variables of the model.

In unit costs by APC, a distinction is made between taught courses (subdegree, undergraduate and taught postgraduate) and research postgraduate courses. This is particularly important in clinical subjects where taught courses generally have high unit costs because of relatively low student-staff ratios, whereas research degrees in these subjects are not likely to have unit costs very different from those of other scientific/technical disciplines. For research students, the unit costs cover the tuition of a research student, but not the cost of doing research per se, which is covered by the research model.

Table 3 presents the available public information on how the unit costs vary across APCs. The humanities are taken as numeraire, and all other unit costs were divided by the unit cost for humanities subjects. The data are given in the form of ranges, since we did not want institutions to conform themselves to the UGC's point estimates regardless of their particular circumstances. (On the other hand, if an institution calculated its unit costs as lying outside the ranges it might well ask why.)

TABLE 3.   Range of Relative Cost Weightings (Teaching) by Academic Program Category

Academic Program Category	Relative Cost Weightings
Clinical medicine	4.8–5.4
Clinical dentistry	5.9
Preclinical studies	2.2–2.5
Subjects and professions allied to medicine	1.4–2.4
Biological sciences	1.3–3.8
Physical sciences	1.3–3.2
Engineering and technology	1.2–2.3
Built environment	1.0–1.6
Mathematical science	0.9–1.5
IT and computing science	0.9–1.5
Business and management	0.8–1.6
Social sciences	1.0–1.6
Languages	0.8–1.5
Humanities (excluding languages)	0.9–1.2
Arts, design, and performing arts	1.3–1.8
Education	0.9–1.4

Most subjects are expected to cost more than the humanities, so most of the ranges' upper limits exceed that of the humanities. For example, the unit cost for physical sciences may be three times that of the humanities.

Research

In the research part, for each cost center, the funding formula is based on the three factors already mentioned:

funding element = volume × unit cost × quality

The *volume* is the FTE number of research-active academics in a given cost center. This number is determined by multiplying the number of academics estimated to be on duty during the year of funding, by the fraction of research-active academics in the cost center as determined by the research assessment exercise (discussed later). Only those academic staff in grades from professor to assistant lecturer whose salaries were wholly supported from general funds are counted.

The *unit cost* is the cost of one FTE research-active academic in the cost center concerned. As in teaching, the unit cost for research in a given center was expressed as relative to that of a low cost, reference cost center. Again, the absolute cost of this reference center is one of the variables of the model. Broadly, the unit cost for research will depend on the cost to an institution's general funds of the time which an academic spends on average on research, and of the support, both technical and equipment, which he or she needs to carry out that research in the cost center concerned, together with an appropriate share of the institution's central costs.

Regarding the *quality* factor, for this first research assessment exercise, the factor was set at 1. The exercise only determined, therefore, the number of FTE academics carrying out research judged to be satisfactory.

Unit Costs

Unit costs are obviously of central importance, because they directly determine or scale the overall recurrent budget of each institution. The setting of unit costs is primarily a policy matter without a mechanistic solution. Setting high unit costs enables an institution to employ more academics per student, to pay the academics more, to equip them better, and to allow more research to be done by an institution at its own discretion using its own funds. The provision of more funds does not guarantee a higher quality graduate but should help. On the other hand, the funding authority might opt for more students at a lower overall unit cost (and be prepared to sacrifice quality to some extent) or for an increase of both quantity *and* quality.

The new model can deal with whatever situation policy dictates. Thus, for teaching, the model can calculate the cost of a given number of students (in different subjects etc.) for given unit costs; or, equally, it can be used to determine the cost per student for a given overall budget and number of students. Further, by changing the balance between the unit costs given by student for teaching and by academic staff member for research, the total funding of one institution can be changed with respect to another, within constant overall funds.

We tried to determine historic unit costs both by mode and level and by subject (i.e., APC and CC). Ideally, unit costs should be determined for each combination of mode and level. In practice, however, this proved difficult to do with much precision on the information available. Nevertheless, historic data on these relative costs were sought from institutions, and some broad conclusions could be drawn for the model.

We covered only the four modes and four levels already mentioned. The greatest varieties of modes were found, not surprisingly, in the old polytechnics, which had many part-time courses, often at subdegree level and sometimes involving evening classes—but these other modes were subsumed into the four chosen.

In order to calculate the historic unit costs by academic program category for the teaching model and by cost center for the research model, we first divide an institution's direct, departmental expenditure from general funds for each cost center between the teaching and research functions. This information was sought in the returns from each institution as part of the overall annual data collection exercise. The institutions provided the data, but none found it an easy task. The teaching-research balance can be estimated in other ways:

> *from the research assessment exercise,* which gives the fraction of research-active academics in each cost center for each institution. These fractions do not, of course, give the proportion of time spent by a research-active academic on research—which may be of the order 30 percent to 50 percent, and will depend on research patterns in the cost center concerned. However, by making certain assumptions about the fraction of time spent on research by a research-active academic, and assuming that the teaching and research costs are in proportion to the time spent on average by academics on the two functions, an estimate may be made of the teaching-research split of funds;

from diary exercises already conducted in Hong Kong (notably for clinical medicine), and in the United Kingdom.

After determining the teaching-research split for a given institution—which is inevitably partly a matter of judgment for all concerned—the next step is to assign the institution's central expenditure to each cost center. This provides the full expenditure—direct and indirect—of that cost center. Ideally, each element of central costs should be assigned to individual cost centers according to the detailed use made by that cost center of that function, considering both teaching and research. In practice, however, there will always be a substantial central expenditure that must be assigned by some arithmetical process or another. If the unit costs determined for different institutions are to be compared, a consistent way must be found to distribute the central expenditure. This is sometimes done by using one or the other of the following two keys:

the cost center's total *direct* expenditure;
the weighted FTE student load numbers (the numbers weighted by
    mode and level) for the cost center.

Each of these approaches gives substantially different overall unit costs for each cost center, especially when subjects with very low student-staff ratios are involved, such as medicine. Thus, we decided for relative simplicity to use a combination of each of these two keys, applied appropriately and differently to the teaching and the research expenditures. (Of course the greater the extent to which an institution assigns the broadest possible range of costs to departments, the smaller will be the unallocated central costs which must be assigned by this rough-and-ready procedure.)

To find the teaching unit cost per FTE student *for a given cost center*, we divide the total (direct plus indirect) expenditure on teaching in that cost center by the weighted FTE number of students. In this, we assume in calculating the weighted FTE numbers, the relative unit costs by level and mode used elsewhere in the model. For the funding model, however, we need *the unit costs by academic program category*, not by cost center. To obtain this, we must work back through a (weighted FTE) load matrix for that institution.

The research unit cost for a cost center is the total (direct plus indirect) cost of research in that cost center divided by the FTE number of research-active academics. Note that the relative unit costs for teaching and research will necessarily be different for a given subject (APC or CC), because the teaching unit cost will depend, inter alia, on student-staff ratios, whereas the research unit cost of research depends essentially on the costs of an academic staff member doing the research.

This process gives historic unit costs for each institution. Average unit costs across all institutions may then be calculated as follows: for teaching, by APC, weighted according to the number of students in each institution; and similarly, for research, by cost center, weighted by the FTE numbers of research-active academics. Provision is also made for other professional activities.

These unit costs are historic because they can only be calculated for the latest year for which full expenditure data are available from institutions through the CDCF (1992–93 in this case). However, what are needed are unit costs appropriate for the period for which the funding is to be given—starting, here, in 1995–96.

How can the historical unit costs be updated? Fortunately, the *relative* unit costs need only be changed from year to year for policy reasons, or because of some systematic shift in relative teaching costs. However, the *absolute* costs may change over that period, depending on a number of factors such as inflation, efficiency changes, and perhaps a general tendency to higher student-staff ratios. The model easily takes account of these absolute changes by changing the value of two single parameters: the cost of teaching a full-time undergraduate in the teaching reference APC, and the cost of a typical research-active academic in the research reference cost center. Account must also be taken of the absolute cost of other professional activities.

The values of relative and absolute unit costs finally used in the model will depend not only on historical data, but also on careful consideration of the costs of teaching and research elsewhere, and on the judgment of the funding body. No fully mechanistic solution can be satisfactory.

Research Assessment Exercise (RAE)

The first research exercise, which formed the basis of allocating research funds for the triennium 1995–98, covered research activities for the academic year 1992–93. Because research had not previously been systematically assessed in the Hong Kong institutions, this exercise was aimed at assessing the quantity of research being done. Research quality was only assessed to a quality threshold of satisfactory; in future years, the exercise will be modified to bring more attention to quality and its reward.

Institutions were first asked to map their departments and research units into a common list of cost centers. Then, for each cost center, institutions were asked to nominate a list of academic staff active in research. Nominated researchers are those academic staff who have produced significant levels of research output in the past four years. The UGC was careful to specify that not all academic staff should be nominated: those whose activities are devoted almost entirely to keeping up with their field and preparing materials for local classroom use would be viewed as devoting themselves entirely to the institution's teaching program. No stigma would be attached to staff not nominated for research. The UGC provided an exception for young researchers, stating that those who had been appointed within the past three years, had less than three years of active research experience before the appointment, and were regarded as possessing strong research potential should be nominated regardless of the amount of outputs produced to date.

Each nominated researcher chose three best outputs to present to the review panels. Research was broadly defined to include traditional academic research (refereed and unrefereed publications), contract research, art objects, performances, designs, and other creative works. (Institutions could also list interdisciplinary research programs in a special table provided for that purpose.) The panels were composed of experienced researchers from appropriate academic fields. They rated each output as either 1 (satisfactory) or 0 (unsatisfactory). Because the nature of research varies so widely across different fields, each panel was asked to develop its own assessment criteria pertinent to the conduct and pattern of research in its area. Panels worked within a common framework but set their own quality thresholds. Each nominated researcher could thus score a total of 0 to 3 points, a 3 automatically qualified the nominee as an active researcher. A 1 or a 2 score required individual assessment, especially in the cases of young researchers and researchers with few but important outputs. Therefore the total number of active researchers provided a rough measure of a cost center's total volume of research.

The funding for research was calculated by multiplying the number of active researchers in each field by a factor that takes into account the cost of research in that field. In addition, the funding formula provided a fixed per capita figure for all academic staff to help fund the time that they may be expected spend in professional activities the RAE was unable to assess. This extra funding was considered necessary because so few submissions were supplied in the areas of applied research and other professional and creative activities, even though the UGC had defined research very widely. In the future, the UGC expects to be able to gauge these activities more effectively.

Conclusion

This chapter describes the design and usage principles associated with higher education funding models of the type used by government agencies and system officers to distribute funds among institutions and campuses. Then we illuminate the principles' applications by describing the Hong Kong University Grants Committee model, in whose development we participated.

We identified five major issues as being important for funding model design and usage:

1. The choice of analysis units for modeling: the model should be neither so aggregative as to submerge important structural elements nor so detailed as to place impossible demands on data collection and user judgment.
2. Whether research represents a separate output: we believe departmental research and instruction should be unbundled for funding though not accounting purposes.
3. How unit cost is determined: cost analysis lies at the heart of funding model development and good analysis will be useful for planning regardless of the type of model constructed.
4. Whether to base the model on actual, predicted, or target enrollments: while some funding agencies use actual or predicted enrollments, the trend is toward "purchasing" desired enrollment levels— i.e., to base funding on target enrollments.
5. Use of judgmentally determined performance assessment factors: funding should be based on performance, on quality as well as quantity; this requires that some kind of judgmental assessment should enter the funding equation.

The application of these principles is illuminated in our description of the Hong Kong funding model. The model has materially improved the University Grants Committee's ability to allocate funds on a rational basis. In addition, because the Hong Kong model is implemented in a desktop computer spreadsheet environment, we can assert that the modeling technology lies within the reach of every higher education system.

CHAPTER 11

Global Accounts

Gordon Winston

The financial accounts of a college or university do not report economic information for the institution as a whole, as one would expect. Instead, the college is divided up into separate activities, and a separate set of financial accounts—income statement and balance sheet—is reported for each of those activities. Each is treated as if it were a separate firm (Garner 1991). Often complex loans and transfers between those firms are recorded in each set of accounts. The system is called fund accounting. Eight or nine fund accounts and their interwoven transfers typically make up the annual financial statement for even a small and simple college.

Fund accounts have come to remind one of the old saw about the weather—that everyone complains but no one does anything about it.[1] This chapter describes the results of a five-year effort to organize the basic economic information about a college's performance in a different and more useful way. The result is a set of global accounts that present an *encompassing*—all-inclusive, complete, integrated—view of a college's eco-

Reprinted from *Planning for Higher Education* 20, no. 4 (1992): 1–16. Reprinted by permission of the Society for College and University Planning. The structure of this analysis was developed between 1986 and 1988 and given an important shot of practicality during my stint as provost at Williams from 1988 to 1990. The support of the Andrew W. Mellon Foundation through its support, in turn, of the Williams Project on the Economics of Higher Education is gratefully acknowledged. William Bowen, Shaun Buckler, Keith Finan, George Goethals, David Healy, Robinson Hollister, George Keller, Duncan Mann, Charles Mott, Saeed Mughal, Will Reed, Joseph Rice, Morton Schapiro, David Schulte, and Winthrop Wassenar gave me valuable insights into these issues with considerable improvement in the quality of the analysis and understanding. I am especially indebted to Harold Bierman, Roger Bolton, David Booth, Anne MacEachern, and Michael McPherson. Needless to say, I did not take all of their good advice.

1. That is not quite accurate. Almost twenty years ago, Bierman and Hofstedt showed how misleading conventional budget deficits can be, using an analysis similar in some ways to that of this paper. Their effort got them an Andy Rooney segment on CBS, a front-page *Wall Street Journal* article titled "Ten Eastern Colleges Accused of Crying Wolf in Reporting Deficits: Two Cornell Accounting Profs Contend the Schools Conceal Gains in 'Financial Condition,'" and strenuous objections from comptrollers and presidents. But there has been little lasting effect.

nomic activities and status. It is the kind of information essential to the governance of the college, the kind the board of trustees, the faculty oversight committee, and the top administrators need. It describes the economic effects of a year's activities and most specifically their effect on the college's real wealth. The structure of the global accounts is the antithesis of that of the fund accounts that *divides* a college into a set of *discrete*—self-contained, balkanized—accounting entities. Global accounts bring information about the whole of the college together. Their aim is to be accurate, clear, and accessible to those who are not steeped in fund accounting.

Fund Accounts

Fund accounting has a long and honorable tradition of service to government and nonprofit institutions, and there are still important questions that only fund accounts—or something like them—can answer. The question addressed in this chapter is the inadequacy of fund accounts to provide the sole or primary way to frame economic information for colleges and universities. The main problems with using fund accounts as the primary way of describing the economic performance of colleges and universities appear to be the following (which are clearly related and all derive from the balkanization of the college's activities):

1. Fund accounts obscure an overall, global understanding of an institution's economic performance.
2. Fund accounts are hard to read and understand—*inaccessible* without a significant investment of time—with their mass of detailed information repeated separately for each fund and the often complex transfers and interactions among funds.
3. One result of balkanization and inaccessibility is a focus of attention on understandable information even though it is partial and may be marginally relevant or even misleading, like operating budget deficits, endowment wealth, or an endowment payout rate. The operating budget often leaves out a third or more of all current economic activity, budget deficits or surpluses are easily manipulated, and the endowment (and quasi-endowment) is only a fraction of total wealth in even the best endowed schools.[2]
4. A worrisome result would appear to be an inherent temptation—usually resisted but always present—to present misleading information. It may happen unintentionally, but funds are potential shells that invite shell games because their complexity induces some parts of the accounts to be ignored while other parts are given unwarranted attention. In moving $5 million of current spending off the operating

---

2. Winston 1988.

budget in the 1980s, for instance, Williams markedly reduced the apparent, but not the actual, growth of its operating expenditures; Carleton reported large current expenditures in their endowment fund instead of the current fund; Swarthmore noted its forty years of exactly balanced operating budgets,[3] apparently achieved by transferring to the budget, after the fact, whatever was needed to cover operating expenses; MIT and Harvard followed the same convention in the 1970s (Bierman and Hofstedt 1973).

5. It is important for the broader understanding of higher education that fund accounting reduces comparability among schools and even for a single school over time.

The original rationale for fund accounts in colleges was that they made it easier to monitor performance in specific areas supported by outside agents, by donors or governments who gave funds to the college for restricted purposes and needed to know if those purposes were being well served and managed.[4] But while that stewardship role remains, it does not justify the use of fund accounts as the primary way of organizing economic information. Efforts to make fund accounting serve purposes of both stewardship and governance—by using ratio analysis, for instance (Chabotar 1989)—have been only partly successful since they retain the shortcomings of fund account data. On the other hand, global accounts that define the context and inform the governance of a college will always need to be complemented by subaccounts, fitted within that inclusive global reporting, that deal with the more detailed information essential to management and that identify restrictions on the use of funds.

Global Accounts

The basic structure of the global accounts is simple. For a year's economic activity, three elemental economic facts are reported:

1. How much the college took in, in total, from all sources
2. What it did with that money
3. The effect of these activities on the institution's real wealth

---

3. "The 1986–87 fiscal year was the fortieth consecutive year in which the College operated with a balanced budget" (Swarthmore College 1987, 17).

4. "In the absence of [the] implicit regulator [of profits], regulation of the allocation and utilization of financial resources of nonbusiness organizations is often achieved by the imposition of stringent controls . . . legally imposed . . . or . . . imposed through formal action of the governing board . . . [and] also . . . directly . . . by the individual or groups that contribute such resources . . . the donor. . . . In order to account for these legally imposed, externally imposed, and self-imposed restrictions or limitations . . . nonbusiness organizations have generally adopted the concepts of fund accounting" (Harried, Imdieke, and Smith 1985, 722).

That is the essential framework of global accounts.[5] What is centrally important is that they completely encompass the institution's activities: no flow or
claim between the college and an outside agent—of income, expenditure,
saving, assets, or liabilities—should be left out. And no financial flows or
claims simply between funds should be included.

The hope in constructing global accounts, initially, was that they would
only reorganize the economic information already reported in the fund accounts. Global accounts were derived from audited, published information,
largely by combining fund activities and eliminating double counting among
them (Winston 1988). And that worked, at first. Indeed, a major question was
whether the approach that generated global accounts from Williams' published fund accounts would work, too, for other schools, a question that was
answered when Duncan Mann and I were able to create global accounts for
Wellesley, Carleton, Swarthmore, and, for contrast, the State University system of New York (Winston and Mann in preparation). The result was an
accounting of the year's total income, total current spending, and total real
financial saving—the change in financial wealth.

But not all wealth. It has become increasingly clear that global accounts
that simply reorganize existing information create a useful set of global financial records that monitor real financial wealth, but they share the shortcoming
of the fund accounts in being inadequate to the incorporation of physical
capital wealth. Neither one can account for all of an institution's wealth: at
Williams, for example, they ignore more than half of its $645 million of net
worth.

So the set of genuinely global accounts presented here, while still heavily
dependent on a reorganization of published information, augments those data
with a more realistic treatment of land, plant, and equipment (a treatment very
much in the spirit of the current literature on capital planning in colleges
(Dunn 1989; Probasco 1991)). For some potential users, these full global
accounts may go too far; not everyone is ready to monitor all of his or her
institution's wealth. One can retreat to the halfway house of global financial
accounts, a system that is no worse then conventional accounting in its neglect
of capital wealth and is a whole lot better in dealing with the other problems of
fund accounting noted above. So considerable improvement lies in using the
global financial accounts, even if they are importantly incomplete. (Table 1 is
repeated in appendix A as table 1-A to show the same college in the abbrevi-
ated form of a global financial account, but the rest of the text will deal with
the fully global accounts that include all institutional wealth.)

In a significant and encouraging recent development, Harvard's new

---

5. It is also the underlying framework—often honored in the breach—of the familiar
income statement and balance sheet.

annual *Financial Report* treats the physical capital stock much as described below, even though that increased realism raised their reported operating expenses by $77 million and gave them a $42 million budget deficit (Harvard University 1992). Harvard's decision not only reduces the risk to other schools of adopting these innovations in reporting economic information, but it indicates another way for an institution to move *toward* fully global accounts without embracing them all at once.

A caveat before describing the global accounts in detail. Their application is more immediately appropriate to most private than to most public institutions. The reason, of course, is the often Byzantine arrangements of responsibility, ownership, and governance that have grown up between public colleges and state and local agencies, arrangements that can affect, inter alia, the ownership of the school's capital stock, responsibility for tuition levels, salaries and fringe benefits, and even control over the use of any endowment wealth. So the scope of responsibility and control may sometimes be very different from that implied by these accounts. It remains, however, that global accounts or something quite like them are essential to public institutions if anyone is to know the real costs of public education and the effects of a state's policies on its educational wealth.

How the elements of global accounts work to form a coherent system of information will be clearer if they are embedded in a concrete example, so two years' data are presented in table 1.[6] Consider the components in turn.

College Income

The income elements in table 1 are fairly straightforward at a small school, but a few comments are useful, nonetheless. The list of income sources is exhaustive: all income flowing into the college during the year is included, whether it comes from students,[7] donors, government, borrowers of the college's wealth, or purchasers of services from the college. Gift and grant income in table 1 is separated according to donors' wishes to recognize that part of gift income is intended to expand the college's wealth and that that part is potentially different from gifts that donors intend should be used at the discretion of the college. Asset earnings include interest, dividends, and

---

6. These are similar to historical data from Williams' published sources, so no legal issues are raised by their use here. In the description of an economic plan below, pains are taken to present transparently unrealistic and uninformative planning parameters to illustrate only the structure of the plan and nothing of Williams' expectations or intentions.

7. Tuition and fee income in these accounts is gross. An alternative would leave institutional student aid out of both income and expenditures and report as income only net tuition and fees.

TABLE 1. Global Accounts

	1989–1990	1990–1991
1. College income		
Tuition and fees	$29,262,691	$32,543,540
Gifts and grants		
To endowment	7,066,669	8,744,806
To plant	1,016,397	713,124
All other	12,664,824	13,951,045
Asset income		
Interest and dividends	17,039,521	15,859,257
Appreciation	18,582,670	6,873,486
Sales, services, and other	1,950,970	2,724,059
Auxiliary income	11,599,559	11,862,813
Total college income	99,183,301	93,272,130
2. Current expenditures		
Operating budget expenditures	62,425,303	66,924,329
Other current expenditures	6,304,914	5,634,728
Less current account maintenance	703,276	642,167
Total current expenditures	68,026,941	71,916,890
3. Additions to capital stock		
Investment in new plant	9,334,326	2,310,285
Less deferred maintenance		
Real depreciation	7,500,000	8,097,195
Less maintenance spending		
In current account	703,276	642,167
In plant fund	3,477,560	4,639,692
Total deferred maintenance	3,319,164	2,815,336
Total additions to capital	6,015,162	(505,051)
4. Operating costs		
Current expenditures	68,026,941	71,916,890
Real depreciation	7,500,000	8,097,195
Total operating costs	75,526,941	80,014,085
5. Wealth end of year		
Financial wealth		
Assets	346,203,972	358,726,081
Less liabilities	50,596,648	49,355,661
Net financial wealth	295,607,324	309,370,420
[Endowment value]	[333,553,551]	[341,572,081]
Physical capital wealth		
Replacement value	323,887,799	341,438,861
Less accumulated deferred maintenance	3,319,164	6,290,686
Net physical wealth	320,568,635	335,148,175
Net worth	616,175,959	644,518,595

capital gains or losses (whether realized or not).[8] Auxiliary income, in a small liberal arts college, consists largely of student charges for room and board; for a university, that line would be both larger and more complicated, as would sales, services, and other, the catchall income line here.

Current Expenditures

Current expenditures in the global accounts is both a more and a less inclusive category than spending from the current fund, in fund accounting: it includes all current expenditures, and it excludes maintenance spending. Current expenditures are included whether they appear within the operating budget or elsewhere in the current fund, the capital budget, the endowment fund, or somewhere else in the fund accounts. So in a global accounting, there is no opportunity to reduce the apparent level or growth of current expenditures by shifting some of them from a closely monitored area like the operating budget to a less scrutinized part of the accounts, like off-budget current fund or endowment fund spending. Spending on the maintenance of the plant and equipment is excluded because it is not a current expenditure: it is spending that buys a durable good—the restoration, renovation, and adaptation[9] of the physical plant.[10]

Additions to the Capital Stock

Predictably, the greatest departure from conventional reporting comes in the global accounts' treatment of the physical capital stock, since that aspect of college management and college wealth is so effectively neglected in fund accounting. The purpose of global accounting of the capital stock is to report its real value and record the effects of the year's activities on that value. It serves, too, to inform a more accurate measure of the college's operating costs that recognizes both current spending and real depreciation of the college's physical wealth.

Additions to the capital stock are simply the year's gross investment in

---

8. While this is logically necessary because Williams accounts its financial assets at market value, it would be desirable even if they did not.

9. *Adaption* refers to action to offset depreciation due to *obsolescence*, in the trilogy described long ago by Terborg. The other sources are depreciation due to *use* and depreciation due to the *elements*—these would be addressed by *renovation* spending as used here.

10. Under present practice, some of renovation and adaptation is embedded in current spending, but the largest part of renovation and adaption spending typically appears as capital spending (labeled *investment in plant*), so only a relatively small adjustment to reported current spending is usually needed to purge total current expenditures of what is more accurately capital spending. At Williams, the maintenance part of current expenditures was only $703,000 in 1989–90 and $642,000 in 1990–91.

new plant less any value lost through deterioration of the capital stock—the year's deferred maintenance. Investment in new plant is uncomplicated: it includes all additions and acquisitions of new land, plant, and equipment that will augment the capital stock. Deferred maintenance describes how much of the year's real depreciation of the capital stock was not repaired or renovated—by how much the physical plant was allowed to deteriorate over the year.[11] Given depreciation, repairs and renovation reduce deferred mainte-nance. Deferred maintenance is not a money expenditure, per se, of course, but it is an expenditure of part of the capital stock—consequent on time and its use in production—and therefore a very real cost of the year's operations. The recognition of deferred maintenance is essential if the full effect of the year's activities on the value of the college's wealth are to be reported.

Real depreciation is an estimate of the potential amount of capital stock worn out or used up in the course of the year's operations—the amount it would have depreciated had there been no repairs, renovation, or adaption. The emphasis on *real* depreciation is intended to distinguish this estimate of *actual* decline in the value of a capital stock over the course of the year, due to time and its use, from the more familiar but quite different matter of income tax liability in a for-profit firm: for many, that is what depreciation has come to mean, both in accounting and the public mind. In the global accounts, it is pure economic depreciation.

Finally, maintenance spending, as noted above, is much the same as investment in new plant—it increases the value of durable capital through renovation and adaption—so it is treated the same in the global accounts. To the small amount of such spending found in the current account is added that portion of a conventional investment in plant entry that in fact pays for renovation and adaption.

In table 1, real depreciation was estimated as 2.5 percent of the $324 million capital stock with which 1990–91 started, or $8.1 million.[12] But since that was offset in 1990–91 by an estimated $4.6 million of maintenance spending from the capital budget and another $.64 million from the operating

---

11. *Deferred maintenance* is often used to describe the accumulated result of past failure to spend enough on maintenance to offset real depreciation. It reduces the value of a stock variable. Here we use the phrase, too, to describe a flow—the extent to which this year's maintenance spending failed to offset this year's depreciation. As usual, this year's flow is an increment to the previously accumulated stock. Note that there is nothing necessarily pejorative about deferred maintenance: it often is advisable to let physical capital depreciate.

12. The 2.5 percent is a conservative estimate. Economists (Schultz 1960; O'Neill 1971) have put it at 2 percent of the replacement value of plant and equipment per year, but estimates more carefully done by university capital planners get 1.5–2.5 percent for renovation and another .5–1.5 percent for adaption (Dunn 1989). So the 2.5 percent used in the text and tables appears to be a conservative estimate of total depreciation and therefore of the spending needed to eliminate all deferred maintenance.

budget, deferred maintenance for the year is estimated, with rounding, as $2.8 million.[13] If current spending on maintenance had been $8.1 million for the year, deferred maintenance would, of course, have been zero.

Additions to the capital stock are the net result of all this: investment in new plant is augmented by maintenance spending and reduced by depreciation. Additions to the capital stock will be positive when new plant and maintenance, together, are larger than real depreciation and negative when they are overwhelmed by the year's depreciation.

Operating Costs

In the global accounts, the year's total real operating costs are reported directly. To total current expenditures is added the year's depreciation of physical plant. So both forms of current spending are recognized as operating costs: current expenditures of the usual sort (less maintenance spending) and current spending of the capital stock through depreciation. Together, these describe the costs of the year's operations.[14]

Wealth: Assets and Liabilities

Assets and liabilities, together, describe the sta.. of a college's wealth at the end of each year. They are the college's stock variables. Two aspects of the reporting of assets in global accounts should be noted. One is de-emphasis of the college's endowment: it shows up in table 1 as a parenthetical notation sandwiched into the list of assets and liabilities that make up the college's wealth. The reason for this dismissive treatment is, simply, that the endowment has come erroneously to be seen as synonymous with total financial wealth. While that was nearly true when colleges had very few nonendow-

---

13. An important departure from the facilities planning literature lies in the fact that the global accounts identify the year's deferred maintenance without implying that it must therefore be prevented; the *recognition* of the cost of real depreciation is not the same thing as *funding* it. See Dunn 1989 or Probasco 1991.

14. An issue lurks under the surface here: it is the classic neglect of the opportunity cost of capital as a real cost of production in colleges and universities (and nonprofits in general). So it is inaccurate to call total current costs *total* when they leave out, in the case of Williams, roughly $30 million a year of real costs of production—half again as much as is typically reported (Winston 1991). Two facts might recommend that we continue to leave them out, however: (1) the global accounts are concerned with the total flows of income and spending by the institution from and to outside agents, so it may be permissible to neglect a real cost of production that is paid, by virtue of the college's ownership of its capital stock, back to itself as imputed income, even though the resulting accounts seriously distort the *costs* of production; and (2) it may be strategically unwise to try to persuade people of the good sense of both the global accounts and an accounting of capital costs at the same time, though a more courageous effort would take on both at once.

ment financial assets and, importantly, very little debt aside from some stray accounts payable, it is not true for many colleges now. Again, Williams' numbers are instructive. In 1989, its endowment had a market value of some $307 million, but the college also had another $22 million in nonendowment assets[15] for total financial assets of $329 million (Williams College 1991). But those assets were encumbered by some $51 million in debt. So the global accounts report net financial wealth of $278 million—total financial assets less total liabilities—as the appropriate measure of the college's financial wealth. In 1990, the endowment was up to $334 million but net financial wealth only to $296 million.

The other important differences in global accounts' wealth reporting are that physical capital assets—land and plant and equipment—are (1) accounted for in current replacement values rather than in the book values that the college originally paid for them and (2) adjusted for accumulated deferred maintenance. At Williams, which is an old school, one major instructional building with seven large classrooms and 13,000 square feet has a book value of less than $50,000 and one faculty residence, not large but pleasant, is valued at $850 (Williams College 1991). Most other campuses would offer similar examples of the distortions inherent in using book values. So while the estimates of replacement values inevitably involve some guesswork, they are clearly a whole lot closer to the truth than are historical values. Accumulated deferred maintenance is treated as an offset against the replacement value of the physical assets, leaving net physical wealth as the measure of value of the capital stock. Table 1 assumes that there was no deferred maintenance before 1989–90, so there is little immediate difference between capital assets and net physical wealth; but table 4 below shows that over a long period, deferred maintenance will significantly reduce the college's net physical wealth— Yale's current pressing problem (*New York Times*, February 3, 1992).

Because financial and physical assets and liabilities are measured in the same current value terms, they can be added together to report the college's total wealth, its total net worth. We are adding apples and apples. For many purposes, it is essential to distinguish between these two forms of wealth (and savings), but for others, it is useful to recognize total wealth, regardless of its form. In table 1, reporting a total 1991 wealth of $645 million tells a very different and more complete story than either reporting an endowment of $342 million or financial wealth of $309 million.

---

15. Though they may differ from endowment assets in other ways, the defining characteristic of these financial assets is that they are "owned," within the college, by a fund other than the endowment fund.

Savings and Wealth: Flow-Stock Relationships

The usual tautological accounting relationships between economic flows and stocks apply to global accounts: *savings* is the difference between income and spending over the period; any change in wealth between two dates equals and must be due to savings over that period; net worth (wealth) at the beginning of a period plus income minus spending has to equal net worth at the end of the period. Of course, real depreciation must be added to current expenditures to account fully for the year's total spending. This done, the stock-flow identity holds for total savings and wealth (net worth) as well as for financial and physical savings and wealth separately. It is just as relevant to global accounts as it is to one's checking account.[16]

Operating and Capital Budgets

Operating and capital budgets are embedded in the global accounts, serving their managerial and planning functions but firmly in the context of the college's overall activities. So total operating expenditures, the bottom line in an operating budget like that of table 2, appears in the global accounts as a component of current spending (the largest). The effect, then, of operating budget performance on the college's wealth is incorporated immediately and directly. Though it is not made explicit here, the same is true for a capital budget that is mapped directly into the global accounts in the form of either new investment or as current spending on renovation and adaption.

---

16. But with one awkwardness caused by the use of current market or replacement values for physical capital wealth in an inflationary environment. It lies in the need for an inflation adjustment to the value of the physical capital stock from year to year that does not (as would be strictly appropriate) appear here as nominal income. Strict adherence to the tautology would have to report the gain in physical asset value due to inflation as income (a physical capital gain) and then assign all of that income to savings, thereby justifying the increase in the nominal value of the capital stock. But since that portion of income is always saved and serves only to keep the replacement value of the capital stock in current dollars, the better choice seems to be to introduce an apparent violation of the stock-flow tautology rather than insert a large piece of funny money income explicitly into the body of the accounts. So the replacement value of physical capital reflects inflation within each year as well as showing the effect of net investment. As presented in table 1, then, the tautology applies directly to financial savings and wealth but not to physical capital or total savings and wealth, unless inflation-induced physical capital gains income is included. (For the reader who would like to confirm this relationship, the replacement value of the capital stock was $300,000,000 in 1989 while the inflation rate was (rounded) 4.85 percent over 1989–90 and 4.71 percent over 1990–91, so the inflation adjustments in replacement value are $14,553,473 and $15,240,777 in 1989–90 and 1990–91, respectively. With these, net physical wealth and net worth at the beginning of each period plus savings and inflation adjustment will equal net physical wealth and net worth at the end of the period.)

TABLE 2. Global Accounts: Current Expenditure Component

	1989–90	1990–91
Operating budget		
Salary pools		
Faculty	$10,194,014	$11,415,331
Administrative/Prof	6,029,465	6,315,789
Weekly	11,568,273	12,101,430
Total salary pools	27,791,752	29,832,550
Fringe benefits	7,258,226	7,816,225
Financial aid	6,517,892	7,719,186
Other restricted spending	2,720,321	3,505,429
Managers' budgets	18,137,112	18,050,939
Total operating budget expenses	62,425,303	66,924,329
Other current expenditures	6,304,914	5,634,728
Less maintenance spending in current account	703,276	642,167
Total current expenditures	68,026,941	71,916,890

Note that while operating *expenditures* are reported in a line in the global accounts, operating *revenues* do not appear. The reason is, simply, that a college's decision on how much of its total income to allocate to an operating budget as revenue is an internal and essentially arbitrary one. That decision may be influenced by some accumulated tradition—tuition and fees, for instance, may all go to the operating budget while only some gifts and a formulaic portion of asset income do—but a college can, by assignment and transfer of its income to and from the budget, make a budget deficit or surplus virtually anything it wants to be including, Swarthmore and others have shown, always exactly zero.[17] Clarity is served, then, by focusing the global accounts on *spending* in the operating budget—or more broadly, on all current spending—as it encompasses an important set of activities in the college's educational enterprise. Attention to the arbitrary assignment of operating budget *revenues*—the result of shifting money between pockets—and the consequent budget deficits or surpluses can be replaced by attention to real

17. In addition to Bierman and Hofstedt's brief fame for showing that budget deficits are often highly misleading—when MIT reported a $5 million deficit, they actually saved $100 million; Princeton's reported $1.5 million deficit went with $151 million in savings; and Harvard's $1.4 million deficit coincided with $314 million in savings, inter alia—a number of others have tried to sound the same warning. William Nordhaus, economist and provost at Yale from 1986 to 1988, for instance, cautioned against relying on operating budget deficits and surpluses because "actions are generally taken to produce a balanced budget" (Nordhaus 1989, 10).

current spending and to actual performance relative to an approved spending plan.[18]

Using Global Accounts

The global accounts structure was first used to organize a historical review of Williams' economic behavior to provide a descriptive context for evaluating present and future performance (Winston 1988). It was done at the height of the public criticisms of cost growth in higher education when it was deemed wise to know how present performance compared with the past. We were able to generate long data series[19] on income levels and changes in its composition; on spending, its composition, and real rates of growth; and on real saving and its distribution between financial and physical capital wealth. The result provided a foundation for economic policies.

But the broader significance of global accounts appears to lie in their ability to describe, monitor, and evaluate a college's current economic performance and in the structure they give to economic planning.

Monitoring and Evaluating Economic Performance

The global accounts do not force any specific criteria of performance evaluation on a college except implicitly in describing the totality of the school's economic activity, but they do make it especially easy to monitor the effects on its real wealth on the college's behavior and the economic circumstances it operates in: the difference between income and current spending is savings (or dissavings), and that, dollar for dollar, increases (or decreases) wealth. And global accounts make it easy to break that down to monitor, separately, the effects of college behavior on financial wealth and on physical capital wealth. There are good reasons why a governing board might consider a dollar saved in a liquid financial asset to be very different from a dollar saved in constructing or renovating a building; both are savings, but their different forms carry quite different implications for future flexibility, costs, returns, and perfor-

---

18. Operating revenues are structurally a lot like a child's allowance—the part of family income the parents assign for the child to spend. Whether or not the child can get by on, or even save from, the allowance is not an uninteresting question or one always viewed with dispassion. But it would be a mistake of some significance if the parents (or their creditors) were to represent the child's deficit or surplus on the child's allowance as a measure of the family's economic fortunes for the week. So, in the context of higher education, a number of Princeton faculty members were vocally unimpressed with the university's recent and much publicized operating budget deficits, convinced that there had to be more going on there than met the eye (Lyall 1989). Global accounts make it clear that there was.

19. Initially, for the thirty years since Williams was a small, all-male, fraternity-centered college.

mance. Even at the level of total savings, a board may think it wise to maintain real wealth or to increase it or to spend some of it down.[20] Or it may prefer only to monitor real wealth or income or spending or their components, rather than to define explicit policies in those respects. These are all decisions on which the structure of the global accounts is agnostic.

Using data from table 1, table 3 illustrates one sort of evaluative summary that global accounts can produce to describe, in the broadest terms, a college's performance for a year.[21] Other summary data could be generated, but these are especially useful in informing broad questions of strategy and governance.

The first line of table 3—savings, or the gain or loss of real wealth—is, in a sense, the bottom line of the global accounts. It describes the change in total real wealth that results from the college's activities for the year, recognizing all its sources of income, all its expenditures on current account and new capital and maintenance, all the depreciation of its physical capital stock, and the contrary effects of inflation in eroding the real value of its financial wealth while increasing the nominal value of its physical wealth. In this fundamental measure, the fortunes of the college illustrated in table 3 declined by some $11 million between 1989–90 and 1990–91, from real savings of $10.2 million to real dissavings of $.7 million.

The next four lines of table 3 address two of the many questions that might be asked about the year's total real savings. The first two lines describe the distribution of total real savings between financial and physical wealth. Physical wealth fared better than did financial wealth in 1989–90 but had a slightly larger decline in 1990–91. The next two lines ask what would have happened to savings without the gifts that were targeted to increase wealth. Some of the increase in wealth on line 1 was the result of the explicit intentions of donors who gave the college money for the purpose of increasing its wealth, so that component might well be separated out from any change in wealth, savings, that was due, instead, to the college's decisions and external circumstances during the year. Without the gifts to wealth (to endowment and plant) of $8 and $9 million in the two years, the college would have saved in other ways some $2.1 million in the good year and lost a bit more than $10 million in the bad one. Again, governing boards would differ in their evaluation of these facts: had the school's performance led to neither savings nor dissavings in those years, that might be considered good work by a board

---

20. The four alternative objectives that Dunn described for endowment wealth are relevant in this broader context of total wealth: (1) protect its nominal value, (2) protect its purchasing power—its real value, (3) have wealth grow as fast as operating expenses, or (4) increase wealth per student as fast as that of competing or peer institutions (Dunn 1991, 34–35).

21. The details of getting from table 1 to table 3 are included in the table in appendix B.

TABLE 3. **Global Accounts Summary**

	1989–90	1990–91
1. Savings—Gain (or loss) of total real wealth	$10,171,785	($651,954)
Gain (or loss) of real financial wealth	$4,156,623	($146,923)
Gain (or loss) of real physical wealth	$6,015,162	($505,051)
Gifts to increase real wealth	$8,083,066	$9,457,930
Savings to increase real wealth	$2,088,719	($10,109,904)
2. Income	$99,183,301	$93,272,130
Real growth rate	−3.26%	−10.19%
3. Spending		
Operating costs	$75,526,941	$80,014,085
Deferred maintenance	$3,319,164	$2,815,336
Investment in new plant	$9,334,326	$2,310,285
Real growth rates:		
Operating costs	4.51%	1.18%
Deferred maintenance	36.27%	−18.99%
Investment in new plant	4.35%	−76.36%
4. Savings—Gain (or loss) of total real wealth, using smoothed asset income	$7,276,151	$8,600,747

interested in real wealth maintenance while it would be considered poor performance by a board that wanted, say, to catch up to Amherst or Swarthmore in wealth per student. So again, the global accounts are agnostic on policy aims.

College income is reported next in table 3 in current dollars while its growth is reported in real terms, adjusted for inflation; together they monitor the flow of total resources into the school over the year.

Direct monitoring of costs and spending levels and their real growth, as presented in the third section of table 3, is a response to the criticisms of higher education in the 1980s and the conviction that real spending growth should be watched closely, both in detailed categories and broadly. Operating costs include both current expenditures and real depreciation as reported in table 1. The year's deferred maintenance is reported as a separate line because of its usual neglect and its potential for causing serious long-term mischief. A board might adopt the policy that deferred maintenance should always be zero (giving top priority to protection of physical plant, whatever it costs in other objectives), or it might feel that deferred maintenance is simply one important aspect of performance that needs to be monitored attentively—a board might conclude that deferring maintenance, like any other reduction in savings, can sometimes provide money to do other, more important, things. Again, global accounts inform policy by defining required maintenance spending and showing the cost of not doing it. Investment in new plant describes only spending for new physical capital.

The last section of table 3 addresses an evaluation problem for well-endowed schools that report their financial assets at market values and thereby incur potentially large variations in reported income through capital gains and losses caused by market fluctuations: year-to-year comparisons of global performance will be hard to interpret if major changes in asset market value have dominated the numbers. So in this last section of the table, the effect of the year's activities on the college's wealth are reexamined using a five-year moving average of asset income instead of actual asset income for each year: that smooths out the volatile element while still reflecting its underlying changes in a subdued form. These data for 1989–90 and 1990–91 illustrate the effect nicely. Between the two years, the school's capital gains income fell by almost $12 million, so much of the striking difference in the effects of performance on real wealth between the two years was due to that sharp (and uncontrollable) decline in income and not, as it might first appear, to the way the college was run in the latter year. Indeed, the effect of operations on real wealth was, with smoothed income, better in the second year: without that abrupt decline in asset income, reductions in deferred maintenance and the growth of current spending would have increased savings by $1.3 million in 1990–91.

The Global Economic Plan

Global accounts easily provide the framework for an economic planning model that has the same inclusive scope and the same ability to integrate detailed management subplans while showing the global economic implications of the school's intended behavior and anticipated circumstances. Tables 4 to 6 illustrate such a model. Table 4 is a basic global economic plan; table 5 is a subaccount giving more detail on planned current spending, the operating budget; and table 6 gives the sort of evaluative summary data just described, here extended to include anticipated future performance over the period of the plan. All values are in 1992 dollars with an assumed 5 percent inflation rate, and past accumulation of deferred maintenance is arbitrarily set at zero at the beginning of 1989–90. All planned and projected values are rounded.

Two years of historical performance data—1989–90 and 1990–91—are the starting point for projections of both anticipated circumstances (inflation, asset market conditions, etc.) and planned college behavior (staffing, salaries, tuitions, resource allocation, etc.). The heart of a planning process is, of course, the thoughtful specification of these planning parameters—projections of future intentions, plans, and expectations. But in terms of the plan *structure* that is at issue here, after the college has decided on those planning parameters—how it wants and expects the components of the accounts to change in the future—a global economic plan will show the effects of that behavior on the college's real wealth over the period of the plan. It is, then, a consistency-and-implications model: the pieces have to fit together over any year, and they have to fit together from one period to the next, satisfying the truism that wealth at the beginning of the period plus income less spending has to equal wealth at the end of the period; each period's performance is anchored in the past year's and the projections are anchored in the most recent history. The result is neither an optimization model nor an equilibrium model. It can be made into a long-run financial equilibrium model if a constant rate of growth of wealth is imposed, but that remains an option and not a characteristic. It is hoped that its more modest logical structure may well be of greater practical value than the more abstract alternatives in actual planning, administration, and governance. The global plan takes the concrete form of a Lotus spreadsheet that is easy to use to ask, repeatedly, the question, What will be the economic implications of the following behavior, now and in the future?

The data in tables 4 through 6 are based on tables 1 through 3, but it is important that they carry no implication about future plans or projections for any actual school. They are illustrative only of the structure of the economic plan. To make that very clear, planning parameter values in these tables have been entered as caricatures—most either as the constant rate of growth of 6 percent (nominal) or as a constant nominal quantity[22]—with the hope that that high level of artificiality will make it starkly clear that these tables deal only with model structure and no privileged information is conveyed.

A cost of that artificiality, though, is that the numbers in these tables are less revealing of an actual planning exercise than they would be with more realistic parameter values. Nonetheless, they show that if a college, starting with the historical performance described in the first two columns, were to plan its spending and anticipate income as described by these rates and levels, it would wind up as described in the last four columns: it would see increasing yearly dissavings, the loss of more real financial wealth than physical wealth, an increased underlying dissavings that is hidden in part by gifts intended to increase wealth, real income growth hovering around zero with real operating costs that are increasing modestly, declining real new investment, and declining but still positive real deferred maintenance. If that pattern of behavior (and circumstances) continued until the academic year 2001–2, the college would

---

22. In practice, three kinds of parameter values might be used to describe plans and projections: (1) rates of growth (constant or changing from one year to the next), (2) levels (constant in real or nominal terms or changing over time), and (3) functionally dependent parameters reflecting things like the way institutional need-based financial aid expenses depend on tuition decisions.

TABLE 4. Global Economic Plan (current dollars, inflation rate 5%)

	1989–90	1990–91	Plan Parameters	Planned 1991–92	Planned 1992–93	Planned 1993–94	Projected 2001–02
1. College income							
Tuition and fees	$ 29,262,691	$ 32,543,540	6.0%	$ 34,500,000	$ 36,600,000	$ 38,800,000	$ 61,800,000
Gifts and grants							
To endowment	7,066,669	8,744,806	$9M	9,000,000	9,000,000	9,000,000	9,000,000
To plant	1,016,397	713,124	$1M	1,000,000	1,000,000	1,000,000	1,000,000
All other	12,664,824	13,951,045	$14M	14,000,000	14,000,000	14,000,000	14,000,000
Asset income							
Interest and dividends	17,039,521	15,859,257	6.0%	16,800,000	17,800,000	18,900,000	30,100,000
Appreciation	18,582,670	6,873,486	6.0%	7,300,000	7,700,000	8,200,000	13,000,000
Sales, services, and other	1,950,970	2,724,059	6.0%	2,900,000	3,100,000	3,200,000	5,200,000
Auxiliary income	11,599,559	11,862,813	6.0%	12,600,000	13,300,000	14,100,000	22,500,000
Total college income	99,183,301	93,272,130		98,100,000	102,500,000	107,200,000	156,600,000
2. Current expenditures							
Operating budget expenditures	62,425,303	66,924,329	On Table 5	70,900,000	75,200,000	79,700,000	127,000,000
Other current expenditures	6,304,914	5,634,728	On Table 5	6,000,000	6,300,000	6,700,000	10,700,000
Less current account maintenance	703,276	642,167	$650,00	650,000	650,000	650,000	650,000
Total current expenditures	68,026,941	71,916,890		76,300,000	80,900,000	85,800,000	137,100,000

3. Additions to capital stock							
Investment in new plant	9,334,326	2,310,285	$7 M constant	2,100,000	2,100,000	2,200,000	2,600,000
Less deferred maintenance							
Real depreciation	7,500,000	8,097,195	2.5% K-stock	8,500,000	9,000,000	9,500,000	14,600,000
less maintenance spending:							
In Current Account	703,276	642,167	$650,000	650,000	650,000	650,000	650,000
In Plant Fund	3,477,560	4,639,692	6.0%	4,900,000	5,200,000	5,500,000	8,800,000
Total deferred maintenance	3,319,164	2,815,336		2,950,000	3,150,000	3,350,000	5,150,000
Total additions to capital	6,015,162	(505,051)		(850,000)	(1,050,000)	(1,150,000)	(2,550,000)
4. Operating costs:							
Current expenditures	68,026,941	71,916,890	As above	76,300,000	80,900,000	85,800,000	137,100,000
Real depreciation	7,500,000	8,097,195	As above	8,500,000	9,000,000	9,500,000	14,600,000
Total operating costs	75,526,941	80,014,085		84,800,000	89,900,000	95,300,000	151,700,000
5. Wealth end of year							
Financial wealth							
Assets	346,203,972	358,726,081		373,500,000	387,100,000	400,200,000	481,100,000
Less liabilities	50,596,648	49,355,661	$50M	50,000,000	50,000,000	50,000,000	50,000,000
Net financial wealth	295,607,324	309,370,420		323,500,000	337,100,000	350,200,000	431,100,000
[Endowment value]	[333,553,551]	[341,572,081]	$350M	[350,000,000]	[350,000,000]	[350,000,000]	[350,000,000]
Physical capital wealth							
Replacement value	323,887,799	341,438,861		360,600,000	380,800,000	402,000,000	617,000,000
Less accumulated deferred maintenance	3,319,164	6,290,686		9,600,000	13,200,000	17,200,000	66,200,000
Net physical wealth	320,568,635	335,148,175		351,000,000	367,600,000	384,800,000	550,800,000
Net worth	616,175,959	664,518,515		674,500,000	704,700,000	735,000,000	981,900,000

TABLE 5. Global Economic Plan: Current Expenditure Component

	1989–90	1990–91	Plan Parameters	1991–92	1992–93	1993–94	2001–02
Operating budget							
Salary pools							
Faculty	$10,194,014	$11,415,331	6.0%	$12,100,000	$12,800,000	$13,600,000	$21,700,000
Administrative and professional	6,029,465	6,315,789	6.0%	6,700,000	7,100,000	7,500,000	12,000,000
Weekly	11,568,273	12,101,430	6.0%	12,800,000	13,600,000	14,400,000	23,000,000
Total salary pools	27,791,752	29,832,550		31,600,000	33,500,000	35,500,000	56,600,000
Fringe benefits	7,258,226	7,816,225	6.0%	8,300,000	8,800,000	9,300,000	14,800,000
Financial aid	6,517,892	7,719,186	6.0%	8,200,000	8,700,000	9,200,000	14,700,000
Other restricted spending	2,720,321	3,505,429	6.0%	3,700,000	3,900,000	4,200,000	6,700,000
Managers' budgets	18,137,112	18,050,939	6.0%	19,100,000	20,300,000	21,500,000	34,300,000
Total operating budget expenses	62,425,303	66,924,329		70,900,000	75,200,000	79,700,000	127,000,000
Other current expenditures	6,304,914	5,634,728	6.0%	6,000,000	6,300,000	6,700,000	10,700,000
Less maintenance spending in current account	703,276	642,167	$650,000	650,000	650,000	650,000	650,000
Total current expenditures	68,026,941	71,916,890		76,300,000	80,900,000	85,800,000	137,100,000

TABLE 6. Global Economic Plan: Summary (current dollars, inflation rate 5 percent)

	1989–90	1990–91	Plan Parameters	1991–92	1992–93	1993–94	2001–02
1. Savings—gain (or loss) of total real wealth	$10,171,785	($651,974)		($2,200,000)	($3,600,000)	($4,900,000)	($16,300,000)
Gain (or loss) of real financial wealth	$4,156,623	($146,923)		($1,300,000)	($2,600,000)	($3,800,000)	($13,700,000)
Gain (or loss) of real physical wealth	$6,015,162	($505,051)	Details	($900,000)	($1,000,000)	($1,200,000)	($2,600,000)
Gifts to increase real wealth	$8,083,066	$9,457,930		$10,000,000	$10,000,000	$10,000,000	$10,000,000
Savings to increase real wealth	$2,088,719	($10,109,904)		($12,200,000)	($13,600,000)	($14,900,000)	($26,300,000)
2. Income	$99,183,301	$93,272,130	on	$98,100,000	$102,500,000	$107,200,000	$156,600,000
Real growth rate	–3.26%	–10.19%		0.12%	–0.45%	–0.39%	0.03%
3. Spending			tables				
Operating costs	$75,526,941	$80,014,085		$84,800,000	$89,900,000	$95,300,000	$151,700,000
Deferred maintenance	$3,319,164	$2,815,336		$3,000,000	$3,200,000	$3,300,000	$5,200,000
Investment in new plant	$9,334,326	$2,310,285	4	$2,100,000	$2,100,000	$2,200,000	$2,600,000
Real growth rates							
Operating costs	4.51%	1.18%	and	0.93%	0.96%	0.95%	0.93%
Deferred maintenance	36.27%	–18.99%		0.40%	1.13%	1.02%	0.26%
Investment in new plant	4.35%	–76.36%	5	–14.18%	–2.25%	–2.32%	–3.10%
4. Savings—Gain (or loss) of total real wealth (using smoothed asset income)	$7,276,151	$8,600,747		$2,600,000	$4,000,000	($2,000,000)	($17,100,000)
5. Accumulated deferred maintenance	$3,319,164	$6,290,686		$9,600,000	$13,200,000	$17,200,000	$66,200,000

find itself dissaving at an annual real rate of $16 million, despite $10 million a year in gifts intended to increase its wealth. Most of that dissavings would take the form of drawing down financial assets, but there would still be an accumulated deferred maintenance of some $66 million or a bit less than 10 percent of its capital stock (all in 2002 dollars). A governing board, looking at these results, would have to conclude that the projected behavior under the projected circumstances is not sustainable. The elimination of asset income volatility makes a significant difference in the evaluation of short-run performance, but, predictably, it has a declining effect on the evaluation of smoothly projected future performance. So the plan reveals that something more fundamental than asset income volatility is producing unsustainable results.

Given the artificiality of these numbers, the results of these plan projections probably do not deserve much more discussion, but they should serve to give a sense of the kind of strategic information that is generated by the global plan: it is, most generally, a description of the future resource implications of the behavior and circumstances envisioned by the college.

Premises and Promise

The premise of the global accounts has been that a college's administration or governing board *wants* to have meaningful and accessible economic information about the college's performance, but that may sometimes be naive. That the operating budget can be a political document is often acknowledged and usually described as regrettable, but it is also of considerable value in avoiding questions and discussions that might be time consuming, tedious, and challenging to administrative decisions. The fact that fund accounts can selectively hide or reveal transactions is often convenient. So is the emphasis on endowment wealth, as though there were no other kind of financial assets and no offsetting debt. And so on. But the difficulty with the manipulation of economic information or selective optimism in its reporting is the old one that plagues any departure from scrupulous efforts to report the economic facts: that the first victim of distorted economic information is often the author of those distortions. It is simply hard to manage a place if you do not know what is going on. This is a lesson learned and relearned in contexts ranging from the Soviet planned economy to the current gyrations of state and city budgets in New York. Unfortunately, as the government parallel suggests, governors and mayors change and so do college administrations, increasing the temptation those transients face to keep their economic numbers looking good and let the sober facts show up eventually "but not on my watch."

But more positively, and more importantly, global accounts appear to represent a marked improvement over fund accounting both in informing the long-run policy issues that confront colleges and universities and in monitoring their most basic economic performance. The information these accounts present has proven to be the sort that induces and encourages the discussion of strategic fundamentals, of issues that are basic to the governance of the institution, issues that take the form of the question, If we keep on doing what we are doing, or what we are planning to do next year, what will happen to our economic wealth? Such elemental questions are not so readily induced or addressed by the kind of economic information now readily available to colleges and universities.

Global accounts describe the effect of a year's activities, actual or planned, on all of the college's real wealth, on the distribution of that wealth between financial and physical assets, on deferred maintenance, and on levels and real growth of income from its various sources and of spending on its various objectives, this in an environment of inflation with its opposing effects on the values of financial and physical wealth. Global accounts describe the whole of an institution; their data are designed to avoid omissions and partial truths, to be clear and accessible, and to direct attention to the most basic economic implications of a college's behavior.

APPENDIX A

TABLE 1-A. Global Financial Accounts

	1989–90	1990–91
1. College income		
Tuition and fees	$ 29,262,691	$ 32,543,540
Gifts and grants		
To endowment	7,066,669	8,744,806
To plant	1,016,397	713,124
All other	12,664,824	13,951,045
Asset income		
Interest and dividends	17,039,521	15,859,257
Appreciation	18,582,670	6,873,486
Sales, services, and other	1,950,970	2,724,059
Auxiliary income	11,599,559	11,862,813
Total college income	99,183,301	93,272,130
2. Current expenditures		
Operating budget expenditures	62,425,303	66,924,329
Other current expenditures	6,304,914	5,634,728
Less current account maintenance	703,276	642,167
Total current expenditures	68,026,941	71,916,890
3. Capital expenditures		
Investment in new plant	9,334,326	2,310,285
Maintenance in current account	703,276	642,167
Maintenance in plant fund	3,477,560	4,639,692
Total additions to capital	13,515,162	7,592,144

(Continued)

TABLE 1-A.—Continued

	1989–90	1990–91
4. Financial wealth end of year		
Assets	346,203,972	358,726,081
[Endowment value]	[333,553,551]	[341,572,081]
Less liabilities	50,596,648	49,355,661
Net financial wealth	295,607,324	309,370,420
5. Financial savings		
Total financial savings	17,641,198	13,763,096
Breakeven savings (inflation offset)	13,484,575	13,910,019
Real financial savings	4,156,623	(146,923)
Real net of gifts to endowment	(2,910,046)	(8,891,729)

APPENDIX B

Performance Calculations

	1989–90	1990–91
Savings—gain (or loss) of real wealth	$10,171,785	($651,974)
Total real savings: $Y-X-[hK^*(t-1)-(mc+mk)]+iK^*(t-1)$	$38,209,833	$28,498,822
Breakeven savings: $iNFW(t-1)+iK^*(t-1)$	$28,038,048	$29,150,796
Gain (or loss) of real financial wealth—Real savings	$4,156,623	($146,923)
Total financial savings $Y-X-K$	$17,641,198	$13,763,096
Breakeven savings (inflation offset) $i(NFW)(t-1)$	$13,484,575	$13,910,019
Gain (or loss) of physical wealth—Real savings	$6,015,162	($505,051)
Total physical capital savings: $K-[hK^*(t-1)-(mc+mk)]+iK^*(t-1)$	$20,568,635	$14,735,726
Breakeven savings (inflation offset): $iK^*(t-1)$	$14,553,473	$15,240,777
Composition of savings		
Financial savings	41%	23%
Physical savings	59%	77%
With smoothed asset income		
Savings—gain (or loss) of total real wealth, smoothed	$7,276,151	$ 8,600,747
Total savings	$35,314,199	$37,751,543
Gain (or loss) of real financial wealth	$1,260,989	$ 9,105,798
Total financial savings, smoothed	$14,745,564	$23,015,817
Spending		
Deferred maintenance: $hK^*(t-1)-(mc+mk)$	$3,319,164	$ 2,815,336
Real yearly growth	36.27%	−18.99%
Current expenditures: $X-(mc+mk)$	$68,026,941	$71,916,890
Real yearly growth	4.72%	0.97%
Operating costs: $X-(mc+mk)+hK^*(t-1)$	$75,526,941	$80,014,085
Real yearly growth	4.51%	1.18%
Investment in new plant	$9,334,326	$ 2,310,285
Real yearly growth	4.35%	−76.36%

Note: K = new investment; K^* = replacement value of capital stock; h = depreciation rate; mc and mk = maintenance spending in current and capital-budget, respectively (both included in X); i = inflation rate; Y = income; X = (current expenditures + mc + mk); $(t-1)$ = end of previous period.

REFERENCES

Bierman, Harold Jr., and Thomas R. Hofstedt. "University Accounting (Alternative Measures of Ivy League Deficits)." *Non-Profit Report,* May 1973, 14–23.

Chabotar, Kent John. "Financial Ratio Analysis Comes to Nonprofits." *Journal of Higher Education* 60, no. 2 (March/April 1989), 188–208.

Dunn, John A., Jr. *Financial Planning Guidelines for Facilities Renewal and Adaption.* Ann Arbor: The Society for College and University Planning, 1989.

Dunn, John A., Jr. "How Colleges Should Handle Their Endowment." *Planning for Higher Education* 19, no. 3 (Spring 1991).

Garner, C. William. *Accounting and Budgeting in Public and Nonprofit Organizations.* San Francisco: Jossey-Bass Publishers, 1991, chapter 2 ("The Role of Funds").

Harried, Andrew A., Leroy F. Imdieke, and Ralph E. Smith. *Advanced Accounting.* 3d ed. New York: John Wiley and Sons, Inc., 1985.

Harvard University. *Financial Report to the Board of Overseers of Harvard College.* Cambridge, MA: Harvard University, 1992.

Lyall, Sarah. "Strife over Style and Substance Tests Princeton's Leader." *New York Times,* December 4, 1989, B1.

Nordhaus, William. "Evaluating the Risks for Specific Institutions." Yale University, March 14, 1989.

O'Neill, June. *Resource Use in Higher Education: Trends in Output and Inputs, 1930 to 1967.* A Technical Report Sponsored by the Carnegie Commission on Higher Education. Berkeley: The Carnegie Commission on Higher Education, 1971.

Probasco, Jack. "Crumbling Campuses: What Are the Real Costs?" *Business Officer* 25, no. 5 (November 1991), 48–51.

Schultz, Theodore W. "Capital Formation by Education." *Journal of Political Economy* 68, no. 6 (December 1960): 571–83.

Swarthmore College. "The Treasurer's Report 1986–87." In *The President's Report, 1986–87.* Swarthmore: Swarthmore College, 1987.

Williams College. "The Treasurer's Report 1990–91." Williamstown, MA: Williams College, 1991.

Winston, Gordon C. "Total College Income: An Economic Overview of Williams College, 1956–57 to 1986–87." Williams College, April 10, 1988.

———. "Why Are Capital Costs Ignored by Colleges and Universities and What Are the Prospects for Change?" Williams Project on the Economics of Higher Education, Discussion Paper No. 14. July 1991.

Winston, Gordon C., and Duncan Mann. *Global Accounts: Reorganizing Economic Information for Colleges and Universities.* Unpublished.

CHAPTER 12

Value Responsibility Budgeting

William F. Massy

We began this book by presenting the argument for resource allocation reform in higher education. Reform usually involves decentralization: the empowerment of operating units to achieve institutional and societal goals. We have discussed the theory of decision making in nonprofit entities, the principle of decentralization, and the problem of aligning operating unit and funding agency incentives. Economic Agency Theory offers three ways of mitigating the last problem: maintaining *specific responsibility* (SpR) through regulation; devolving *pricing responsibility* (PriR) through price-based incentives; and assigning *overall value responsibility* (OVR), the overall responsibility for producing value as defined by the principal. Other chapters have described efforts to reengineer resource allocation systems within higher education institutions and in other contexts. Throughout the book, we have described design principles that should guide budget process reengineering such as the treatment of capital and the development of funding models and global accounts. Drawing on these materials, we now propose an integrated performance-based budgeting system—*value responsibility budgeting* (VRB).

Balancing intrinsic values with market forces emerged as one of the key elements in resource allocation design. Centralized systems (e.g., line-item budgeting) do a poor job because they fail to maximize intrinsic values and cannot adapt to changes in the educational marketplace. As discussed in chapter 2, *performance responsibility budgeting* (PRB) and *revenue responsibility budgeting* (RRB) represent the polar extremes of decentralization. PRB focuses mainly on intrinsic values: funds are provided in blocks to operating units according to their recent performance and future prospects and are assessed in relation to the institution's mission, vision, and goals. The central administration retains responsibility for revenue management—for adapting to market forces. RRB devolves virtually all revenues directly to the operating

293

units, who assume the revenue management responsibility. Both systems relax line-item and categorical spending restrictions and thus permit operating units to decide their own expenditure trade-offs.

While either decentralization approach usually represents an improvement over centralized budgeting, neither is problem free. PRB skirts the problem of externalities, which arises when the costs or benefits associated with a unit's actions may impact other units as described in chapter 3. In an ideal world, PRB would police incentive incompatibilities by withholding funds from units that pursue their own goals at the expense of the central institution. Experience, however, proves that punishing such behavior is difficult. Operating units believe they own the prior year's budget base, and they argue for equitable consideration vis-à-vis other units within the institution. Few administrations possess sufficient performance information to make the case for differential treatment; hence, incremental allocations tend to vary only marginally. This leads operating units to consider most of their costs as fixed and inhibits the units from responding to market forces.

On the other hand, RRB encourages entrepreneurship but may shortchange intrinsic values relative to market forces. Revenue devolution also limits the central administration's ability to influence operating unit behavior to further the central mission, vision, and goals of the institution when they differ from those at the local level. While taxes and subventions can in principle provide such influence, the property rights principle often prevents this from happening in practice. Units assert ownership of revenue streams and the expenditures funded by subventions, thwarting performance-based funding adjustments.

Needed is a system that will empower operating units while maximizing incentive compatibility and retaining central influence on operating unit goals. Such a system should engender a sense of urgency within operating units about responding to market forces, while not opening the way to unbridled entrepreneurship with its long-run corrosive consequences on intrinsic academic values and on the control of externalities. Chapter 8 considered one design approach: the *program related group* (PRG) concept, based on health care's *diagnosis-related groups* (DRG). PRGs would carry revenue responsibility to the level of the operating unit. If carefully designed, they would embody institutional mission, vision, goals, and other intrinsic values, and PRGs would avoid the problem of externalities. In terms of economic agency theory, use of PRGs would provide a combination of pricing responsibility and overall value responsibility. At present, however, higher education is unable to define, much less to implement, a system of PRGs. Therefore, we offer in this chapter a budgeting system, VRB, that combines elements of

PRB and RRB to produce the desired features of both while minimizing the undesirable ones—a system that almost any institution could implement now.

Value Responsibility

Value responsibility budgeting adopts pricing responsibility principles for some institutional activities, specific responsibility principles for a few others, and value responsibility principles everywhere else. VRB can be applied at any level in the responsibility chain, from government allocations for systems or campuses all the way down to school allocations for academic and support service departments.

Implementing value responsibility budgeting requires that one develop: (1) a revenue-attribution model like the ones used in RRB, (2) a cost-attribution model like the one described in chapter 10, (3) a supplementary incentives and regulation model, and (4) a performance-based block allocation system for the central administration's remaining funds. The four models closely follow the tenets of nonprofit budgeting theory and economic agency theory, presented in chapter 3.

The exposition of VRB will be aided by simulating several annual budgeting cycles for a hypothetical institution, "SimU." Assume that SimU is a small public institution with two academic responsibility centers ("School Alpha" and "School Beta"), two general funded support centers ("Academic Support Services and Administration" and "Plant O&M"), plus a number of auxiliaries and service centers. In addition to obtaining tuition revenue and state support, SimU relies on a modest sponsored research program, a small endowment, and an annual gift flow. To keep the example as simple as possible I have lumped together all the academic support service and administrative functions: in a real institution, they would be divided into a number of separate responsibility centers. Despite these and other simplifications, the example contains all the elements necessary for applying VRB to virtually any institution—large or small, public or private.

The Revenue-Attribution Model

Value responsibility budgeting resembles revenue responsibility budgeting in that some revenues are assigned to responsibility centers; however, the provost will withhold revenues that cannot be attributed to a particular center or that appear likely to produce externality or value incongruity problems. Hence the first step in designing a VRB system is to categorize the institution's revenues according to the following three-way classification: (1) attributable and assigned to a center; (2) at least partly attributable to a center but withheld (we will call these "associated revenues" to distinguish them from assigned revenues); and (3) not attributable to a center.

Table 1 presents the revenue breakdowns between the assigned and associated categories for School Alpha in simulated year 1. (The sums are in thousands of dollars unless otherwise indicated.) Had SimU been a real institution, it might have used the following decision rules in making the breakdowns:

1. *Tuition and fees:* first divide the revenue stream into general and specific categories, and then subdivide them as to assignability.

   Specific: tuition and fees from special programs like continuing education, workforce training, and professional education. Such programs usually are initiated and predominantly staffed by individual centers, so 100 percent of the revenues are assigned.

   General: all other tuition and fee revenue. First determine the average revenue per course unit for (*a*) undergraduate, (*b*)

TABLE 1.   Revenue Breakdown for a Responsibility Center School Alpha, Year 1

	Assigned	Associated	Total
Tuition & fees	$1,250	$300	$1,550
General	$1,000	$300	$1,300
Specific	$250	$0	$250
State appropriations	$4,880	$2,750	$7,630
General	$3,980	$1,500	$5,480
Specific	$900	$1,250	$2,150
Sponsored research	$2,000	$971	$2,971
Direct	$2,000	$0	$2,000
Indirect	$0	$971	$971
Endowment payout	$350	$0	$350
Restricted	$350	$0	$350
Unrestricted	$0	$0	$0
Current gifts	$50	$20	$70
Restricted	$50	$0	$50
Unrestricted	$0	$20	$20
Other income	$15	$35	$50
Gross total	$8,545	$4,076	$12,621
Less financial aid	$0	$260	$260
Net total	$8,545	$3,816	$12,361

professional, and (*c*) other graduate students; then allocate according to the following table:

	Own major	Other major	No major
Units taught by this center	assign	associate	associate

While other schemes could be devised, this one balances incentives in ways that may cancel out the worst externalities observed in conventional RRB systems (where 100 percent of tuition is assigned).

The center gets assigned-revenue credit for all units it teaches to its own majors, giving it a strong incentive to attract majors. Revenue from units taught to other centers' majors and students who have not yet declared a major become associated with this center; while not as powerful as a revenue assignment, association nevertheless will count in the center's favor at budget time.

The scheme provides a positive incentive for teaching undergraduate general education courses and service courses for other majors. The provost, however, can discourage destructive competition and duplication by judgmentally discounting the resulting associated revenue. The strong incentive to teach to one's own majors might lead to inappropriate limits on student choice and failure to take advantage of other centers' capacities. However, the department will be penalized in the "marketplace for majors," which provides a built-in regulatory mechanism.

2. *State appropriations:* (*a*) allocate according to the decision rule for tuition and fees if the state allocates funds according to the number of units taught; (*b*) assign to the center that fulfills the condition if the state appropriates on the basis of faculty or staff lines or for particular purposes; (*c*) do not attribute to any center if the state appropriates in a lump sum.

3. *Sponsored research:* (*a*) assign direct expenditures to the unit owning the project; (*b*) associate overhead recovery with the owning unit. The center that employs the faculty principal investigator owns the project; additional decision rules will be needed to accommodate joint appointments and multiple principal investigators.

4. *Endowment payout:* endowment earnings appropriated by the

institution for current purposes. (As discussed in chapter 4, pay-out may consist of dividends and interest or be the result of apply-ing an endowment spending rule.) The decision rule is: (*a*) assign the payout from restricted endowment to the center meeting the condition; (*b*) do not attribute unrestricted endowment payout.

5. *Current gifts:* (*a*) assign restricted gifts to the center meeting the condition; (*b*) associate unrestricted gifts if a policy presumption exists that the gift, though legally unrestricted, results from the activities of a particular center—as when an alumna from a par-ticular school contributes to the institution's annual fund, for example; (*c*) do not attribute the remaining unrestricted gifts. A more complex decision rule might be developed for alumni of more than one school and other complex cases.

6. *Other income:* miscellaneous revenue classified according to the particular conditions involved.

7. *Financial aid:* while financial aid could be apportioned according to the rule used for tuition and fees, SimU has decided to associ-ate the whole sum rather than assign part of it. This rule reflects the principle that the whole institution carries the financial aid burden, but that schools should be reminded about the aid liabili-ties produced by their enrollments. Eschewing assignment also helps avoid arguments about whose students are the most needy.

As can be seen from the table, the revenue totals are defined as gross and net of financial aid. SimU considers aid to be a discount from revenue rather than an expense, so most subsequent calculations will be based on the net figure.

Table 2 rolls up revenue to the level of the whole institution, again for simulated year 1. The first two columns were obtained by summing the assigned and associated revenues of the various responsibility cen-ters. The third column represents unattributed revenue, which does not enter the individual center calculations. As can be seen from the table, the unattributed revenue comes from state appropriations, endowment payout, and gifts.

The Cost-Attribution Model

The main difference between the VRB and RRB cost-attribution mod-els lies in the use of variable costs instead of average costs. The standard RRB overhead-allocation model, however, could be substituted for the variable-cost model without losing VRB's other advantages.

I shall begin by discussing the sources and uses of funds for simulated School Alpha. (Readers who are familiar with overhead cost bases and rate calculations may wish to skip down to the discussion of how to estimate variable costs.) Starting from this base, we will work our way through the various cost attribution processes that produce tables showing SimU's overall cost structure.

Table 3 presents School Alpha's year 1 data. Looking first to the funds sources, we see that assigned revenue comes directly from table 1. The block allocations, incentive awards, and categorical allocations do not affect cost attribution, so we can defer their definitions. On the other hand, sales to other units do affect cost attribution, as do most of the funds-uses categories.

TABLE 2. Institutional Revenue Breakdown, Year 1

	Dollars				Percentage		
	Assign	Assoc	Other	Total	Assign	Assoc	Other
Tuition and fees	$2,250	$1,500	$0	$3,750	60%	40%	0%
Less financial aid	$0	($650)	$0	($650)	0%	100%	0%
Net tuition and fees	$2,250	$850	$0	$3,100	73%	27%	0%
State appropriations	$8,380	$13,350	$3,300	$25,030	33%	53%	13%
Sponsored research	$3,000	$1,457	$0	$4,457	67%	33%	0%
Endowment income	$850	$0	$7,121	$7,971	11%	0%	89%
Current gifts	$125	$50	$2,100	$2,275	5%	2%	92%
Other income	$780	$1,020	$0	$1,800	43%	57%	0%
Total (net revenue)	$15,385	$16,727	$12,521	$44,633	34.5%	37.5%	28.1%

TABLE 3. Sources and Uses of Funds School Alpha, Year 1

Sources of Funds		Uses of Funds	
		Prior year plus cost-rise:	
Assigned revenue	$8,545	External	$13,451
Base block allocation	$14,040	Service centers & auxiliaries	$744
Incremental block allocation	$0	School Beta	$264
Excepted incentive awards	$0	AcadSS & adm	$528
Categorical allocations	$0	Plant O&M	$1,055
Sales to other centers	$317	Budget adjustments	$0
Total sources	$22,902	Other:	
		Incentive surcharges	$0
Surplus (deficit)	$364	Overhead charges	$6,495
		Total uses	$22,537
Activity bases:			
Allocation base	$13,451	Allocation base: research	$1,710
Charging base	$15,725	Charging base: research	$2,000

VRB divides funds uses into three major categories: *prior year plus cost-rise, budget adjustments,* and *other.* As the name suggests, the first category represents the cost of the prior year's activities adjusted for inflation and real cost-rise. The second category, budget adjustments, represents decisions made by the school in order to balance its budget— no budget adjustment was needed in year 1, so discussion of that process can be deferred. In the third group, incentive surcharges fall into the same category as incentive awards (to be discussed later), but overhead charges lie at the core of the cost-attribution model.

Allocation and Charging Bases. Cost attribution proceeds in two steps: (1) determining allocations, and (2) applying charges. As in any overhead-distribution methodology, the first step apportions costs among organizational units and activities. This produces a charging rate, which is used in the second step to distribute the costs to units and projects. The cost-apportionment and cost-distribution processes require an *allocation base* and a *charging base,* as shown at the bottom of table 3. Both bases are built up from School Alpha's funds uses; they refer only to direct academic activities, so department administration costs are excluded. The research bases separate *sponsored research* from the other direct activity, *instruction and departmental research;* the latter's bases can be obtained by subtracting the sponsored research bases from the overall bases.

To understand the differences between the allocation and charging bases, we must look at the school's sales to other units and its purchases from other units and service centers. Table 3 itemizes purchases from other units, beginning with "Service centers and auxiliaries" (shortened to "services centers" in the discussion) and ending with "Plant O&M." All other expenditures go to external entities—for example, employees and outside vendors. To sort out the relevant relationships, I will assume that SimU has adopted the following policies:

1. Provider-center prices will include overhead so they can easily be benchmarked against outside suppliers (which also include overhead). Therefore, the prices charged by the service centers, School Beta, Academic Support Services and Administration, and Plant O&M include overhead.
2. Purchases from provider-centers will not be included in the purchasing center's overhead allocation base, since these activities already contain overhead loadings. That is, School Alpha's allocation base excludes the aforementioned purchases, which means that the resulting overhead rate for the school will be lower than would be the case had they been included.

3. Purchases from provider-centers will be included in the school's charging base in order to avoid undesirable favoritism compared to outside vendors. Sales to other centers will be excluded, however, so that no cost element is charged overhead more than once. Therefore, School Alpha's charging base equals the sum of prior year plus cost-rise and budget adjustments, minus sales to other centers.

The research bases embody the additional assumption, made mostly for convenience, that no research is included in sales to other units. Hence the research charging base equals the direct sponsored research line in table 1. However, research expenditures are assumed to include purchases from other centers on a pro rata basis.

Rate Calculations. The top portion of table 4 presents the institution-level step-down calculation for allocating year 1 average costs to responsi-

TABLE 4. Overhead Stepdown Schedules, Year 1

Average Cost Allocations	Base	D&I	O&M	AS&A	ADA	Total	Rate
Depreciation and interest[a]	$3,600	($3,600)					
Plant O&M	$6,449	$180	($6,629)				
Academic support & adm	$6,488	$720	$1,396	($8,604)			
Academic department admin.	$2,183	$504	$977	$358	($4,022)		
Total overhead	$18,721						
Instr. & dept'l research	$25,938	$1,998	$3,873	$7,169	$3,601	$16,641	64.2%
Sponsored research	$3,000	$126	$244	$839	$422	$1,631	54.4%
I&R overhead						$18,272	63.1%
Svc. ctrs. & auxiliaries	$1,445	$72	$140	$237	$0	$449	31.1%

Variable Cost Allocations	Base	D&I	O&M	AS&A	ADA	Total	Rate
Depreciation and interest[a]	$3,600	($3,600)					
Plant O&M	$4,837	$180	($5,017)				
Academic support & adm	$3,244	$720	$1,056	($5,020)			
Academic department admin.	$546	$504	$739	$209	($1,998)		
Total variable overhead	$12,227						
Instr. & dept'l research	$25,938	$1,998	$2,931	$4,183	$1,789	$10,901	42.0%
Sponsored research	$3,000	$126	$185	$490	$209	$1,010	33.7%
I&R variable overhead						$11,911	41.2%
Svc. ctrs. & auxiliaries	$1,445	$72	$106	$138	$0	$316	21.9%
Fixed overhead						$6,494	

[a]Depreciable asset base at the end of the base year and years 1, 2, and 3 (in millions) are $80, $90, $90, $90, respectively.

bility centers and activities. (The resulting overhead rates will apply to year 2.) The first column presents the allocation bases for the various responsibility centers. It also contains figures for "Depreciation and interest on plant debt" and "Academic department administration"—the latter being carved out as a proportion of School Alpha's and School Beta's expenditures. (The rest of the schools' expenditures show up as instruction and research.) Total overhead is shown as a subtotal, following the four overhead line items.

The step-down proceeds according to these steps:

1. The depreciation and interest line is allocated in column 2, proportional to the net assignable square feet of building space used by each center and activity.
2. The plant O&M allocation is added to the plant O&M base to produce the figure for loaded plant O&M cost shown at the top of column 3. This cost is allocated among the remaining rows, again proportional to net assignable square footage.
3. The process is repeated for academic support and administration and academic department administration, this time using percentages of total cost rather than building space to make the allocations. Academic department administration does not benefit service centers, so that allocation is zero.
4. The allocations to the "direct cost" categories (rows 6–8) are summed across the table, and then divided by their respective charging bases to obtain the charging rates shown in the last column. The figures in the "total" line are based only on the "Instruction and departmental research" and "Sponsored research" lines. Summing the totals for "Instruction and research overhead" and "Service centers and auxiliaries" produces the "Total overhead" subtotal shown in column 1.

The average-cost overhead rate for sponsored research multiplies sponsored-research direct revenue to obtain research-overhead recovery. (The rate is reduced by 10 percent to account for negotiation losses.) The other rates are shown for comparison with RRB, but they are not used in VRB.

Cost allocations in VRB key off the not-for-profit decision rule presented in chapter 3, so they should be based on variable cost rather than average cost. The lower portion of table 4 presents the variable-cost step-down calculations. They are identical to the average-cost calculation except that the allocation bases for plant O&M, academic support and administration, and academic department administration have been multiplied by a variable-cost factor that represents the proportion of the center's costs that vary with output.

The variable-cost allocation table contains a line labeled "Fixed overhead," which equals the difference between "Total overhead" and "Total variable overhead." Thus it represents the sums expended by the overhead responsibility centers that will not be collected through the variable-cost charging rate.

Estimating variable cost. Unlike manufacturing firms, colleges and universities do not estimate variable-cost factors on a regular basis. The following method, however, proved effective in trials by the Stanford University Business and Finance division:

1. Segment administrative and support costs by organizational subunit (within a given responsibility center), down to the point where the costs of individual function become reasonably apparent. (The Stanford groupings had been developed earlier for segmenting research overhead according to OMB Circular A-21.) Once the variable costs for the subunits have been determined, they can be rolled up to produce variable-cost estimates for the responsibility center as a whole.

2. Determine what output measure to use for each unit; for example, consider using accounting transactions in the controller's office, net square feet for plant O&M, and landscaped acres for grounds maintenance. In our experience, the appropriate output measure becomes apparent when activities are segmented to a sufficiently detailed level.

3. Determine the output range and time frame to be used in deciding whether each unit's costs are fixed or variable. The output range should be large enough to require the unit to adjust its production process—for example, a 5 percent change in transaction volume might require an accounting unit to add staff, whereas a 1 percent change might be accommodated using existing resources. The time frame should be long enough to permit the unit to adjust to the new output level but not so long as to permit wholesale restructuring. In general, the objective is to approximate the slope of the average cost curve (based on current production methods) for significant and permanent output changes.

4. For each unit, estimate the ratio of variable to fixed cost (the "variable cost ratio"). Many units will spend most of their time processing transactions or delivering services: for example, payroll, accounts payable, benefits counseling, building and grounds

maintenance, and student health services. Their costs are variable except for supervision: for example, an accounts payable office with one supervisor and nine processors would have about 90 percent variable cost. Other units will be engaged mainly in policy determination, information systems development and maintenance, legal work, and other activities that do not vary with output in identifiable ways: their costs would be classified as fixed. A few units may defy analysis. For example, the employee relations office may write policy manuals and perform institution-wide collective bargaining (fixed), handle employee grievances (variable), and counsel supervisors (mixed). Such units may be subdivided, or the variable-cost ratio may be assessed by judgment.

Every new administration and support service expenditure generates a variable cost as seen by the deans and other unit managers. The variable-cost ratios should be reviewed periodically—for example, once every five years—with the variable-cost ratios being held constant during the interim. The review will provide all stakeholders an opportunity to scrutinize the institution's cost structure—indeed, the exercise could include a zero-based analysis of the overhead activities themselves in addition to their partitioning into fixed and variable components. (The reviews might be performed on a rolling basis, so that one-fifth of the support units are evaluated each year.) Changing the variable-cost ratios will change the overhead charging rate; however, responsibility centers can be immunized from such changes through offsetting adjustments to their block allocations. The adjustments would prevent windfalls or sudden hurt due to resetting the variable-cost ratios, whereas future decisions would be governed by the new charging rates.

While generalizations about the ratio of variable to fixed costs are hazardous, my experience suggests that more costs are variable than one might think. Of course, the ratio will vary by activity. For SimU, I have assumed only 25 percent of academic department administration to be variable: small departments will have only a chair and secretary (fixed cost), though larger ones have a more elaborated and variable infrastructure. I have assumed 67 percent of administration and academic support to be variable and 90 percent of depreciation and plant O&M to be variable.

The variable-cost ratios for depreciation and plant O&M reflect the cost of square footage used by the responsibility centers, without regard to the fact that total space may be fixed in the short run. The 90 percent figure represents the opportunity loss associated with each centers' space utilization. One might wish to exclude depreciation and interest when allocating costs to individual programs and projects, however, since the smaller figure probably will produce the desired incentives without burdening the activities too heavily.

Pros and Cons of Variable Cost Overhead. The nonprofit enterprise decision rule presented earlier provides the driving impetus for variable-cost overhead rates. Variable-cost rates add complexity, however, and they may reduce the visibility of fixed costs. These are important issues, so we shall digress slightly to consider the pros and cons of variable-cost overhead in more detail.

Complexity makes it harder for stakeholders to understand and therefore to support a variable-cost allocation system. Variable overhead calculations do add a new layer of analytical complexity, but this is offset by greater conceptual clarity. In my many discussions of overhead allocation with deans and faculty, I have rarely found it difficult to explain how new academic programs produce variable overheads or why the institution should attribute these extra costs to the programs causing them. Explaining why new programs should be burdened with a share of fixed costs encounters great resistance, however, since the respondents don't see how their actions change the central administration's economic position.

Variable-cost overhead rates are considerably smaller than the ones based on average costs. For example, if School Alpha adds two gift-funded staff members costing (say) $100,000 for compensation, benefits, and local office support, it would incur an overhead charge of $41,200 based on the variable-cost allocation compared to $63,100 based on the conventional average-cost allocation. If the average-cost rate were to be applied, the school would contribute $21,900 to the institution's fixed-cost base—that is, the central administration would have that much more to money to reallocate. While the extra money might seem attractive, obtaining it violates the nonprofit enterprise optimality principle. Under an average-cost system, an activity whose marginal value plus marginal revenue exceeds its marginal cost may be inhibited by the extra payment to the central administration, which produces a "deadweight loss" analogous to that of a sales tax in the general economy. As noted earlier, such a tax inevitably encounters resistance from deans, department heads, and faculty, whereas variable-cost charges—while never popular—can be defended logically.

Experience with revenue responsibility budgeting indicates that deans and other managers take a strong interest in overhead rates and thus help discipline administrative and support budgets. If we eliminate fixed costs from the overhead rates that responsibility centers pay, will they lose the discipline? This is an important question, but I believe the answer is "no" for the following reasons:

Every addition to overhead will involve responsibility center co-payments, starting when the rates are revised the following year. The co-payment will equal the variable-cost factor for the support unit in question multiplied by the expenditure change. Likewise, every overhead saving will involve a dividend for responsibility centers in the form of reduced rates.

Changes to the "Total fixed cost" line in table 4 will be reflected dollar for dollar in the sums available for distribution to responsibility centers through the block allocations (described later). Therefore, stakeholders will have no difficulty in tracking fixed costs and applying appropriate pressure to support-unit budgets.

Finally, applying variable-cost principles to overhead allocation should make the prices of services provided by one responsibility center to another more comparable to those of equivalent services that might obtained from external vendors. Universities have high fixed costs because they must deal with multiple constituencies and complex policy matters. Allocating these fixed costs to internally produced services can make the services noncompetitive with those obtainable outside, since the outside suppliers typically do not have to deal with equivalent complexity. Internally produced services should not be given a price advantage. Although empirical research on university versus for-profit fixed costs is lacking, variable-cost overhead may produce a more level playing field than average-cost allocations.

The Supplementary Incentives and Regulation Model

As developed so far, value responsibility budgeting includes powerful price-oriented incentives based on revenue assignments and variable overhead charges. VRB's other major feature, performance responsibility, will be considered in the next section. Now I shall introduce the possibility of supplementary price-based incentives and specific regulation. Adopting VRB does not oblige one to use any of these, but they represent a potentially useful addition to the resource allocator's armamentarium.

Suppose SimU's provost wants to discourage responsibility centers from using a certain type of input—an older type of printing service, for example, which is currently low priced but likely to leave its users in a technological cul-de-sac. While the provost could prohibit responsibility centers from using the service, that would require a disempowering and possibly bureaucratic process. A simpler way, one more compatible with VRB principles, would be to penalize use of the service by augmenting its price.

The "incentive surcharge" introduced in table 3 provides the desired penalty. The provost announces a "tax" on purchases of services whose use is discouraged and describes the reasons why this represents good policy. Activities for which the service has high current value will continue to make use of it, but others will stop. The same logic might be applied to certain types of part-time faculty, who may be inexpensive and expedient but damaging to educational quality. Subsidies also can be used to provide positive incentives, for example, to encourage the use of a new technology. (A subsidy can be represented as a negative surcharge.) SimU accounts for the surcharges separately in order to keep them clearly in view and to avoid contaminating its overhead distributions with these deviations from true variable cost. As shown in the table, incentive surcharges appear "below the line" and thus are not included in either the overhead allocation or charging bases.

Our second supplementary price-based incentive operates on the responsibility center's outputs. Suppose the provost wants to encourage a particular set of outcomes that she values more highly than the responsibility centers do—the classic principal-agent problem. Schools might be less sensitive to minority educational attainment than the institution as a whole, for example, or they may favor lengthening time to the doctoral degree whereas the provost might wish to see it shortened. Once again, a financial incentive can be used in place of specific regulation.

The "incentive award" shown in table 1 provides the desired outcome-based incentive. The provost offers to pay a certain sum for each output event a responsibility center achieves, such as a bachelors degree attained by a disadvantaged student in five years or less or a doctorate achieved in four years. These dollars augment those earned in blocks or through assigned revenues. The sums can be used for any legitimate purpose, including faculty development. As in the case of incentive surcharges, the incentive awards are accounted for separately. They do not enter the overhead base calculations directly, although the expenditures they fund do enter in the usual way.

Finally, the provost may wish to limit a responsibility center's discretion by issuing certain funds in the form of a "categorical allocation" (also introduced in table 4). This might be a good approach if the institution wants to upgrade a certain type of equipment or provide remedial language training, for example. The center must spend the money for the intended purpose, just as if the funds were a restricted grant from an external sponsor. In the language of principal-agent theory, categorical allocations represent a form of specific regulation. They can be effective in assuring the central administration that particular goals are achieved, but if used too broadly categorical allocations become disempowering and defeat the purposes of value responsibility budgeting.

Performance-Based Block Allocations

Certain principles of accountability lie at the heart of value responsibility budgeting. The National Commission on the Responsibility for Financing Higher Education articulates this four-point program:

1. *Agree on the tasks that need to be accomplished: the goals of the enterprise.* Accountability is impossible without clarity about objectives, so care must be taken to articulate the institution's mission and develop a vision of how that mission can be achieved. The vision should be well understood and widely accepted within the organization, since effective performance is unlikely without agreement about the tasks' importance.
2. *Ensure that the available resources are sufficient to complete the tasks successfully.* If resources are insufficient, those called upon for implementation may throw up their hands in frustration or despair. A serious incongruity requires that the central authority allocate more resources or revise the vision.
3. *Provide the enterprise with the authority it needs to be effective, and then let the enterprise do the job without interference.* Professors possess specialized knowledge, and they become frustrated when denied the opportunity to make the decisions for which they are qualified. Therefore, academic productivity depends heavily upon empowerment. The benefits of empowerment extend beyond the professoriate; for example, U.S. industry is discovering that self-directed work teams can be far more productive than equivalent but closely supervised units.
4. *Define a set of measurements to indicate how well the enterprise is doing relative to its goals, and follow up by tracking these measurements.* No accountability system that lacks effective performance measures will work for long. Without such measures, differences of objectives between the central authority and the academic unit will drive the system out of control. Indeed, any behavioral system that lacks feedback will tend to drift.[1]

---

1. Adapted from "Making College Affordable Again," report by the National Commission on Responsibilities for Financing Postsecondary Education (February 1993), 56–57.

Implementing these principles requires close cooperation and trust between the parties. The principal and agent must contract with each other about objectives, resources, and measures, and the principal must develop confidence in the agent's ability and willingness to perform. Cooperation and trust do not spring forth automatically. They arise from effective planning and assessment processes, pursued in good faith by both parties over a period of time. Specific regulations and price-based incentives of the kinds discussed in the two previous sections usually represent arms-length transactions: they do not necessarily build cooperation and trust, and they actually may undermine it.

VRB builds accountability through a process of planning and negotiation leading to performance-based block allocations as in PRB. The process can be described simply, though the negotiations and the calculations leading up to them may be complex.

1. Determine the *discretionary revenue* available for allocation. Discretionary revenue represents the sum available for judgmental allocation, after providing for previous commitments to responsibility centers and other needs.
   a. Project gross and net revenues, and then estimate the sums to be received from the responsibility centers as overhead charges and incentive surcharges. Turning to table 5, we see that SimU estimates year 1 net revenue at $44,633 and overhead charges at $13,877. Note that the overhead recoveries double count a portion of net revenues. However, these sums can be allocated by the central administration, so they should be included in the *available funds* figure.
   b. Subtract projected assigned revenues, interest on debt, funded depreciation, and other transfers. I have assumed that SimU funds depreciation, transferring the sums to a capital reserve from which future construction can be financed. (The "other transfers" line can be viewed as an additional contribution to the capital reserve.) Then subtract any expected incentive awards and categorical allocations to operating units, to obtain the sum available for block allocations. These set-asides reduce the funds available for block allocation from $58,511 to $37,464.
   c. Project the responsibility centers' *base block allocations* and subtract them from the net available funds. The projection proceeds by: (i) adding the previous year's incremental block allocation (discussed below) to the preceding year's base

allocation; (ii) adding estimated inflation and real cost-rise; and (iii) subtracting any sums to be withheld for reallocation. Responsibility centers will receive the projected base block allocation, plus or minus the year's incremental allocation.

d. The *reallocation factor* represents the percentage of the prior year's block that responsibility centers should be able to save through productivity gains—that is, by investing in technology, working smarter, or eliminating low-priority activities.

TABLE 5.   Sources and Uses of Funds, Central Administration

	Base year	Year 1	Year 2	Year 3
Sources of funds				
Total revenue	$44,353	$45,283	$45,811	$46,750
Less financial aid	($490)	($650)	($735)	($826)
Net total revenue	$43,863	$44,633	$45,076	$45,924
Overhead charges	$13,503	$13,877	$14,545	$15,076
Incentive surcharges	$0	$0	$634	$662
Available funds	$57,367	$58,511	$60,255	$61,663
Uses of funds				
Revenue assigned	$14,857	$15,385	$16,223	$16,423
Interest on debt	$2,000	$750	$0	$0
Funded depreciation	$2,000	$2,000	$2,250	$2,250
Other transfers	$2,000	$2,210	$2,332	$2,460
Expected incentive awards	$665	$702	$1,340	$1,414
Categorical allocations	$0	$0	$300	$317
Net available funds	$35,844	$37,464	$37,811	$38,800
Base block allocations	$35,900	$37,336	$38,784	$39,386
School Alpha	$13,500	$14,040	$14,602	14,686
School Beta	$13,100	$13,624	$14,269	$14,840
AcadSS and Adm	$6,800	$7,072	$7,380	$7,325
Plant O&M	$2,500	$2,600	$2,534	$2,535
Discretionary revenue		$128	($974)	($586)
Incremental allocations:				
School Alpha		$0	($500)	($125)
School Beta		$100	$0	($150)
AcadSS and Adm		$25	($350)	($200)
Plant O&M		($170)	($100)	($150)
Other transfers		$100	$0	$0
Surplus (deficit)	($56)	$73	($24)	$39
Accumulation or use of reserves				
Beginning reserve balance	$2,000	$1,944	$2,018	$1,994
Accumulation (use)	($56)	$73	($24)	$39
Ending reserve balance	$1,944	$2,018	$1,994	$2,033
Fixed overhead applicable to the year		$6,203	$6,494	$6,628

(The assessment is made as a matter of policy; center management must find the savings.) Figures in the 1–2 percent range seem reasonable as a general proposition, and I have assumed that SimU uses 1.5 percent. Note that the reallocation factor does not include any downsizing that may be needed to cope with financial stringency; that would be taken care of through negative block-incremental allocations.

Turning back to table 5, we see that SimU expects discretionary revenues of $128 thousand for year 1, with red ink projected for years 2 and 3. (The source of the red ink will be discussed below.) The base year contains no discretionary revenue figure, since that block already includes all budget adjustments. SimU's 1.5 percent reallocation factor deducts $539 thousand from the year 1 base block allocation, $600 thousand from the year 2 allocation, and $582 thousand from the year 3 allocation.

2. Determine the *incremental block allocation* for each responsibility center, plus the amount of any additional transfers. Apportioning discretionary revenue provides the provost with her best opportunity to influence responsibility center behavior. The process might go something like this:

   a. Prior to the main budget process, the provost reviews her discussions with school deans, faculty, and support service directors about institutional goals, how the particular center should work to further them, and how the center's achievements measure up against the goals. Such discussions should proceed continuously throughout the year; however, they should be brought to summation just prior to the budget season.

   b. The provost asks each dean or director to present a number of planning scenarios, based on projections for assigned revenue and other income sources, the relevant direct and indirect cost factors, and alternative assumptions about the center's incremental block allocation. One such assumption will be a zero incremental allocation. Other assumptions will be based on the center's prebudget conference, where the year's total discretionary revenue and the provost's preliminary thinking about priorities are revealed. This conference provides the provost with an opportunity to state her opening position in the year's budget negotiation—for example, by saying what objectives and activities she would like to see included in the center's plans. The planning scenarios will delineate programs, actions, and expected accomplishments for the ensuing year, and also provide a three- to five-year projection for establishing perspective.

c. The provost reviews the responsibility centers' planning scenarios, confers with the deans and directors as individuals and in group settings, and makes her allocation decisions. While the decision criteria cannot be stated in advance, she will consider: (i) the quality of the center's plans—for example, in terms of data, logic, and consistency; (ii) the plans' congruence with stated institutional goals; (iii) the center's past performance record in delivering on its promises; (iv) whether it has been a good "institutional citizen," cooperating as needed with other units and the central administration; (v) the amount of associated revenue the center generates; (vi) its other resources—for example, from assigned revenue, sponsored research, and gifts; and (vii) whether the center is encountering extraordinary problems that might require special consideration.

One usually will emphasize items i through v, since these contribute most to value responsibility. Too much emphasis on vi and vii will undermine VRB by undermining the centers' willingness to own its financial problems. In times of large revenue shifts or externally caused difficulties, however, the provost will want to compensate for them via the block allocation. SimU's hypothetical discretionary revenue and incremental block allocations are shown in the lower portion of table 5. The incremental allocation figures reflect the provost's judgments, discussed above. When added to the projected base allocations, they produce the center's total block funding for the year. The negative discretionary revenues in years 2 and 3 force budget reductions rather than provide growth opportunities in those years.

I have imagined that SimU anticipates problems with its state appropriation and plans to mitigate them by increasing tuition and sponsored research. Both tuition and research contain large assigned-revenue components. Therefore, assigned revenue will grow faster than total revenue, producing a squeeze on discretionary revenue. Following normal university practice, the provost has responded by cutting the administration in year 1 while continuing to fund modest budget increases for the academic units. (Fortunately, SimU's debt will be paid off by the end of year 1, although a new building scheduled to come on line in year 2 will add to depreciation charges.) Should the squeeze accelerate as projected, the schools will shoulder budget base reductions in years 2 and 3. The provost also has decided to institute surcharges on auxiliary faculty salaries; this salary line had been growing faster than enrollments and sponsored research, and she felt that the schools should shift the teaching workload back toward the regular faculty. Following these decisions, SimU projected modest deficits in years 1 and 2 and a small surplus in year 3.

Table 6 traces the projections back to School Alpha. The school's assigned revenue grows by about 6.3 percent between the base year and year 1, which is more than three times as fast as net total revenue for the institution as a whole. Thus the school can produce a balanced budget for the year even without an incremental block allocation. The provost

TABLE 6. Projected Sources and Uses of Funds and Budget Adjustments: School Alpha

	Base Year	Year 1	Year 2	Year 3
Sources of funds				
Assigned revenue	$8,039	$8,545	$9,099	$9,445
Base block allocation	$13,500	$14,040	$14,602	$14,686
Incremental block allocation		$0	($500)	($125)
Expected incentive awards	$0	$0	$600	$633
Categorical allocations	$0	$0	$150	$158
Sales to other centers	$300	$317	$334	$352
Total sources	$21,839	$22,902	$24,285	$25,149
Uses of funds				
Prior year plus cost-rise				
External	$12,750	$13,451	$14,191	$14,952
Service centers & auxiliaries	$1,000	$744	$929	$907
School Beta	$250	$264	$278	$294
AcadSS & adm	$500	$528	$557	$587
Plant O&M	$1,000	$1,055	$1,113	$1,174
Budget adjustments		$0	($20)	($300)
Other:				
Incentive surcharges	$0	$0	$354	$366
Overhead charges	$6,308	$6,495	$6,888	$7,166
Total uses	$21,808	$22,537	$24,290	$25,146
Surplus (deficit)	$31	$364	($5)	$3
Budget adjustments		$0	($20)	($300)
Accum. or use of reserves		$0	$0	$0
Beginning reserve balance	$1,500	$1,531	$1,895	$1,890
Accumulation (use)	$31	$364	($5)	$3
Ending reserve balance	$1,531	$1,895	$1,890	$1,893
Percent of total expenditures				
Budget adjustment		0.00%	(0.09%)	(1.24%)
Year-to-year change		3.34%	7.78%	3.52%
Surplus (deficit)	0.14%	1.62%	(0.02%)	0.01%
Ending reserve balance	7.02%	8.41%	7.78%	7.53%

reminded the dean, however, that the tuition gain will come from a policy change rather the school's own performance in the marketplace, so that he should expect a $500 thousand block-allocation cut in year 2. The prospect of such a large financial problem tipped the scales in a close faculty vote on whether to participate in the provost's teaching improvement program (TIP), which enabled the dean to project an incentive award payment of $600 thousand.

The school's budget adjustment figures, shown in the box, represent the dean's response to projected financial conditions—that is, his main controllable variable. He adjusts the figures until the "surplus" line produces satisfactory values. (The budget adjustments are repeated further up the table and thus are included in the surplus line.) The school projects a $20 thousand downward budget adjustment and a small deficit in year 2. Should SimU's financial problems persist into year 3, the school will have to cut its budget by $300 thousand to cope with a further block-allocation reduction and other income variations.

School Alpha's financial results are summarized at the bottom of table 6. The summaries are couched as percentages of expenditures in order to provide perspective in relation to the school's operating base. For example, the aforementioned $300 thousand budget reduction represents only 1.24 percent of expenditures, hardly a daunting figure.

Table 7 rolls the financial summaries up to the institutional level. The provost has managed to avoid significant deficits by the central administration and in the consolidated budget. Reserves are declining as a percentage of expenditures, however, and continuation of deficits at the school level might present problems even if SimU's central budget remains in balance. The distribution of revenues by source and distribution of expenditures by responsibility center (which can easily be mapped into expenditures by function) provide important strategic information that can be compared with similar results from other institutions. For example, Barbara Taylor, Joel Meyerson, and I provide benchmark data that can be used for such purposes.[2]

Summary of VRB

Value responsibility attempts to balance intrinsic values and market forces. Response to market forces is achieved through what economic agency theory calls price responsibility—that is, price incentives. VRB tracks all price effects; it filters the effects judgmentally when exter-

2. Barbara E. Taylor, Joel W. Meyerson, and William F. Massy, *Strategic Indicators for Higher Education* (Princeton, NJ: Peterson's, 1993).

TABLE 7. Central Administration Information Summary

	Base Year	Year 1	Year 2	Year 3
Incremental allocations (% of base blocks)		0.15%	(2.5%)	(1.6%)
Budget adjustment as a percent of expenditures				
School Alpha		0.00%	−0.08%	−1.19%
School Beta		−0.93%	−1.77%	0.00%
AcadSS and Adm		0.00%	−3.10%	−6.60%
Plant O&M		−2.18%	−3.55%	−2.77%
Surplus (deficit) & ending reserves as a percent of expenditures				
Central administration				
Surplus (deficit)	(0.1%)	0.13%	0.00%	0.04%
Ending reserve balance	3.48%	3.50%	3.28%	3.21%
Responsibility centers				
School Alpha	0.14%	1.62%	0.00%	0.01%
School Beta	(0.5%)	(0.4%)	0.06%	0.00%
AcadSS and Adm	(0.1%)	1.17%	(0.5%)	0.08%
Plant O&M	0.65%	0.09%	(0.1%)	0.00%
Consolidated				
Surplus (deficit)	(0.2%)	0.81%	(0.1%)	0.05%
Ending reserve balance	8.96%	9.53%	8.91%	8.66%
Block/net associated revenues				
School Alpha	361.59%	367.88%	346.35%	310.50%
School Beta	310.26%	307.66%	309.08%	306.37%
School Alpha/School Beta	116.55%	119.57%	112.06%	101.35%
Net revenue/Total institutional net revenues				
Tuition & fees (net)	4.70%	6.95%	7.74%	8.28%
State appropriations	59.62%	56.08%	52.52%	50.65%
Sponsored research	9.63%	9.99%	11.40%	11.66%
Endowment payout	17.23%	17.86%	18.66%	19.32%
Current gifts	4.94%	5.10%	5.47%	5.72%
Other income	3.89%	4.03%	4.21%	4.36%
Expenditures/Total institutional expenditures				
School Alpha	38.98%	39.11%	39.98%	40.02%
School Beta	32.56%	32.55%	32.52%	32.79%
AcadSS and Adm	16.43%	16.40%	15.93%	15.68%
Plant O&M	12.03%	11.94%	11.58%	11.51%
Total academic	71.54%	71.67%	72.50%	72.81%
Overhead Rates				
Average cost rates				
Instr. & dept'l research	64.0%	64.0%	64.2%	63.2%
Sponsored research	54.0%	54.0%	54.4%	52.4%
Variable cost rates				
Instruction and research	41.5%	41.3%	41.2%	40.8%
Service centers	18.0%	18.5%	21.9%	20.2%

nalities or conflicts with institutional values are at issue and transmits the effects directly to operating units in other cases. Price effects stimulate vigilance about marketplace changes. Operating units have every incentive to be entrepreneurial when they receive the benefits directly, and in other cases the units are constantly reminded about the revenue changes they influence. Units also are constantly reminded of the institution's mission, vision, and goals, and are urged to conform their plans to the institution's value system. Available performance measures are used to assess operating unit outcomes, and greater or fewer resources will flow to the unit as a consequence of these judgments.

VRB differs from RRB in that revenues are not devolved to units when institutional values or externalities are at issue. Rather than assessing a tax on all revenues, VRB addresses value and externality conflicts up front, before ownership of the revenue stream is transferred. One might say this does little but change the terms of dialogue between central administration and operating units; but, as we have seen throughout this book, the terms of dialogue are critical. Requests for extended revenue ownership should be met with explanations of institutional values and externalities: a decision to grant the request would be accompanied by agreements on how to mitigate any conflicts, and a negative decision would be made in context of a familiar set of arguments. Such an approach differs significantly from the one in RRB, where full revenue ownership is granted at the outset and arguments about taxes revolve around taking away what the operating units already own.

VRB differs from the typical PRB implementation in two ways. First, the existence of a full-blown revenue-attribution model permits revenue considerations to inform judgments about block allocations. (This was Jon Strauss's point, in chap. 7, when he described the use of departmental financial statements in an institution that had not adopted RRB.) Second, VRB deducts a productivity improvement target from prior year's block allocations before deciding on the new year's allocations. This generates a pool of funds for reallocation even when total revenues aren't rising faster than inflation, and it also establishes the idea that operating units are expected to improve their productivity continuously.

VRB also incorporates variable-cost overhead, chargeable to all expenditures regardless of funds source. (RRB systems generally use average-cost overhead, and PRB systems apply overhead only to restricted-fund expenditures if at all.) In the plant area, variable costs are taken as including the opportunity cost of building space utilization in order to incorporate the capital dimension in operating-unit planning. Variable-cost overhead tends to produce optimal decisions, as shown by the nonprofit decision rule described in chapter 3, whereas average-cost overhead distorts decision making. While variable-cost systems are more difficult to develop than average-cost systems, variable-cost systems are easier to justify and, in my opinion, well worth the effort.

Stanford University's new budgeting protocol incorporates some of the features of VRB. (Stanford had been operating under a variant of PRB, adopted in the early 1980s.[3]) For example, the university no longer adjusts for cost-rise in projecting the prior year's block allocations to schools.[4] This makes 100 percent of the cost-rise available for reallocation. Allocations now are made in context of the consolidated budget and capital budget, not just the operating budget (mostly unrestricted funds) as heretofore.[5] The university also has developed a costing model to determine contribution margins at the departmental level,[6] which can be used as described in chapter 7. The Medical School and the Graduate School of Business have operated on a revenue responsibility basis for many years. While full revenue responsibility for other schools is not likely (nor desirable), the devolution of some additional revenue responsibility as called for in VRB seems likely.

Resource-Based Incentives and Academic Quality

One issue remains controversial in VRB, just as in PRB, whatever the method used to assess performance. Is it effective to punish low-performing academic programs by reducing their budget allocations? And even if effective, is it equitable to do so? I have participated in meetings where this issue was debated heatedly and then resolved in favor of rewarding high-performing programs but *not* punishing low-performing ones. Our discussion of value responsibility budgeting would not be complete without consideration of the principles and pitfalls associated with performance-based funding.

While the idea that funding should depend on performance has wide appeal, controversy arises when one addresses program design. The controversy revolves around the following plausible but mutually contradictory propositions:

---

3. William F. Massy, "Budget Decentralization at Stanford University," *Planning for Higher Education* 18, no. 2: 39–55.

4. Stanford University, "The Stanford University Budget Plan: 1994/95" (Office of the Provost, June, 1994), 2.

5. Ibid., 3 and 9.

6. Dan Rodas, Geoffrey Cox, and Joy Mundy, "Applying Gross Margin Analysis in a Research University" (NACUBO, *Executive Strategies,* forthcoming in 1995).

1. One should tilt investments more toward high-performing units (institutions, schools, or departments) than low-performing ones, other things being equal: this reflects the "high-assay principle," mentioned in chapter 1.
2. One shouldn't penalize subpar performers by reducing their budgets: "reduced funding will only degrade quality, and that's not fair to the students or faculty involved."
3. Rewarding high-performing units with larger budgets (while not reducing the funding for low performers') will, over time, increase cost per unit of output: this might enable critics of performance-based funding to argue, "unit costs are too high already, and the incentive value for possible performance improvement isn't worth the extra expenditures on current high performers."

One cannot simultaneously pursue high-assay investments, forfend the consequences of poor performance, and contain unit cost. Something must give. As we shall see, the "something" should depend on expected academic unit behavior and the restructuring environment within which resource allocation is embedded.

Design and Performance Quality

Our analysis begins with three propositions that, we believe, are self-evident and not controversial.

1. Institutions and funding agencies want to deploy their funds in ways that maximize quality given desired output quantities. Institutions and agencies want to provide incentives that will induce institutions and academic units to make quality-improving choices on their own initiative, rather than regulating quality through micromanagement.
2. Maximum achievable quality varies positively with resources applied: that is, greater funding pushes out the "quality frontier." The concept of a quality frontier is related to that of design quality in manufacturing. Design quality, which characterizes the product's specifications, varies according to the amount and type of labor, materials, and capital utilized, and according to the degree to which the design meets user needs. For example, larger budgets for engineering, materials, capital equipment, and labor hours will, other things being equal, yield

a better product. Even the most effective quality management won't turn a Hyundai into a BMW.

3. How close an academic unit comes to achieving frontier-level quality depends on its objectives and resource-utilization efficiency: institutions, schools, and departments will vary considerably in what we call "performance quality," the degree to which their delivered quality approaches the quality frontier defined by their resources. For purposes of discussion, we consider units that operate close to the frontier and strive continually to improve themselves as *quality conscious*.

Good incentives can improve quality consciousness and thus performance quality but, by themselves, incentives can't remedy defects in design quality. Herein lies the problem underlying our proposition 2: incentive-oriented funding penalties diminish design quality even as they work to improve performance quality.

The choice of incentive program depends on how design quality and performance quality vary with funding levels. For example, will the operating group targeted by the incentive focus on design quality or performance quality when confronted with a potential funding change? Table 8 summarizes these effects for the three basic strategies available to resource allocators: (1) do not link funding with performance (work to enhance quality using other management methods); (2) link funding to performance only in the positive direction relative to baseline funding and quality; and (3) link funding and performance symmetrically relative to the baselines. The three strategies are shown on the rows of the table. The columns depict three possible states of the world: (A) departments have no discretion to vary quality (i.e., delivered quality always equals design quality); (B) departments do have discretion, but most of them currently operate near the quality frontier; and (C) departments have discretion, and a substantial number operate well under the quality frontier. Column A represents a straw man, introduced for purposes of discussion, since the idea that faculty cannot vary the delivered quality of education and research is preposterous.

Reading down the first column, where departments (or schools or institutions) have no discretion over quality, we see that incentives don't matter—and hence that nothing is gained or lost with respect to incentives by choosing one or another linkage strategy. The choice does matter when it comes to meeting the high-assay investment criterion, however. Symmetric linkage meets the criterion most completely, while positive linking meets the criterion only for programs that are above baseline

TABLE 8. Effects of Performance Funding

Funding v. Performance	No Discretion (A) Q = Design Q	Departmental Discretion on Quality	
		(B) Q = Frontier	(C) Q < Frontier
No linkage with performance	Incentives don't matter Fails on investment criterion	No incentive for maintaining Q Fails on investment criterion	No incentive for improving Q Fails on investment criterion
Positive linkage with performance: rewards only	Incentives don't matter Partly meets investment criterion	Provides incentives for exemplary Q Partly meets investment criterion	Provides incentives for improving Q Partly meets investment criterion
Symmetric linkage with performance: rewards and penalties	Incentives don't matter Fully meets investment criterion Can't fall into the "quality trap"	Provides full incentives Fully meets investment criterion Won't fall into the "quality trap"	Provides full incentives Fully meets investment criterion May fall into the "quality trap"

quality levels. (The same observations apply to the other two columns in the table.) We also note, in the first column under symmetric linkage, that departments "can't fall into the quality trap," which will be discussed in connection with the table's last column.

Incentive differences play a stronger role when we move on to the second column, where departments do influence delivered quality but where delivered quality tends to be close to the frontier. A no-linkage strategy doesn't hurt one's ability to spur quality improvement—since departments are doing well already—but one nevertheless forgoes the opportunity to reinforce commitment to quality through the resource allocation system. The positive-linkage strategy offers incentives for outstanding performance: departments close to but not quite at the quality frontier—which is never known with precision anyway—may try to become exemplary. Programs that offer a small number of prizes for outstanding performance fall into this category. Finally, symmetric linkage adds a powerful incentive to maintain quality, since departments would predict that a falloff in performance would lead to funding losses.

In the table's third column, departments behave in ways that deliver quality at significantly lower levels than would be delivered at the quality frontier. The no-linkage strategy provides no incentive to improve in this case—which, alas, is probably the most realistic one. The positive-linkage strategy does provide an incentive for improvement, provided the enhancements needed to obtain the extra resources are sufficiently realistic for at least some departments to qualify if they become quality conscious.

The Quality Trap

The biggest question arises in connection with the lower right-hand cell of table 8: the application of symmetric linkage to a situation where few departments are quality conscious and some are rather deficient in delivered quality. The system will provide incentives for improvement, but departments that fail to improve—that do not make the transition to quality consciousness—will end up with less funding. For these institutions, less funding may well produce even lower quality as the old methods are applied with fewer resources. Further rounds of funding withdrawal may follow, in which case the department can be said to have fallen into a "quality trap": where capacity and morale disintegrate to the point where quality improvement is out of the question. This possibility drives the concern about the symmetric linkage of funding with performance. Notice that departments cannot fall into the quality trap when they cannot influence delivered quality (col. A), and that they are not likely to fall into the trap if they are quality conscious and already operate at high quality levels.

The key question underlying the choice of linkage strategy, then, is whether departments, schools, or institutions will respond favorably to a combined carrot-and-stick strategy, or whether most will feel the full force of the stick. The former case produces a win-win result, in that quality consciousness and delivered quality will improve, and funding will be more closely aligned with effectiveness. Success in applying the symmetric linkage strategy, however, will depend upon whether those targeted by the incentives possess the capacity to transform themselves, and whether sufficient insights about quality and the facilitation services needed to support the growth of quality consciousness are readily available.

Our recent field research suggests that the necessary conditions for the needed transformations are present in only a minority of departments and institutions.[7] To the extent this is true, a "motivate and forget" strategy—wherein symmetric linkage is implemented without a concurrent program of quality motivation and facilitation—could be quite dangerous. The critics may be right in urging caution, but an effective quality program run in parallel with symmetric performance-based funding can mitigate the problem. Moreover, performance-based funding may be necessary to provide the incentives required for a quality program to be taken seriously.

Conclusion

Our first purpose in writing this book was to focus attention on higher education resource allocation processes: to emphasize that such processes need to be carefully designed, not just allowed to evolve. Academic-program knowledge and good judgment are necessary but not sufficient conditions for good outcomes. Increasing numbers of institutions are considering how to reengineer resource allocation processes as part of their overall restructuring efforts—such efforts are necessary to accommodate permanent changes in higher education's social, demographic, economic, and technological environment. These institutions are working to decentralize resource allocation without abdicating accountability.

Our second purpose was to present the theoretical underpinnings

---

7. Cf.: William F. Massy, Andrea K. Wilger, and Carol Colbeck, "Overcoming 'Hollowed' Collegiality," *Change* 26, no. 4 (July-August 1994): 10–20; William F. Massy and Andrea K. Wilger, "Improving Productivity." *Change* 27, no. 4 (July/August 1995): 10–20; and Andrea K. Wilger and Janice Pang, "Faculty Views on Curriculum" (paper presented at the Third Annual AAHE Conference on Faculty Roles and Responsibilities; Phoenix, January, 1995).

needed to design good resource allocation processes: for example, productivity principles, organizational design, the theory of economic decision making in nonprofit organizations, agency theory, and externalities. In so doing, we focused on the need to balance intrinsic values and market forces, since institutions that consider only values are vulnerable to changing market conditions and those that become too entrepreneurial will dilute their defining character as *academic* institutions.

Our third purpose was to present examples of decentralized resource allocation processes and process elements—building blocks from which to construct good processes—from higher education and elsewhere. This led us to consider the two polar types of decentralized budgeting processes (PRB and RRB), capital decisions, accounting system and funding model design, resource allocation in health care, and examples of decentralized allocation at the governmental level (in Britain) and within particular institutions (mainly RRB).

In this final chapter we have proposed a budgeting approach that combines the positive aspects of PRB and RRB while skirting their main problems. We also examined the linkage between resource allocation reform and academic restructuring at the grassroots level, a connection that must be planned carefully lest departments fall into the quality trap.

We hope this collection of essays will stimulate thinking about resource allocation processes at all levels: from departments to schools to institutions to systemwide offices to governmental funding agencies. We do not claim to have all the answers, and what works in a particular context will depend upon the particular circumstances in any case. A framework for thinking about problems and a vocabulary for discussing them has proved essential for organizational transformation, and we have tried to present such a framework and vocabulary. We wish our readers well in their transformation efforts.

Index

Academic Program Categories (APCs), 257, 260
Academic units: protected from market fluctuations, 30; VRB and quality of, 317–22. *See also* Higher education
Agency theory, 75–77, 293
Allocation bases, 300–301. *See also* Resource allocation
Analysis units, 247–48
Anthony, Robert, 98, 101
Atkinson, Harry, 12
AUCF (Average Unit of Council Funding), 226
"Available funds" projections, 130

Base block allocations, 309–10
Baumol, William J., 51–52
Behavioral prototyping, 181–82
Biller, Robert, 180–81
Black box model: elements of, 66–85; unpacking the, 57–66; used for higher education, 49
Blackman, Sue Anne Batey, 51
Bok, Derek, 39
Borrowing: from endowment, 123–25; to increase revenue/income, 122–23
Bowen, Howard, 66
Bowen's law, 4, 9
BPR (business process reengineering), 26
Bright, Craig, 92
British government: emerging educational role of, 223–25;

performance-based funding by, 42–43
British universities: allocation through assessment by, 229–31; assessment of research in, 231–34; assessment of teaching/programs in, 235–39; new allocation model of, 227–29; new funding approach of, 225–27; significance of new allocation by, 239–42. *See also* Higher education
Budget Group (Stanford), 27
Budget growth rate, 132
Budget Incentives Task Force (USC, 1981), 179
Business management. *See* Organization management

California Higher Education Policy Center, 15–16
CAMPUS (Comprehensive Analytical Methods for Planning in University Systems), 12, 246, 248
Capital budgets (global accounts), 277–79
Capital decisions: complications of, 116–17; discounting future utility as, 118–21; on endowment reversibility, 117–18; five options listed for, 115–17; made regarding endowments, 127–29; optimizing liabilities as, 122–29; using integrated financial planning for, 129–36
Capital stock (global accounts), 273–75